Britain and the American Frontier

Britain and the American Frontier 1783-1815

J. LEITCH WRIGHT, JR.

THE UNIVERSITY OF GEORGIA PRESS
ATHENS

Library of Congress Catalog Card Number: 73–90845
International Standard Book Number: 0–8203–0349–6

The University of Georgia Press, Athens 30602

Set in 10 on 13 pt. Mergenthaler Baskerville
Printed in the United States of America

To Nancy

Contents

Illustrations and Maps

Preface

THROUGH a series of historical accidents Britain after the Revolution assumed France's former role in North America. She was established in the Maritime Provinces, along the St. Lawrence and Great Lakes, and her subjects were scattered throughout the Indian country in the Mississippi Valley and in the Floridas. Britons, whether in Canada or the Bahamas, held similar views about the frontier, and their outlook was remarkably like Frontenac's. Looking at North America from the British rather than the American perspective, many events—retention of the forts in the Old Northwest, the Louisiana Purchase, disunionist movements associated with Burr and the Federalists, and British objectives in the War of 1812—sometimes take on a significance different from that generally assumed.

For many reasons there was no lasting Anglo-American accommodation before 1815, and loyalist exiles, who did not regard the verdict of Yorktown and the Paris peace treaty as final, were partly responsible. Their surprisingly resilient bitterness persevered for years in the Indian country, Canada, the Floridas, the Bahamas, Westminster, and Windsor. It is no fairer to ignore the numerous loyalists after the Revolution than to disregard their activities during that conflict. Many of them appear on the ensuing pages whom historians—perhaps wisely—have ignored. Individually they were not so important, but collectively they exercised a lingering pervasive influence. There was a continuous interplay between these loyalists and the British government. As a result the initiative for British policy originated sometimes in London and sometimes in America.

British statesmen after the French Revolution fervently agreed with Burke: republicanism endangered an ordered society, Christianity, and the best in western civilization. The international conflict between radical republicanism and Burke's philosophy frequently marred Anglo-American harmony and helps explain the action of British conservatives and American High Federalists alike. Conservative fear of change was genuine, though alarm may have been based as much on myth as on fact. Again and again Whitehall considered preempting the Mississippi Valley, denying it to French or American republican enthusiasts and isolating French Canadians against Jacobin contagion.

It is sometimes maintained that a common cultural heritage and reviving trade led to an Anglo-American reconciliation after the Revolution. Though cultural and commercial considerations are peripheral to the main thrust of this work, naturally they cannot be ignored in any comprehensive treatment of Anglo-American relations. But one should keep in mind that cultural ties and a thriving trade did not preclude bitterness, rivalry, and lack of unity. The most costly war the United States has ever fought (the Civil War) was between cultural brothers, and if one considers no more than reciprocal trade it is hard to explain Pearl Harbor. It is misleading to project twentieth-century Anglo-American harmony and the spirit of the Roosevelt-Churchill Atlantic Charter back into the decades following the Revolution.

Nineteenth-century nationalism of the Daniel Webster and Theodore Roosevelt stripe did not burn so brightly in the years immediately after the Revolution. Americans may have considered themselves the chosen people, but that did not prevent one elite republic from proliferating into several. And there was the paradox that, though liberty flourished in America after 1783, the policies of George III's allegedly despotic government seemed to many American Indians and Negroes more identified with liberty than measures adopted by the new United States.

Throughout the 1783–1815 period the British government was simultaneously pulled by a desire to reach an accommodation with former colonists and a willingness to ally with various red, white, and black Americans to constrict the boundaries of the new republic or to bring about its downfall. Far less has been written about Britain in this latter regard. Whether her involvement with disunionism was wise depends on one's point of view, but that she failed was of enormous consequence for the future of the United States.

Since this is a study of Britain's policy toward America, I have relied to a considerable extent on British, Canadian, and Bahamian sources. Most historians of the period have utilized American material along with such official correspondence as that of the British minister in the United States. But what the minister in the American capital proclaimed was Britain's official policy and what Charles Jenkinson, Lord Hawkesbury; William Wyndham Grenville; Henry Dundas, Lord Melville; and Robert Banks Jenkinson, the second earl of Liverpool (among the most influential statesmen in London) were up to frequently differed. Fortunately in recent times Bradford Perkins and Charles Ritcheson, among others, have ransacked British archives more diligently than heretofore and have deepened our understanding of British objectives. But for better or worse my findings in respect to the frontier frequently differ from theirs and from those of A. L. Burt who, though he did not use material in Britain, has made an important study of the period that scholars cannot ignore. Distortion of Britain's role in the Old Southwest is but one example of the dangers involved in not adequately using British sources.

Political labels are perplexing. The terms "Whig" and "Tory" were in use during and after the Revolution. At times organized parties existed in Britain: party labels had meaning in the early eighteenth century and again in the mid–nineteenth century. But during the confusing 1783–1815 period I have assumed that party labels made little sense and that one is less likely to be led astray by assuming parties did not exist. The younger Pitt, supposed founder of the second Tory Party, rarely referred to himself as either Whig or Tory, but when he did he counted himself a Whig. Similar distortions occur in America, because many branded as Tories during the Revolution in fact considered themselves Whigs.

Geography also creates problems. Nova Scotia and New Brunswick are sometimes treated as part of Canada in this work, though technically they were distinct royal colonies until well after 1815. There were two Floridas during the period under consideration, and, whatever their fluctuating boundaries, they did not conform to the limits of present day Florida. This study is about the frontier whose exact location at any given moment was hard to pin down. I do not treat the frontier in any Turnerian sense but merely employ this term to indicate areas contiguous to populous American settlements which the United States claimed (or coveted) but where her authority was weak or nonexistent. Territory involved might be in the United States, Spanish Florida, Spanish Louisiana, or British Canada.

I wish to acknowledge the assistance of many institutions and individuals: the staffs of the Library of Congress, the William L. Clements Library, the Henry E. Huntington Library, the New York Public Library, the Columbia University Library, the Florida State University Library, the Public Archives of Canada, the British Museum, the Public Record Office, Bodleian Library, the University of Nottingham Library, the National Maritime Museum, and the National Library of Scotland. I particularly wish to thank R. A. H. Smith of the British Museum for allowing me to use the Grenville Papers which were not arranged for general use by scholars. The Royal Archives at Windsor Castle were consulted through the gracious permission of Her Majesty the Queen. Sir John Johnson, sixth baronet of New York, furnished helpful information concerning his ancestors. Grants from the American Philosophical Society (Johnson Fund) and from Florida State University helped make possible travel in this country and abroad. Harriett Brown, Lynda Gotko, Kathleen Meffert, and Louise Barber carefully typed the manuscript and helped prepare the bibliography. Beth Wright's contribution is manifest throughout.

1 • A New Republic

"OH, GOD! It is all over!" exclaimed Frederick Lord North, pacing up and down and waving his arms.[1] And Cornwallis's surrender at York-town in October 1781 had repercussions on both sides of the Atlantic. Parliament condemned further offensive fighting in America, North's wartime ministry toppled, and the new administration headed by Lord Rockingham (and after his death, by Lord Shelburne) determined to conclude American hostilities, retaining the colonies in a loose federal union if possible, but granting independence if necessary. Britain, beset by rebellion within her empire and at war with major western European powers, made concessions to the Americans, including recognition of their independence. The American diplomats Benja-min Franklin, John Jay, and John Adams had reason to praise the 1783 definitive peace treaty which conceded unconditional independence, the Mississippi River as the western boundary, the Great Lakes as the Canadian boundary, and liberty to continue fishing off Newfound-land. In the Anglo-Spanish peace treaty concluded simultaneously, Britain ceded both Floridas to Spain.[2] The 1783 Paris peace treaties contrasted sharply with those of 1763 signed in the wake of Gen. James Wolfe's victory at Quebec. In 1763 Britain had won everything east of the Mississippi River except New Orleans; now she had lost all to the United States and Spain.

With the granting of independence to the thirteen colonies and the restricting of Britain to thinly populated Canada, 1783 has been called a pivotal date in the development of the British empire: she had lost the bulk of her American colonies, and her most valuable remaining possessions were in the East. Undoubtedly the Indian Ocean became the focus of the New Empire, but 1783 was not the precise date mark-ing the demise of the American empire and the rise of a new one in the East. It was after 1783 that Lord Cornwallis and his successors es-tablished British *raj* throughout the Indian subcontinent's interior; and even after 1783 Britain maintained influence in America.

There were two ways of considering Britain's North American role in 1783: one was to stress treaty provisions limiting her to Canada; the other to emphasize the reality of her American position. Since they differed, it is essential to examine the frontier at the end of the Revolution. The primary question was where or what was the American frontier. Members of the Confederation Congress answered this simply by citing peace treaties maintaining that the United States' frontier was Canada on the north, the Mississippi on the west, and the thirty-first parallel on the south. But at the end of 1783 one found almost no American citizens loyal to the new republic in Niagara, the Passamaquoddy Bay Islands, Detroit in the north, Natchez on the Mississippi, and along the thirty-first parallel.

The best way to assess the frontier is to determine where frontiersmen actually lived, and the Appalachian Mountains rather than the Mississippi is a better frame of reference. Though this mountain barrier had deterred Americans from going into the Ohio Valley before the end of the French and Indian War, hardy Americans began settling in the West at the war's end. Two decades later at the conclusion of the Revolution, they migrated through the Cumberland Gap or down the Ohio River by the thousands, astounding observers on both sides of the Atlantic. The population of the United States in 1783 was 2,389,000, of which about 56,000 persons were west of the mountains;[3] in 1790 the total population was 3,929,000 of which 221,000 inhabitants were in the West.[4] Despite an increase of some 165,000 during the 1780s and the founding or expansion of new towns—Marietta and Cincinnati on the Ohio River, Lexington in Kentucky, and Knoxville and Nashville in Tennessee—the fact remains that the West was enormous, some 422,000 square miles, and the population density was only .13 per square mile in 1783. American frontiersmen were not evenly distributed but concentrated on the upper Ohio, Tennessee, and Cumberland rivers. The most pronounced western characteristic in 1783 was that clusters of the fifty-odd thousand frontiersmen around raw, new towns were islands in the forest wilderness. They were closer to Detroit than Richmond, and the broad Mississippi and its tributaries afforded easy access to Spanish New Orleans.

Despite United States census records, the typical westerner at the end of the Revolution was red rather than white. The Indians—the Six Nations of the Iroquois Confederacy in the northeast, the Shawnees and assorted Algonquin tribes in the northwest, the Creeks and their Muskogean brethren in the south, numbering in all some 150,000[5]—with few exceptions had fought against the Americans during the Revolution and had been victorious as often as they had been defeated. They had not been represented in Paris during the 1782–83 peace negotiations where their lands had been reapportioned without their consent. United in a wartime confederation and having experienced no Yorktown, these Indians had their own notions about sovereignty. They controlled much of the West, both above and below the Ohio River, and British influence remained in native councils.

The Anglo-American treaty apparently defined the Canadian boundary from the Atlantic Ocean to the Great Lakes. But at the close of 1783 Canadians were settled on the coast at Passamaquoddy Bay and soon bickering with their republican neighbors about the precise location of Maine's northern boundary. This dispute involved not only coastal islands occupied by Canadians but thousands of square miles of largely uninhabited woodlands. Vermont, with a greater population, was of more immediate concern. Were the approximately 50,000 settlers living in the "New Hampshire Grants" subjects of New Hampshire, or of New York, which also claimed much of this area, or of the sovereign state of Vermont? To small farmers and wealthy land speculators alike, the issue of sovereignty was all important. Northern Vermont leaders (Ethan Allen, ebullient head of the Green Mountain Boys, brothers Ira and Levi, and semiliterate Gov. Thomas Chittenden) asserted that Vermont was independent, that neither New York nor New Hampshire had any claim, and that their title to extensive land holdings was valid. During the Revolution neither New York, New Hampshire, nor the Confederation Congress had recognized Vermont's existence. But the Allens realized that Britain would, and since 1778 they had intrigued to attach Vermont to Canada.[6] British influence was powerful if not paramount at the end of 1783 from the Passamaquoddy Bay Islands in Maine to northern Vermont, to upstate New York (where the British flag still flew at Oswego and Niagara), all of which the United States claimed.

At the end of the Revolution there was as much wrangling over the southern boundary as the northern. Superficially only the United States and Spain were involved. The United States maintained that

West Florida's northern boundary was the thirty-first parallel, while Spain asserted it was farther north: at least thirty-two degrees twenty-six minutes, or at certain points the Tennessee, Cumberland, or Ohio rivers. The Indians occupied most of this disputed area in the Old Southwest, and Spain, ensconced in Louisiana and West Florida and soon peacefully taking possession of East Florida as a result of the 1783 treaty, considered herself guardian of the southern Indians.

Trade was the key to controlling the Indians, and neither Spain nor her Bourbon ally France, was able to furnish the required guns, blankets, and hardware. During the Revolution, even though Spain seized West Florida, British merchants controlled the Indian trade of the Old Southwest. After the Revolution Spain had to rely on these same merchants. White and half-blooded British factors had resided in principal Indian villages for decades before the Revolution, and many of them remained, still wearing their British uniforms and dispensing British wares. These were exchanged for deerskins, which, with or without Spanish approval, were forwarded to British merchants in Pensacola, St. Augustine, or the Bahamas.

Observers examined the European peace treaties and got a fairly clear picture of the limits of the United States. But if one actually trekked through Maine and Vermont in the north, the boundless Indian country in the west, or along the Florida frontier at the end of 1783, he would be struck by the fact that British political and economic influence, though diminished, had not been extinguished. For many years before the American Revolution territorial disputes and questions of sovereignty pertaining to thinly populated areas had been settled not by litigation and reference to treaties but by effective occupation. The Revolution had not altered this.

During the unsettled 1782–83 period frontier issues confronted the British government. Most directly or indirectly concerned the loyalists. Those Americans who had opposed independence and with varying degrees of enthusiasm had supported Britain were a sizable minority. Numerical estimates varied. John Adams claimed they were one-third of the population.[7] A more recent and probably more accurate reckoning is that 20 percent of the whites were loyalists.[8] Even relying on the lower figure meant there were over a half-million loyalists. Many of these had remained passive and had weathered the Revolution relatively undisturbed. But the outspoken ones, who by word and deed had actively supported Britain, had suffered tar and feathers, imprisonment, confiscation of their lands, and vigilante justice from their neighbors. With the signing of the preliminary Anglo-American peace treaty in November 1782, some loyalists assumed the conflict was over and that they could return home. It was quickly apparent upon their return that this was not a good idea because some were hanged or tarred and feathered.

There were tens of thousands of loyalists who did not want to—and indeed could not—return home. Though many ultimately relocated in Quebec, Nova Scotia, and the West Indies, one of the more vexing tasks confronting the British government before the definitive treaty was signed was to find additional refuges. Ministers in the Rockingham and Shelburne administrations and in the Fox-North coalition invariably turned to the frontier where there was an abundance of fertile land and a relatively mild climate.[9]

The frontier was enormous, and Britain was more interested in some parts than in others, one of which was the Old Northwest, bounded by the Ohio on the south and the Mississippi on the west. Command of Detroit and other Great Lakes ports, a close alliance with the Indians who were led by British officers and supplied by British traders, and mounting dissatisfaction of French settlers at Kaskaskia and Vincennes with the Americans, gave Britain effective control over most of the Old Northwest after Yorktown, George Rogers Clark's victories notwithstanding.[10] Much has been made of Benjamin Franklin's suggestion at the Paris peace negotiations and of its fleeting support by Richard Oswald, the British representative, that Britain cede Canada to the United States as a goodwill measure.[11] But Oswald and his mentor, Lord Shelburne, quickly scrapped notions about relinquishing Canada and concentrated on keeping it, perhaps even with its 1774 boundaries extending to the Ohio River. According to George III the supposedly pro-American Shelburne in fact was beginning to trust the French more than the Americans.[12] Entreaties from fur traders and Indian allies were partially responsible during 1782–83 for Britain's considering retention of the Old Northwest or its establishment as a "neutral" buffer state.[13]

A more important reason was concern for the loyalists. As it became apparent that the Americans, despite ambiguous provisions in the preliminary peace treaty, were not going to allow pronounced loyalists to return home or to restore their property, British statesmen began to identify at least part of the Old Northwest as a loyalist refuge.[14] Shelburne's critics, with the loyalists in mind, denounced cession of "the fertile banks of the Ohio, the paradise of America."[15] Col. John Connolly and John F. D. Smyth were loyalists who had been roughly handled because in 1775 they had tried to unleash the western Indians on the rebels. Before and after signing the preliminary treaty they implored Shelburne to retain the Old Northwest.[16] Shelburne was sympathetic and urged the Americans to use the West for loyalist compensation.[17] Franklin, a heavy speculator in western lands who stood to benefit handsomely if Britain retained the Old Northwest, may have been more agreeable to this than his diplomatic dispatches suggested.[18] Eventually Britain relinquished the Old Northwest, not because she did not control most of it but because she had to make concessions in order to obtain peace.

Maine also was associated with the loyalists. Since at least 1778 Britain had regarded this thinly-settled province a likely spot to relocate refugees, and even after Cornwallis's defeat she actively worked to retain possession. Gen. Sir Guy Carleton (the future baron Dorchester) in the fall of 1782 began fortifications on the Penobscot River and expected to expand them. With the backing of George III but not Parliament, Carleton, after concentrating his troops in New York, may have planned to exert British might to secure a more favorable American settlement than the marquis of Rockingham's supporters expected to win at the conference table. British statesmen in Paris worked to extend Nova Scotia's boundary southward to the Kennebec, because Shelburne wanted almost all of Maine. But regardless of what happened in Paris, loyalists continued to settle in northern Maine with every intention of remaining. They were disappointed when they saw that the definitive peace treaty made the more northern Saint Croix the boundary and that Carleton had ceased work on the Penobscot fortifications. Some Maine loyalists moved again; others stayed, particularly on both sides of the Saint Croix and on the Passamaquoddy Bay Is-

lands. They still expected part of Maine (by United States definition) to remain a loyalist refuge.[19]

The loyalists figured prominently in Vermont. From the Revolution's outbreak there had been a sizable loyalist faction, and, after
the initial enthusiasm of Ethan Allen's seizure of Ticonderoga, Vermont had been conspicuous in the Revolution by its passivity. Her
cattle and foodstuffs helped sustain the British in Canada; before
Yorktown, Ethan and Ira Allen, while they were not busy bickering
with New York, New Hampshire, and Congress, found pretexts to
visit upper Lake Champlain, where they negotiated with Britain
about reestablishing royal authority.[20]

Arrangements for Vermont to take its place in the empire were
almost complete when news arrived of Cornwallis's surrender. After several months of hesitation and uncertainty while reviewing
the impact of the defeat in Virginia, both the Allens in Vermont
and, with less fervor, British authorities in Canada and London
again took up the project of attaching Vermont to Canada. Congress in the spring of 1782 once more refused to recognize Vermont, eliciting reports that New York and Vermont were on the
threshold of open warfare, that irate citizens at Walpole and neighboring Connecticut River towns had toasted George III, that Ethan
Allen had publicly declared for Britain, and that large and small
landowners were becoming convinced that only a British connection guaranteed their land titles and economic prosperity.[21] When
Ethan Allen in early summer told Gen. Frederick Haldimand, "I
shall do everything in my power to render this state a British province," the hero of Ticonderoga wanted nothing better than to see British troops again garrisoning that fortress.[22]

British reaction was mixed. Whitehall was cautious partly because each new home secretary was reluctant to make a snap decision. Also, each questioned whether annexing Vermont would en-
danger peace negotiations, even though arrangements could be
clothed in secrecy and verbal understandings and Vermont at first
would merely proclaim her neutrality.[23] But British officials in
America (Haldimand in Canada, Carleton in New York, and loyalists associated with them) who were remote from European peace
negotiations urged Vermont's reunion despite the risks.

No British minister during the 1782–83 period acceded to the Allens' petition, but not one dismissed it outright. Shelburne and his successors in a general way committed themselves to a Vermont connection.[24] Geographical considerations, the foodstuffs and ship masts readily available in Vermont, and pro-British sentiment in this province were compelling reasons for not turning down the request out of hand. After 1781 the loyalists became even more identified with Vermont. Ethan Allen urged them to settle in upper Vermont alongside the considerable number who were already there. He promised them lands on reasonable terms and relief from heavy taxes of neighboring states. Loyalist immigration strengthened the Allens' position, because neither the Allens nor the refugees held any affection for Congress.[25] The Allens, and such loyalists as Benedict Arnold and William Smith, wanted the refugees to resettle in Vermont proper or north of the forty-fifth parallel in Canada,[26] and Britain to retain Dutchman's Point and Pointe au Fer on upper Lake Champlain within Vermont. Lord North in the summer of 1783 refused to encourage Vermonters actively. But influential Britons advocated the opposite course, North would not be in office much longer,[27] and Vermonters and Canadians alike had reason to be optimistic about a closer connection.

Ministers also considered the Floridas and Louisiana. The Floridas, like Canada, had remained loyal during the Revolution, and from the beginning numerous refugees had arrived: West Florida's population had at least doubled; and East Florida's probably had quadrupled.[28] Though 1782 marked an unofficial cease-fire between the Americans and Britain, Anglo-Spanish hostility did not subside. They were at each other's throats in the Bay of Honduras. It was an open question how much Britain would aid the rebellious South American natives. The most dramatic phases of the Franco-Spanish siege of Gibraltar occurred after Yorktown. Spain prepared to take East Florida, while British subjects proposed a descent on West Florida and Louisiana. Spain had been in Louisiana for years and during the Revolution had seized the British colony of West Florida. Acquisition of Spanish territory on the Gulf of Mexico could take some of the sting out of Cornwallis's defeat.

Loyalists, after Yorktown looking on the Floridas and possibly

Louisiana as their future home, demanded an aggressive Gulf Coast campaign against the Spaniards. West Florida refugees—the governor, council members, Indian superintendents, and wealthy planters alike—forced by Spain to flee during 1779–81, bombarded the government with petitions urging such an expedition.[29]

East Florida, in contrast to West Florida, remained under British control throughout the Revolution, and loyalists resettled on the St. Marys and St. Johns rivers expected this province to remain their permanent home. Reports in the spring of 1783 about East Florida's possible cession to Spain provoked dumbfounded settlers to demand that Britain never relinquish Florida. Both Gov. Patrick Tonyn and John Cruden, a North Carolina loyalist now spokesman for St. Marys refugees, contended that it was unfair and unnecessary to give up East Florida.[30] Cruden, when he was not badgering the home government, petitioned Spain to allow the loyalists autonomy on the St. Marys, all the while laying the groundwork for a loyalist refuge in the environs of this river with or without the approval of Spain, Britain, or any other power.[31]

British diplomats—Shelburne and Thomas Townshend (the future viscount Sydney) at Whitehall and Richard Oswald, Benjamin Vaughan, and Henry Strachey in Paris—during 1782–83 pondered the merits of a campaign against West Florida and Louisiana and hoped to retain East Florida. Oswald, owning Florida acres, had a personal interest.[32] Loyalists could be accommodated in East Florida or resettled in West Florida and Louisiana with little expense to the Crown. When ministers in London or Cruden in Charleston looked for someone to lead an expedition against Spanish Gulf Coast possessions, they invariably turned to John Murray, the peppery earl of Dunmore. Because of Cornwallis's misfortune Dunmore had not resumed his Virginia governorship, and he stopped off in Charleston early in 1782 to consult with Cruden and Gen. Alexander Leslie about a Spanish campaign. A British Gulf Coast colony would benefit not only white loyalists but also black ones. Numbering many thousands in Carolina, slaves of loyalist masters and blacks recently liberated from their rebel owners could be armed to help recapture Louisiana and West Florida. Given land and their freedom if they did not already have it, armed black and white loyalists, Dunmore asserted, could hold Florida and Louisiana against Spain, the United States, or anybody. Dunmore hesitated no more then about arming blacks than in 1775 when he had deployed his Ethiopian Regiment in Virginia.[33]

British ministers assumed that, through force or negotiation, part or all of the Floridas and Louisiana would end up under British control, and Americans made the same assumption. John Jay and Benjamin Franklin realized that whoever acquired West Florida, it was not going to be the United States. Spain treated the Gulf of Mexico as a Spanish lake and refused Americans free navigation of the Mississippi. The Americans had no enthusiasm for seeing Dunmore and other Tories at the Mississippi's mouth, but if they conceded free navigation, as they indicated they would, then better British loyalists than Spaniards.[34] Military and diplomatic exigencies resulted in Spain's retaining West Florida and quietly taking possession of East Florida. But even after the signing of the 1783 peacy treaty, the dream of the Floridas and possibly Louisiana as loyalist asylums did not die: Cruden and his embittered followers remained on the St. Marys for many months; loyalists continued to come into West Florida even though now it belonged to Spain; British merchants, legally or not, still managed the southern fur trade; and, though Dunmore returned to Britain, the Floridas and Louisiana were foremost in his mind. Many others, from the humblest packhorse Indian trader, to uprooted loyalist small farmers, to British nobility claiming lands, shared Dunmore's views.

The numerous loyalists on the frontier were mainly concerned about acquiring farmland in return for that confiscated by the Americans. But prominent loyalists thought in grander terms than mere small farms. Land speculation was a vital part of Britain's entanglement in the frontier. One reason why ex-Governor Peter Chester of West Florida, Gov. Patrick Tonyn and Thomas Brown in East Florida, diplomats Townshend, Oswald, and Strachey in Europe were so interested in the Floridas during 1782–83 was the fact that they or their kinsmen owned extensive lands in these colonies.[35] At the end of the Revolution Oswald's overseer was working almost two hundred slaves on part of Oswald's forty thousand East Florida acres, and because of his losses here, Oswald counted himself a suffering Florida loyalist.[36] Dunmore, who according to his reckoning had lost almost four million acres elsewhere, expected to be partially reimbursed in the Floridas or Louisiana.[37] The main reason the Allen clique wanted to resettle loyalists in northern Vermont was to uphold land titles.

Ambitious speculators had divided and redivided virgin lands west of the mountains by overlapping claims. The proposed royal colony of Vandalia south of the Ohio River, lying largely in present-day Kentucky and West Virginia, was the most ambitious, and in 1783 distraught loyalist shareholders endeavored to retain their princely grant.[38] The best way was for the crown to retain title to the West in the peace treaties, or, if this were relinquished, to establish loyalists in Vandalia paving the way for ultimate restoration of royal authority. Loyalist shareholders of the Illinois–Wabash Company recognized the advantages of loyalists' settling in the Illinois country on their grant.[39] Indian agent and land speculator Alexander McKee had fled from Pittsburgh to Detroit abandoning thousands of western acres.[40] John Connolly, forced to relocate in Canada, claimed part of the new town at Lexington, Kentucky, and lands ranging from the Gulf of Mexico to Canada.[41] Family and in-laws of the late Sir William Johnson—his son Sir John Johnson, his nephew Guy Johnson, his son-in-law Daniel Claus, and others in the Johnson clan—had been forced to leave the Mohawk Valley and scatter along the Canadian frontier. The Johnsons, claiming lands in New York and the West,[42] along with others forced to relocate in Canada, the Bahamas, Britain, or among the western Indians, wanted to make good their claims to western lands by having the British flag eventually fly over the territory in question.

Land speculation and loyalist relocation were inseparable from the Indian question. Loyalists had been received literally with open arms by the Indians: Sir William Johnson's Mohawk Valley progeny was as often red as white; McKee's wife was a Shawnee; James Colbert in a real sense was father of the Chickasaw nation; and the wealthy Georgia Tory, Lachlan McGillivray, had a Creek wife and at least one mestizo son. Binding the loyalists and Indians together was their common bitterness toward the Americans. The loyalists detested the rebels because they had drawn their swords against

George III; the Indians resented the rebels because it was they who most conspicuously encroached on Indian lands. An Indian dream, going back years before the Revolution, was to play down tribal differences and create a confederation to contain the Americans. During the Revolution British Indian superintendents, Sir John Johnson at Niagara, Alexander McKee at Detroit, Thomas Brown in the Floridas, wanted the Indians to drive the Americans across the mountains while British regulars drubbed them in the East. In a vague way thinking Indians realized that their loyalist advisers probably were just as hungry for Indian lands as the rebels. But common rancor toward the Americans drew them together.

At the end of the Revolution the Indian dream of uniting the diverse tribes was as strong as ever. Though it is misleading to consider the Indians scattered in semiautonomous villages completely united at any time, there was remarkable cooperation and solidarity. In 1782 and 1783 hundreds of Cherokees and southern Indians came to Detroit and similar British posts where authorities handsomely entertained them and bestowed presents.[43] At the same time Brown put on a fireworks display to awe a large Shawnee-Iroquois delegation that arrived at St. Augustine.[44] Whether the fireworks or Brown's poll—rebels had scalped him three times—most impressed the Indians is not recorded. When the Cherokees, Shawnees, Mohawks, and Creeks ranged throughout the West, it is safe to assume that as they passed through the scattered villages and spoke in council squares, they urged unity.

Yorktown led to a vague Anglo-American cease fire, and in the two-year interval before signing the definitive treaty, Britain attempted to limit hostilities not only on the Atlantic Seaboard but also in the West. But not a single Indian had surrendered at Yorktown; no Indian representative was at the Paris peace conferences; more united than ever, they regarded themselves as independent and in no wise bound by European treaties. The Indians upon occasion had been defeated: the Cherokees and the Delawares among others had received hard wartime knocks.[45] But on the whole the Indians had inflicted as much damage as they had sustained, a point not disputed by Kentucky survivors of the Battle of Blue Licks, by Col. William Crawford, captured near the Sandusky River and burned at the stake, or by Daniel Boone who had not come to Detroit in 1778 as a tourist.[46]

Though the British government in 1782 committed itself to defensive operations against the Americans, it was not possible for ministers to snap their fingers and quiet the frontier. The Indians had the final say-so. When Whitehall urged the Indians to follow the redcoats' example and remain on the defensive, its counsel might have been followed if the Americans had reciprocated. Though Washington reduced hostilities in the East to a minimum, the same did not apply to the frontier.

According to the Americans, the Indians were not British subjects but wards of the United States living on American soil. If there had been confusion about this during the Revolution, both the preliminary and definitive treaties reaffirmed the United States' position, clearly marking the Mississippi as the western boundary.[47] The Indians in 1783 insisted their boundary was not the Mississippi but was delineated by assorted pre-Revolutionary treaties. The 1768 Treaty of Fort Stanwix had fixed the Ohio as the boundary for the northern Indians while the 1773 Treaty of Augusta had established the upper Ogeechee as the Creek boundary in the south.[48] If the Americans respected these and similar pre-Revolutionary treaties, there could be peace; if the Americans did not recognize these boundaries—and they most emphatically did not—then no conciliatory Whitehall policy would be reflected in Indian councils.

Dismayed Britons at the end of the Revolution assumed that their North American empire had almost disappeared. Most of them resolved to abide by the unpopular peace treaties, and it appeared that Britain no longer had to concern herself about managing affairs on the frontier. But in 1783 it was risky to speculate about any fixed policy because of the constant making and unmaking of ministries. There were five during 1782–83, and in December 1783 many wagered with Charles James Fox that William Pitt's new administration would not last a week.[49]

While the Union Jack flew over Detroit, Niagara, St. Augustine, and numerous lesser frontier posts, Britain, willingly or not, was involved in frontier affairs. At the end of 1783 she still traded with and gave presents to the Indians throughout the West, partly to reward them for wartime services, partly to enable them to defend their lands, and especially to retain their goodwill. Alienating the Indians would jeopardize the lives of thousands of British subjects from Canada to Florida. Abruptly withdrawing support would substantiate opposition charges that Britain had shamefully abandoned her wartime allies both above and below the Ohio.[50]

Neither Canadian nor Florida governors could figure out Britain's Indian policy in 1783. Whitehall sent out confusing orders: withdraw traders from the interior, but continue to dispense presents liberally; bind the Indians firmly to the king's interest, but insure that they are at peace with the Americans.[51] Canadian and Floridian authorities raised disturbing questions such as exactly what Britain should do if Georgians occupied the Oconee lands[52] or American frontiersmen settled north of the Ohio,[53] but got no answers.

While Britain had posts on the American frontier from Canada to Florida and traded with and gave presents to the Indians, those in authority in London had to contend with frontier issues. Besides the Indians there were loyalists, humble farmers, wealthy planters, Indian traders, and land speculators stretched out along the frontier from the St. Marys to the Saint Croix. Britain in 1783 did not or could not ignore the condition of these displaced refugees. It was meaningless to speak of any fixed British policy. Only time would tell whether she could disentangle herself or whether forces over which she had little control would make events on the Ohio, the Mississippi, the Onion River in Vermont, and the Chattahoochee in Georgia still of import at Whitehall.

2 • British Indecision

AMID lavish dinners and the exchange of compliments and gifts, diplomats representing Britain, France, the United States, Spain, and Holland signed the various peace treaties in September 1783. The key provision of the Anglo-American treaty stipulated that the colonies were independent. After signing the definitive treaty, and in some cases sooner, British troops began withdrawing from Charleston, Savannah, and New York. George III might have smiled when he heard reports of how departing redcoats greased New York City's flagpole just before Washington's soldiers tried to take down the Union Jack and raise Old Glory; but by the fall of 1783 there was no doubt in the king's mind that British troops had to withdraw and that Old Glory was to wave over this city.[1]

The king did not formally ratify the Anglo-American treaty until April 9, 1784, some seven months later.[2] Delay was due more to poor communications than royal petulance. The Americans, because of difficulties in assembling sufficient delegates in Congress and because the port of New York froze over, were to blame. After many months the ratified American treaty arrived in Europe; George III, who previously may have considered flouting Parliament's will, now accepted independence and promptly signed his copy. Then the two parties exchanged ratified treaties in Paris.[3] Until George III ratified the Anglo-American treaty and both signed copies were exchanged, Britain was not legally bound. Though she waived technicalities and demonstrated her good faith by evacuating New York and other seaboard ports, in a narrow sense her troops did not have to leave these eastern ports or the West. During the winter of 1783–84 no British soldier at Oswego, Detroit, or Michilimackinac dared grease the flagpole because the Union Jack was regularly raised, and though the ceremony was not appreciated by the Americans, it was perfectly legal.

British politics were erratic during that winter, and if the government had a frontier policy it was to abide by the treaty as interpreted by Britons rather than Americans. Because of the delay in ratification and the treaty's vague phrasing, ministers assumed Britain had months to withdraw all forces from the northern forts. The Americans themselves as late as August 1783 were on the verge of agreeing in principle that redcoats had to evacuate coastal ports within three months but could take up to three years to leave the frontier forts.[4] It was natural that British statesmen did not much bother themselves about the frontier: the treaty constricted Canada's boundaries; this province was thinly inhabited, over half of its population French, and it was a financial drain. Furthermore, in the southeast Florida was to be given up.

When ministers grappled with fundamental policies toward America they usually were concerned with the seaboard where Americans were rather than the frontier where, with few exceptions, they were not. The chief controversy was whether to relax the navigation acts and grant the United States commercial concessions. This was an important issue affecting British economic prosperity and the well-being of her navy and merchant marine, but ministers who dealt with colonial matters immediately after the Revolution looked even more to the Orient than North America. Heated debates over Fox's India Bill in 1783 and Pitt's alternate bill the following year were in the limelight.[5]

Though eyes turned eastward and Britain's shrunken North American empire seemed of little consideration, Britain during the winter of 1783–84 occupied the northern posts. Her flag flew at St. Augustine. All along the frontier the Indians still looked to the British, and Vermonters continued to petition for a close connection or outright union. The government had to deal with these matters, though apparently ministers could dispose of them quickly.

Because of the political confusion in London, it is desirable to digress briefly and take a closer look at the nature of postwar British politics. Yorktown and the ensuing peace treaties had created havoc. Frederick Lord North's administration, identified with the views of George III and a harsh policy toward the rebellious colonies, had fallen and had been replaced first by the marquis of Rockingham's ministry and then by several others in rapid succession. From North's downfall in March 1782 until the relative stability of the Pitt administration in 1784 political chaos reigned.

Whether the views of the earl of Shelburne, the marquis of Rockingham, Charles James Fox, Lord North, or William Pitt were decisive,
whether department heads independently contrived policies without reference to the prime minister, or whether George III, despite
Yorktown's shockwaves, continued to exert a powerful, if not a
dominant influence on major decisions are fundamental considerations.

Edmund Burke and critics of Lord North and the "king's
friends" had charged that a dissolute ministry, corrupted by secret
service money and sinecures, had caused a disastrous war and loss
of the thirteen colonies. After North's downfall his successors had
dissolved the office of secretary of state for the colonies and the
Board of Trade. With the colonies independent these govern-
mental branches were not so necessary, and abolition reduced
patronage and sinecures. The secretary of state for home affairs
assumed supervision of the remaining colonies in March 1782, and
two years later an unpaid, apparently temporary Committee of
Council appointed for the Consideration of All Matters Relating to
Trade and Foreign Plantations was created to assist him. This body,
reconstituted as the Committee of Council for Trade in 1786, pop-
ularly styled the Board of Trade, assumed most functions of the
pre-Revolutionary Board of Trade, and in 1791 its head officially
became a member of the cabinet.[6] After the Revolution the home
secretary and those in the new Board of Trade by virtue of their
offices were the ones who most concerned themselves with overall
colonial policy as well as administrative details.

The nature of the relationship between the home secretary and
the prime minister was not easy to perceive, and one is never sure
whether Home Secretary Thomas Townshend, viscount Sydney's
dispatches to colonial officials after the Revolution contained his
independent ideas or merely reflected the views of William Pitt,
the cabinet, or the king. It is misleading to think of the prime minister, the cabinet, and ministerial solidarity in twentieth-century
terms. Though a mediocre minister, Sydney (and other ministers as
well) often acted as if his department were semiautonomous and he
did not have to bow to the wishes of the prime minister. After the
Revolution the king, the prime minister, and the secretaries of state

still shared political power, and government by departments had not ceased with North's retirement.

Sydney, Charles Jenkinson (created Baron Hawkesbury in 1786), and those at the Board of Trade were responsible to both George III and Pitt. Despite the debacle of the American Revolution and North's downfall, the strong-willed George III was no figurehead. He had threatened to defy Parliament in 1782 and precipitate a constitutional crisis, and he only gradually lost power in the post-Revolutionary years.[7] The king, because of royal patronage and his role in military and diplomatic concerns, still wielded authority in colonial matters. Members of the royal family, notably the king's favorite brother, the Duke of Gloucester, and two of his sons, the Dukes of Kent and York, all holding positions of trust in the army or close friends of those who did, displayed interest in the American frontier. At any given moment after 1783 at least one of them was on speaking terms with the king and in a position to advise him without reference to Pitt. Jenkinson, who eventually headed the new Board of Trade and joined the ministry, had been leader of the "king's friends" in Parliament during the Revolution. An effective administrator, influential and ambitious, Jenkinson, better known as Lord Hawkesbury, was still the king's man, not Pitt's. Upon occasion Jenkinson and Sydney recommended and implemented colonial policies which ran counter to Pitt's views—but not to those of George III.

Parliament, having burned its fingers with the Stamp Act, the Tea Act, and similar legislation, was less inclined after the Revolution to meddle in American colonial affairs, thereby strengthening the king's hand and that of individual ministers. That Parliament remained relatively passive after the Revolution concerning American problems, that the younger Pitt did not have the same passion for colonial matters as his father, and that there was no ministerial solidarity made the roles of the home secretary, the reconstructed Board of Trade, and George III most influential.[8] So far it has been assumed that colonial policy was always conceived in London. But at times doubt existed whether courtly statesmen in Britain or discontented loyalists, alienated United States political and military leaders, illiterate frontiersmen, and royal governors in America were forging British policy.

After the Revolution a select group in Britain, pondering the United States' role in the new order, reflected not only on the populated East and the commercial treaty but also on the frontier. Many of them had detailed knowledge making them as outstanding after the Revolution as before. Numbered in this group were ministers or subministers: Home Secretary Sydney, and Lord Hawkesbury and Henry Dundas at the Board of Trade. Certain Parliament members regarded themselves as frontier experts: George Johnstone, West Florida's contentious ex-governor, knew that most of both Floridas had changed little from De Soto's day; Gov. John Murray, fourth earl of Dunmore was a veteran of the campaign against the Shawnees; John Burgoyne and Henry Clinton were among a half dozen officers who had served in America. Gov. Sir Frederick Haldimand and his successor, Sir Guy Carleton, Lord Dorchester, in Canada and Gov. John Maxwell and his successors in the Bahamas, along with their advisors, were usually versed in frontier matters. Loyalist George Chalmers who had been run out of Baltimore in 1775 and subsequently had become chief clerk of the Board of Trade and an eminent antiquarian, William Smith, a New York exile who became chief justice of Quebec and Dorchester's closest advisor, and the former West Florida merchant, John Miller, a member of the Bahamian council, were typical of those who pressured Whitehall not to ignore the American frontier.

They were a minority and though vocal enough were not heard above the clamor over Carlo Khan's (Fox's) bill to reorganize the government of India or diatribes against young Pitt when he became prime minister. After the Revolution few British ministers saw any need for a comprehensive frontier policy, and most interested themselves in specific, short-term exigencies stemming from evacuation. Time was necessary before the voices of Hawkesbury, Dundas, Dorchester, Dunmore, and the loyalists were heard and before Whitehall recognized that the disparate frontier problems were connected and an overall policy was necessary.

Immediately after the Revolution no issue was more complex

than that of the frontier posts stretching from Michilimackinac and Detroit in the west to Niagara, Oswego, and Dutchman's Point farther east. Their function was to guard the St. Lawrence–Great Lakes waterway vital for Canadian commerce and security. Shelburne and Richard Oswald had ceded the Old Northwest, fixed a new boundary, and neither doubted that most posts were south of the line. Though Shelburne and Oswald may not have recognized the implications of their cession, the real question was why, since both Britain and the United States agreed these posts were on American soil, did it take thirteen years for Britain to evacuate them?

Allegedly Britain succumbed to entreaties from Canadian fur traders and other interested parties.[9] When Gen. Friedrich von Steuben in the summer of 1783, citing the preliminary treaty, asked about handing over Detroit and the other forts, Canadian authorities politely but firmly refused.[10] The Americans charged that Gen. Sir Frederick Haldimand, the Canadian governor, had determined to flout the treaty. But the methodical Swiss-born professional soldier was telling the truth when he said he had not yet received Britain's ratification of the definitive treaty or specific orders to evacuate and therefore could not relinquish the posts. Even if the preliminary treaty's wording were retained, it was specified that the posts would be turned over "with all convenient speed."[11] Haldimand made an excellent case for temporarily retaining the disputed posts.

But what is important is that Haldimand's refusal to hand over the posts in the summer of 1783 did not represent a British decision to retain them indefinitely. Such a decision had to be made in London, not Quebec. Early in 1783 Thomas Townshend (Lord Sydney) informed Haldimand that he was studying the sensitive issue of the upper country forts and that he would send appropriate instruction in his next dispatch. Townshend left little doubt that these instructions would enjoin Haldimand to withdraw from posts on United States soil. Within little over a month Townshend was out of office, and no orders were sent.[12] In the late summer George III, more or less reconciled to American independence, maintained that the Canadian boundary line was well drawn.[13]

Early in December North promised to transmit definite instructions for evacuating the forts.[14] Before the month was out North resigned and he, like Townshend, never wrote his dispatch. The general feeling in Whitehall in 1783—which was Haldimand's view also —was that the posts would be turned over to the Americans in the near future.

The Americans were impatient: British forces had departed Charleston and Savannah in 1782 and had begun evacuating New York before September 1783, giving proof that Britain recognized American independence. Since Britain was withdrawing from eastern ports, it seemed only natural for Washington to ask about the posts' delivery. But Haldimand refused to stipulate precisely how and when they would be handed over.[15] The governor parried Washington's request in the summer of 1783 for the obvious reason that he had not seen the definitive treaty—it had not even been signed—and he had doubts about on which side of the boundary some of these posts were located.[16] This is not to say that he had not seen the preliminary treaty, that he did not know about the proposed boundary and the Old Northwest's cession, and that he was not furious or had not tried to obtain modifications. Foremost in his mind was whether his protests to Shelburne and North would have any effect.[17] Better than anyone he recognized the impact that withdrawal would have on Canadian security, the fur trade, Indian relations, and on the loyalists who were continuing to arrive. If Britain had not promptly made preparations to turn over New York it indicated she was duping the Americans and expected to continue the war. New York was near the heart of the new nation with thousands of its citizens in or outside the city anxiously awaiting British departure. The Canadian posts, in contrast, were isolated, and the inhabitants in their vicinity were Indians, redcoats, and loyalists. There was no determined patriot citizenry in Detroit, Niagara, and Oswego resolved to see the Union Jack lowered.

Haldimand hoped that the definitive treaty "will be more satisfactory to us here than the preliminaries."[18] Washington, however, wondered why Britain, who was preparing to hand over New York, was not making similar arrangements for the northern forts. Neither Washington nor any American patriot wanted the preliminary treaty modified, because, as interpreted by Americans, it could hardly have been more favorable.

During the winter of 1783–84 British troops remained at the northern posts as the loyalist population mounted. Until official notice of the definitive peace treaty or direct orders to evacuate, Haldimand knew he had to retain possession. The treaty was not ratified by George III until 1784, and, because of ministerial confusion, Haldimand had received no previous orders to evacuate. And orders or not, the Great Lakes–St. Lawrence system froze over in winter, rendering immediate evacuation difficult if not impossible.

He wanted to occupy the forts indefinitely, but reports indicated that there would be no boundary adjustment in the final treaty, and that, as stipulated, they must be turned over. One might quibble about exactly how long Britain had, but Haldimand, studying United States newspapers and receiving no encouraging word from England, assumed that soon he would have to withdraw.[19] While evading American inquiries about a fixed date for transfer, the Canadian governor ordered the commanders at Detroit, Niagara, and Michilimackinac to pick out appropriate sites across the boundary for relocation.[20] As the Americans during the winter of 1783–84 continued to pester the Canadian governor about a precise date for transfer, Haldimand, snug in the Chateau St. Louis at Quebec, impatiently waited for the St. Lawrence River ice to break up and instructions from Whitehall.

The long awaited mail packet arrived in June, and the elated Haldimand saw that, contrary to his expectations, the new home secretary, Lord Sydney, had liberally interpreted "with all convenient speed."[21] Sydney had written this dispatch on April 8 the day before George III ratified the treaty, and critics have charged that the king and his ministers decided to violate the treaty just before ratifying it.[22] To interpret this dispatch properly, however, it is necessary to consider British politics, ministerial changeovers, and the machinations of pressure groups, and to keep in mind the remoteness of the posts and the time it took to assemble accurate information in London.

As Haldimand had watched the St. Lawrence freeze over during the 1783–84 winter, political turmoil prevailed in London. The Fox-

North coalition fell in December 1783, and the youthful Pitt, not commanding a majority in the Commons but with George III's backing and the independent-minded Sydney as home secretary, tried to fashion a new administration. The Canadian forts were no more the foremost problem for Sydney than they had been for North. Had North remained in power he would have ordered Haldimand to evacuate immediately—which is exactly what Haldimand expected Sydney's dispatch to say.[23] But Sydney was vague: do not hand over the posts immediately but with "all convenient speed," which might mean 1785, 1786, or who knew when.

Sydney differed from his predecessor North; and there is every indication that the ideas in Sydney's April dispatch reflected his thinking and initiative as opposed to Pitt's or George III's. The new home secretary granted Haldimand time for a number of reasons. One was the protests of the British and French Canadian fur traders. Petitioning a succession of ministers in London for at least temporary retention of the forts, these merchants by the winter of 1783–84 were a better organized pressure group, their arguments were more specific and better reasoned, and they influenced Sydney.[24]

But Sydney was no novice in colonial affairs: he had been in the Rockingham and Shelburne ministries as secretary at war and home secretary and had helped negotiate the peace treaties and establish the Canadian boundary. Over the years Shelburne had amassed an enormous amount of data concerning the colonies and their commerce, and one point that had emerged during his 1782–83 administration was that, though the Old Northwest's fur trade was valuable, it was not worth enough to underwrite the expense of garrisoning the forts.[25] Sydney was as aware of this in 1784 as he had been when he served under Shelburne.

Profits from the fur trade were not to be scoffed at. The key issue, however, was whether Britain in 1784 should, in effect, subsidize the Canadian fur traders by retaining the posts, when at the same time this might embroil her in further troubles with the United States. Sydney listened to the Canadian fur traders' remonstrances, but their protests were not why he ordered Haldimand to delay. The Canadian governor was on the verge of relocating these posts on the Canadian side of the boundary, and they could in 1784, as they later did after the 1794 Jay Treaty, help protect the fur trader's interests on the American side of the line.[26]

The Indians, who almost without exception did the hunting and trapping, were entangled with the fur trade and the posts' disposition. It was dangerous both in Canada and in Florida to shower the Indians with munitions and presents, "to take them by the hand," to insist that George III's loyal subjects would fight shoulder to shoulder with them against the Americans, and then abruptly desert them. This had something to do with British honor, a matter of more concern to Indian agents and soldiers directly associated with the natives than to Whitehall. More to the point was the security of British subjects who must bear the brunt of native hostility should Britain leave them in the lurch. Another consideration—not as important in 1784 as during the peace negotiations—was the Mississippi Valley's fate. Though legally Britain was to withdraw, conditions might suddenly change. Evacuating the forts without providing for the Indians would alienate them, a foolish policy if Britain expected to employ the natives again.

Most of the Six Nations in the Mohawk Valley had sided with Britain during the war, though Tuscaroras and Oneidas had aided the Americans.[27] At the Revolution's end many of the Mohawks and a lesser number of the other Iroquois tribes under the leadership of Joseph Brant moved to the Grand River north of Lake Erie in Canada. Warriors from the Six Nations, Britain's most dependable and effective allies during the war, were confused and dismayed by the peace. Indian superintendents ordered them to remain on the defensive. But they "said nothing about taking away [our] axes";[28] would the Indians continue to get British aid or "intirely non?"[29] Canadian authorities urged delay in evacuating the posts to give the Indians time to adjust to their new situation and enjoy the "sweets of the King's protection."[30] Sydney wrestled with the problem of the Six Nations and the other tribes and weighed the effect of an abrupt withdrawal not only on British subjects but also on Americans. As he remarked to Haldimand, the Americans should appreciate temporary British retention because it gave them time to make peace with the natives.[31] This was the ministerial logic that had led to Lexington and Concord.

It is impossible to measure every consideration that motivated

Sydney's ordering a delay. Though the Indian problem and the fur trade influenced his decision, they were not the most important factors. He enjoined Haldimand not to hand over the posts primarily because he claimed the Americans had not honored a single provision in the peace treaty.[32] Though they were an exaggeration, there was truth in his charges. A year or two later Britain linked the fort's retention with American nonpayment of pre-Revolutionary debts, but Sydney was not so concerned about debts in 1784. Not enough time had elapsed for an overall pattern to emerge of Americans' not paying their prewar obligations.

But loyalist persecution represented an immediate treaty violation. Franklin, warning that Americans were not likely to "receive again into our Bosoms those who have been our bitterest enemies," was right.[33] Their lands were not restored and some states still confiscated them. Newly formed associations prevented loyalists from returning home; those venturous ones who did were mistreated, tarred and feathered, even killed.[34] Sydney, a participant in the peace negotiations, knew that the provision stating that Congress would "earnestly recommend" to the states that they restore loyalists' property and cease persecuting them was a face-saving phrase. He therefore realized that when the individual states did not restore loyalist property, technically it was not a treaty violation. But British defenders of the unpopular treaty had insisted that "it would be injurious to the honour of a rising" republic if it did not deal fairly with the loyalists.[35] Though the respective states were not perturbed by slurs on their honor, British subjects resented American actions and regarded them as a violation of the spirit, if not the letter, of the treaty.

The whole question of the loyalists was a sensitive, emotional one, identified with British, if not American, honor. Loyalists, along with merchants and members of Parliament who championed their cause, cited instances of how the Americans continued to persecute loyalists. In a restrictive sense the treaty did not go into effect until after ratification, but Britain had evacuated the seaboard ports before ratification and expected the United States to reciprocate by at least not physically harming the loyalists. Though there were treaty violations enough on both sides, from Sydney's standpoint it was a large issue that the loyalists still were being persecuted. The Commons and public generally sympathized with their sufferings in behalf of the mother country, and if retention of the forts could be used as a lever in behalf of the loyalists, so much the better. The Americans strictly interpreted the treaty in "earnestly recommending" favorable treatment for the loyalists; Britain, in turn, strictly construed evacuating the forts "with all convenient speed." One narrow construction deserved another and to a considerable degree one depended on the other.

It was a paradox, one of many stemming from the Revolution, that Lord North, identified with George III and harsh treatment of the rebels, was for quickly evacuating the forts; while Sydney, a critic of wartime policy, ordered Haldimand to delay. But it is incorrect to infer that just because Sydney ordered the posts' retention, this represented a decision to keep them permanently. Since he had not made up his mind in 1785 about the posts' ultimate fate, it is unlikely he had in 1784.[36] A London newspaper, observing in 1785 that Haldimand's conduct in regard to the posts "has . . . been in some measure approved by ministers,"[37] accurately reflected the confusion, because neither Haldimand, the Americans, nor Sydney himself knew what Britain's long-range policy was. Sydney in April 1784, ordering delay, was buying time, not laying out broad policy; in fact, his thinking about the posts was not radically different from North's. Among other things this delay was a good example of the cumbersomeness of the eighteenth-century British empire, of the difficulty of communications over thousands of miles, and of the time-consuming process of collecting reliable information and acting on it.

Difficulties in evacuating Florida were similar to those along the Canadian border. During and immediately after the Revolution loyalists had migrated to both provinces. In Canada they solicited a delay in handing over the forts; in East Florida they petitioned for a reprieve in delivering this province to Spain. In both colonies there was delay: Spain formally took possession at St. Augustine in June 1784, but it was not until November 1785 that Gov. Patrick Tonyn with the remaining loyalists sailed away.[38] The Indian problem was common to both provinces. Florida merchants, like their

Canadian counterparts, tried to find ways whereby they could still superintend the trade of the Old Southwest; Floridians, like Canadians, were concerned with retaining Indian goodwill, because even after the final evacuation in 1785 there were loyalists in Florida who must suffer if the natives turned against them.[39]

An additional reason to court Indian friendship was the possibility that Britain might recover part or all of the Floridas. Spain more than anything wanted the towering fortress of Gibraltar, bound to the Spanish peninsula by a narrow strip, and during the war and at the conference table had tried unsuccessfully to get it. Spain, still hoping to acquire Gibraltar after 1783, willingly would have swapped Britain part or all of the Floridas and more for this prize.[40] There was a group in Britain—and George III was a member[41]—which still advocated this exchange after 1783. Gibraltar did not have the same significance that it later acquired after the opening of the Suez Canal. For years after the Revolution there were half-hearted, unsuccessful negotiations whereby Britain might end up with at least part of Florida.

If John Cruden, "President of the British American loyalists" in East Florida, had had his way, there would have been no massive evacuation. For two years after the Revolution he remained on the St. Marys River hoping to postpone the exodus: "Rather than accept any of the alternatives in our choice, we will die with our swords in our hands, for we are almost driven to despair."[42] Neither Britain nor Spain supported any of Cruden's proposals, and by the end of 1785 a majority of the loyalists, including Cruden himself, had left for the Bahamas or elsewhere.[43]

But a considerable group, numbering in the hundreds, remained in the vicinity of the St. Marys River on the border of Florida and Georgia. Nominally they became Spanish or United States citizens, but Amelia Island in Florida and Camden County in Georgia were remote from population centers and political authority. When loyalists remained around the St. Marys River, in a vague fashion one of Cruden's schemes was realized. They did not pay much attention to decrees from Augusta or St. Augustine; some owned land on both sides of the boundary and claimed Georgia or Spanish citizenship as suited their convenience. To the annoyance of established authorities, they came uncomfortably close to forming an autonomous loyalist community.[44]

Some Britons suggested delaying East Florida's evacuation because this province was bound up with a larger issue: the fate of Spanish America. There had just been one successful colonial revolt against a mother country (Britain), and during this Revolution British subjects, along with Spanish Creoles and Spanish American Indians, had advocated a second American revolution against Spain.[45] The revolutionary Venezuelan Creole, Francisco de Miranda, visited the British West Indies during the latter stages of the Revolution and the North American mainland in 1783–84 where he mingled with British officers and loyalists, secured a letter of introduction to Haldimand in Canada (whom for some reason he did not visit), and eventually made his way to London. Miranda also hoped to win the support of Alexander Hamilton and Henry Knox.[46] Both Americans and Britons were interested, though for different reasons.

Dunmore, urging a loyalist settlement in the Floridas and Louisiana, associated relocating loyalists in the Floridas with Spanish American rebellion, which in fact had recently broken out in Peru and elsewhere.[47] Sitting in the House of Lords after 1783 he, like his colleagues, had not forgotten either the Floridas or Spanish America. Despite British encouragement of Spanish American revolution, nothing came of it, and East Florida's evacuation continued uninterrupted. But in 1783 as in 1815 or at any intervening period the prospect of a Spanish American revolt and of its effect on the Floridas and on the British who, legally or not, lived in clusters around the St. Marys, Tombigbee, and Tensaw rivers, at Natchez, and in the Indian country, was something that intrigued and not infrequently embarrassed Whitehall.

The Indians might become unmanageable when the redcoats began to withdraw. British subjects who had been in Detroit when Pontiac besieged it in 1763 appreciated the danger. Southern Indians also posed a threat. Thomas Brown went out of his way to entertain them, ply them with presents and rum, insist with incomprehensible logic that Britain would ever "hold them fast by the hand," all the while recognizing that the Indians regaled within

St. Augustine's walls were hostages for British subjects deep in the Indian country.[48]

Trade was at the heart of the relationship between Britain and the natives. Superintendents at Detroit, Michilimackinac, and Niagara continued dispensing supplies on a lavish scale after the Revolution to reassure the Indians and to gain time for a new arrangement, whatever that might be. The commerce of private merchants complemented presents distributed through the Indian department. Manufactures, obtained gratis or in trade, were indispensable to the Indians. The Ohio River roughly divided the Old West, and Canadian merchants and agents usually supplied the natives above this river while their counterparts in Spanish Florida supplied those Indians to the south. Merchants resolved to remain in the Indian country as long as possible.

The forts' retention, even if temporary, was a favorable sign and reinforced the traders' determination to stay in much of the Old Northwest.[49] There was a similar pattern south of the Ohio. British merchants who had been in the Indian country during the Revolution remained. Here Panton, Leslie, and Company stands out. Fleeing from South Carolina and Georgia to East Florida during the Revolution, employees of this firm continued trading with the southern Indians. The incoming Spaniards no less than the British were concerned with the trade's status. The Indians must traffic with some whites; the question was with whom? Spain, unable to furnish the required goods herself, subsequently failed in making a satisfactory arrangement with her French Bourbon ally.[50]

When Panton, Leslie, and Company proposed that it remain in Florida and receive a trade monopoly to manage the Indians in Spain's behalf, Spain had little choice but to accept. William Panton threatened that, unless Spain agreed, he would return to the United States and conduct the trade for them, though it is doubtful whether Georgia or South Carolina would have welcomed "with open arms" these or any Scottish loyalists.[51] Spain, realizing that this firm might manage the trade "for their own benefit and not for ours,"[52] needed Panton as badly as Panton needed Spain. He remained in East Florida and in time established warehouses at St.

Marks, Pensacola, Mobile and on the Mississippi, from which he conducted the trade of the Old Southwest. This firm's main competition came from other loyalist merchants based in the Bahamas (where Panton also had a warehouse) who wanted a share of the southern Indian trade.[53]

Britain's direct political influence on the frontier had diminished after 1783, but as a result of her industrial and commercial superiority, there was no appreciable economic change. The same white or Indian factors of British merchant firms continued trade in the usual fashion, apparently unaffected by recent European treaties. Even after 1783 British Indian agents remained. Those in the south (Alexander McGillivray among the upper Creeks, James Durouzeaux among the Lower Creeks, John McDonald among the Cherokees, James Colbert's sons among the Chickasaws, and many more) no longer were paid by Britain or had commissions but retained considerable prestige.[54] To the north Britain continued her Indian department on a reduced basis. Some employees were in Canada proper; others, such as Alexander McKee and Simon Girty in the vicinity of Detroit or Sir John Johnson and John Butler around Montreal and Niagara, frequently intruded on American soil.[55]

Both Spain and the United States worried about the presence of British merchants and Indian agents in the Indian country. As the British began leaving East Florida Governor Tonyn remarked that the neighboring Indians retained "Deeply rooted, an unextinguishable ardent love . . . to the British name, which may rise into a flame and be improved to advantage"[56]—an observation that applied to almost any tribe on the frontier. Spain and the United States understood this and knew that whoever managed the Indian trade guided the natives' political destinies.

Indian hostility toward Americans permitted British merchants and agents to remain unmolested. The natives, as they listened to reports of how Britain had ceded the Old Northwest and watched Brown prepare to sail away to the Bahamas, first distrusted Britain and felt she had deserted them. But resentment dissipated because the British did not completely withdraw from the Indian country, nor did the overriding American threat diminish. Aware that no single tribe could hold its ground against the Americans, Indians from Maine to Florida worked to strengthen the wartime confederation.[57] Cooperation was indispensable. One did not have to be a sachem to recognize that bows and arrows did not deter the Americans for long. Guns, powder, and hatchets were essential. The Spaniards were unable to furnish them; the Americans were better able and were most anxious, but the Indians knew that with this commerce land cessions would inevitably follow. With no one to turn to but Britain, the Indians begged the traders to stay.

Consciously or subconsciously British subjects, from ministers to semiliterate Indian traders, associated the fur trade, the Indian problem, retention of the northern posts, and Florida's possible re-acquisition with another issue: was the United States going to break up? Loyalists almost to a man hoped so. Only this explains why Chief Justice William Smith was optimistic when he left New York in 1783: he expected to return there or to a neighboring colony and not be greeted by Old Glory.[58] Edward Bancroft, Benjamin Franklin's friend and British spy, reported from Philadelphia at the end of 1783 that it was unlikely the thirteen states could remain united.[59] George III's opposition to sending an accredited minister to the United States and branding any subject willing to accept this post his personal enemy was due partly to the fact that he did not expect the new nation to last.[60] It was not long after the Revolution before Americans themselves openly talked about disunion. Regardless of where one looked there were signs that the United States, seething with factionalism, might disintegrate. For Britons in the Indian country or living along the Canadian border and in Spanish Florida the foremost consideration was subsequent territorial adjustments.

European *philosophes* with scanty knowledge of America but drawing on their concept of natural law postulated that the United States could not succeed because it was impossible for a republic to govern such a large area. Vermont seemed to bear this out. North's August 1783 directive that Canadians, because of the peace treaty, should not openly support Vermonters against neighboring states was not the final word. Before and after the peace treaty the Allen brothers (Ethan, Ira, and Levi) and Thomas Chittenden asked Britain to relax commercial restrictions and allow Vermont free trade with Canada. Ira Allen appeared in Montreal during 1784 renewing this petition.[61] Sydney, more flexible than North not only toward the question of the posts, but also toward Vermont, was not sure what to do.

Making exceptions to the navigation acts in Vermont's favor was complex. Though Shelburne and Pitt flirted with Adam Smith's new theories about free trade, Britain's evolving commercial policy toward the United States was to treat her like any other foreign country and to enforce the navigation acts rigorously. The influence of Hawkesbury, Chalmers, and mercantilists at the Board of Trade and the anti–free trade writings of John Baker Holroyd, baron Sheffield had been decisive.[62] As far as North America was concerned, Britain still regarded the navigation acts as essential for her navy and the rock of the empire. Allen's suggestion to exempt Vermont from commercial restrictions was no simple matter. If Vermont became an integral part of the United States, granting commercial concessions implied that Britain would do the same for the rest of the states. The drift of Britain's policy, however, was in the opposite direction. Neither Congress nor Vermont's neighbors in 1784 officially recognized her, and if she made good her claim for independence, allowing free commerce was altogether a different matter.

The Allens argued that free trade facilitated Vermont's return to the British fold, while Canadian newspapers boldly proclaimed that Vermonters were more attached to Quebec than to Philadelphia.[63] A prosperous Vermont, commercially and politically tied to Canada, could be an example to other New England states suffering economic depression partly because of the navigation acts' restrictions. Sydney was unsure about Vermont because he did not comprehend exactly what was going on, and he granted Haldimand, who understood Vermont about as well as any British officer and was on the scene, limited freedom of action.[64] The Canadian governor in 1784 sanctioned a few commercial concessions, such as the right to export grain and cattle freely via Lake Champlain, and in time extended these privileges.[65]

The British threat of annexing Vermont could make the states pay more attention to Congress' promise to "earnestly recommend" amnesty in behalf of the loyalists. The characteristically ambivalent Sydney sympathized with Vermonters who professed fealty to George III and agreed that they should be permitted to rejoin the empire. He concurred in retention of the Lake Champlain forts partly to insure the well-being of nearby loyalists. Sydney approved Haldimand's initiative concerning the posts and the making of exceptions in the navigation acts, and even the encouraging of ultimate reunion of loyal Vermonters as long as it did not involve Britain in disputes with New York and New Hampshire and violate the peace treaty. Sydney, thousands of miles away, did not elaborate.[66]

Though Britain knew more about Vermont's long history of separatism than about that of any other part of the United States, Vermont's position was not unique. Nantucket Island's whale fishermen, some of whom were loyalists and suffering from the navigation acts, solicited commercial favors or even political reunion.[67] Because of the loyalist sentiment in thinly-settled northeastern Maine, some Britons hoped to attach part of Maine, much more than the disputed islands in Passamaquoddy Bay, to New Brunswick.[68]

A semiautonomous community existed in the Wyoming Valley near the Susquehanna River's headwaters in northern Pennsylvania. Pennsylvania and Connecticut claimed jurisdiction and had battled for years over civil authority. Loyalists of the area fled at the beginning of the Revolution, though some, with their Indian allies, returned and ravaged the valley. After the Revolution a few loyalists came back but perceived that the Paris peace treaty did not protect loyalists returning to the Wyoming Valley. In contrast to Vermont, Maine, Nantucket Island, and the Floridas, there was no loyalist populace urging restoration of British rule. But the Connecticut settlers, their land titles threatened, were fighting a determined but losing battle against Pennsylvania. The Connecticut faction, looking for outside support, eyed Canada. When Gen. Ethan Allen rode into the Wyoming Valley in 1786—as apparently did Capt. Daniel Shays in 1787—to assist fellow Yankees, the possibility of an independent Wyoming Valley allied with Canada did not diminish.[69]

Separatist tendencies appeared in the growing western communities. The mountains, spanned by poor roads and no canals, were a barrier, and as geography linked upper Vermont with the St. Lawrence, it bound the West to the Mississippi and the Great Lakes. Westerners recognized that the Mississippi River and its tributaries afforded the only practicable means of transport and that their bulky exports had to be sent to New Orleans, or with easy portages, to the Great Lakes before being shipped to Europe or the Atlantic seaboard. Easterners did not fully appreciate this. The fruitless 1786 Jay-Gardoqui negotiations with Spain whereby easterners offered to forego free navigation on the Mississippi illustrated the East-West rift. James Monroe's speculations about what binds "they to us when the Mississippi shall be open" reflected an eastern point of view.[70] For westerners the question was how could they remain part of the United States without free navigation.

After the Revolution there were numerous "Spanish conspiracies" in which westerners intrigued to place the West under Spanish dominion in return for free navigation.[71] At the same time, though not as well noted, frontiersmen conspired with Canadians about placing the West under British protection in return for free commerce via the Great Lakes–St. Lawrence route or assistance in taking Spanish Louisiana and Florida to open the Mississippi. James Wilkinson was probably the "Gentleman at the Falls of the Ohio" who wrote a letter reproduced in many newspapers openly hinting at western secession and a Canadian attachment.[72] Britain, according to Wilkinson in a separate private letter, had sought his cooperation since 1783,[73] and the British governor at Detroit had his agent in Tennessee and Kentucky.[74] Tobias Lear, Washington's confidant and private secretary, returning from an inspection of the West, advised his eastern friends that this unruly section would remain in the union fifteen years at best.[75]

It was as easy to draw sectional lines on an east-west as on a north-south axis. Contention smoldered between the southern agrarian slave and the northern commercial states. Thoughtful Americans, not only irascible loyalists but Rufus King, James Monroe, and Theodore Sedgwick, reflected on a division, though they differed whether the Hudson, Delaware, or Potomac river should be the boundary.[76] Regardless of where one looked there was the possibility the United States might collapse. The outbreak of Shays' Rebellion in frontier Massachusetts in 1786 convinced Washington at Mount Vernon and the new Canadian governor, Lord Dorchester, that disintegration had already begun. The all-important question was what changes were in store after the United States' downfall? Surprisingly enough Britain, not by design, still had an important stake in the frontier, and delay and indecision were no longer excusable. Time had run out for Sydney.

3 • Dorchester and Dunmore

THOUGH British troops had evacuated Florida in 1785, they still occupied posts on American soil from upper Lake Champlain to Detroit. It was no longer possible to justify retention as a temporary measure. Two years had allowed time enough to depart, and excuses about the lakes' freezing over in winter, fear of an Indian uprising, and giving the fur traders time to collect their debts were no longer valid. A reason for keeping the posts at first had been to protect the loyalists, but wartime passions had subsided, and instances of persecution and land confiscation were now rare.

If Britain were to retain the forts, she had to reassess her entire American position. Ministers began to look at America in a new light and to recognize, not always clearly, that continued delay represented a new policy. By 1786 Britain publicly warranted occupying the posts because of nonpayment of pre-Revolutionary debts.[1] A pattern had emerged of states, especially Virginia, erecting legal barriers in the way of debt collection. But nonpayment did not evoke as strong feelings as loyalist persecution. The British government, particularly George III, was sympathetic to the loyalists who had lost their property and risked their lives and whose interests had been sacrificed in the peace treaty.

It was not fair to equate loyalists who returned home facing a howling mob and vigilante justice with refusal to honor the debt to a Scottish merchant. One involved money, the other lives of British patriots. During the depression of the 1780s United States as well as British creditors had equal reason to complain. When Britain decided not to observe that part of the treaty respecting the forts and to keep them indefinitely, nonpayment of debts was the excuse, legally a good one with which even Secretary for Foreign Affairs John Jay agreed.[2] But it was not the main reason redcoats remained on American soil. It was becoming apparent to the British government that it was to remain deeply involved in affairs within the United States and that the posts' retention was associated as much with the crumbling of the United States as with the distress of British creditors.

Indians were most immediately concerned with the posts' status and the Old Northwest's fate. Whether the British standard, the United States flag, or that of some autonomous western republic waved over the Old Northwest affected Indians and whites alike and transcended profits from the fur trade. Joseph Brant recognized this. Though his new home was on the Grand River, his influence and that of the Six Nations extended throughout both Canada and the United States. This was due to the fact that much of the Six Nations still lived in western New York and that traditionally the Six Nation confederacy had guided the political life of neighboring tribes.[3] After the Revolution, when he was not at the Grand River or Montreal, he was at Niagara, Sandusky, and Detroit—at the same time Mohawks were among the southern Indians—urging native unity. Because of his position among the Six Nations and their historic role of leadership, he claimed with some exaggeration to be chief spokesman for thousands of Indians. It was several years after the American Revolution before it became obvious that conflict had destroyed the Six Nations' preeminent position and that leadership was passing westward, especially to the angry Shawnees. Brant in 1785 may not have been aware of this development and acted as if little had changed.[4]

An intelligent half-blood, though not likely to win any Latin prizes, he was more literate than the average frontiersmen. The posts' future and that of the Old Northwest was foremost in his mind when he saw the peace treaty. Brant understood what Sir William and Sir John Johnson and other colonial officials recognized: the font of power in the British empire was not in Quebec but in London. If the proper authorities in Britain espoused his cause, the rest would take care of itself. This was what prompted him in the fall of 1785, despite objections of the Indian superintendent, to go to London, and he boarded a vessel carrying the retiring Frederick Haldimand. Brant had to find out at firsthand whether Britain would keep the posts indefinitely and what aid, if any, she would give the Indians on both sides of the boundary.[5] As a loyalist he expected to plead his claim for compensation more effectively in London than on the Grand River.

The London press in December 1785 announced the daring Indian leader's arrival. He was presented to George III at an official levee;[6] newspapers revived the eighteenth-century exploits of the mighty Iroquois;[7] and later the Mohawk chief conferred with Thomas Townshend, Lord Sydney. The meeting with the home secretary was a Johnson family reunion. Along with Brant was Daniel Claus, Sir William's son-in-law; Guy Johnson, Sir William's nephew; and Col. John Butler, Sir William's pre-war advisor and superintendent for the Six Nations.[8] This conference occurred in a period when the government was recognizing that continued occupation of the posts represented not a belated commitment to execute the treaty but a new departure. Brant's arrival and his request for aid to Indians living in the United States pointed this out.

Prolonged occupation of the posts implied that Britain was actively supporting the Indians. Native claims to most of the Old Northwest were based on the 1768 Treaty of Fort Stanwix, concluded under Sir William Johnson's leadership, between the British government and the Six Nations and northwestern tribes. This treaty established the Ohio River as the boundary. The Six Nations and especially the militant chiefs of the northwestern Algonquin tribes argued that they had not been defeated in the Revolution, had signed no new treaty, and that the Ohio remained the boundary. Frontiersmen spreading into the West had better stay south of this river. And they usually did. Brant, the Shawnee Blue Jacket, and similar chiefs with some success had organized a northern confederation with which the southern Indians were associated, and they demanded that land cessions meet general Indian approval. Grants to lands north of the Ohio by bribed, drunken, second-rate chiefs were not binding. The Ohio was the boundary: Americans had no right to venture above it.[9]

One of the points Brant raised in his discussion with the home secretary was what gave Britain the right to cede native lands above the Ohio to the United States, which was another way of asking whether Britain was going to honor Johnson's Fort Stanwix Treaty. At the heart of this was the nature of Indian title to land, something that had never much concerned Britain before. Britain assumed that the royal charters and the right of first discovery gave her title to most of North America. There was the problem of Indians actually on the land. If they had not been defeated in war, then in all fairness, even though they were pagans, they must have some rights.

During the eighteenth century, Britain generally conceded that the

Indians, because they were actually on the land, enjoyed the right of usufruct, the use of the soil, but overall sovereignty resided with the British monarchy.[10] Thus when the Indians in 1768 at Fort Stanwix had ceded lands below the Ohio and elsewhere, what they had been paid for was not their title to these lands—the British monarch already owned them—but rather compensation for relinquishing the right of usufruct. In 1782–83 it never occurred to Shelburne that he did not have the right to give the Old Northwest to the United States, since Britain had owned it since the sixteenth century. What the United States had not acquired by the Treaty of Paris was the Indian claim of usufruct to most of the lands in the Old Northwest. Britain had not purchased this from the Indians and could not give it to the United States.[11]

The Indians did not treat land titles the same way the whites did. They never fully understood what gave the Pope or Christian monarchs the right to their lands. The whites, when they negotiated treaties at Fort Stanwix and elsewhere, might make mental reservations that what they were purchasing was merely the Indians' right of usufruct, not a clear title. Over the years Indians gained much experience in negotiating with the whites and became less naïve.

Before the Revolution Britain did not consider the Indians independent but her wards, and when she "purchased" land from Indian "nations" she was merely acquiring the natives' right to the use of the soil. After the Revolution Britain began to treat Indian land titles somewhat differently. Canadian officials in 1783, thinking in terms of usufruct and hoping to quiet the Indians, maintained that Britain had not really given the Old Northwest to the Americans. It belonged to the Indians, and Britain guaranteed the natives' right to the use of the soil.[12] From this time on Britain, because it suited her interests, leaned more and more toward the position that Indians within the United States were in every way sovereign. She never abandoned the concept of usufruct, because to do so embarrassed her in dealing with Canadian Indians. But when Brant was in London, his and Whitehall's views of Indian sovereignty were closer than at any time in the eighteenth century.

The Mohawk chief, realizing that legal hairsplitting hardly ever settled ownership of sparsely settled American lands, had not come to

Whitehall to dwell on the merits of usufruct. Since Britain agreed in principle that the Ohio was the proper boundary, he wanted to know exactly how much aid to expect.[13] There is no detailed account of Brant's conversation with Sydney, but Brant became convinced by Sydney or someone else that troops were going to remain in the posts indefinitely—an encouraging sign. The Canadian Indian department, though reduced in numbers, would continue to minister to the natives below the boundary. If Britain were to justify this—and she never seriously tried—it would have been hard not to argue that the Indians within the United States were completely independent. Presents from the Canadian Indian agents and trade with Canadian merchants allowed the Indians to acquire arms and powder for the hunt or for use against the Americans.

Brant was reasonably satisfied with these commercial arrangements, but he was unhappy about others. One was Britain's reluctance to use troops to defend the Ohio. British soldiers had ranged throughout the Old Northwest during the war, fighting side by side with the Indians, and Brant wanted to keep it that way. If sovereign Indian "nations" invited redcoats among them, it was perfectly legal. It could also ignite hostilities with the United States, and Sydney refused to risk putting British soldiers on the Ohio to guarantee an Indian boundary. Redcoats remained in the Old Northwest, but at Detroit, Michilimackinac, and Niagara rather than on the Ohio. If the United States' troops moved against these posts, Britain would meet them with force. While denying open military assistance to the Indians, Sydney did not abandon them to the mercy of the Americans.[14] This illustrated Britain's moderately aggressive policy related to the premise that the American boundary set in 1783 was not sacrosanct.

There were different reactions to Brant's London visit. Sydney, thinking about the posts' retention, Brant's half pay, his £1500 compensation as a loyalist, and larger sums given to his sister and the Mohawks, maintained that the native chieftain departed reasonably content.[15] General Haldimand visited Brant and, because of controversy over compensation for war losses and Britain's uncertain commitment to the Treaty of Fort Stanwix, felt the government had not done enough for her wartime allies and that Brant had a right to be uneasy.[16] Publicity attended the Mohawk's visit. John Rigaud painted his picture, and the press reviewed the history of the Six Nations and commented on the valiant leader of the Indian confederacy stretching from the Mohawks to the Creeks.[17] A newspaper questioned American pretensions "that the forts on their back settlements were by the late treaty to be given up."[18] and that the United States "so remarkable for wisdom, should even entertain the most distant idea of founding a claim to their [Indian] lands on the late treaty."[19]

Brant, accompanying the new Canadian governor, Sir Guy Carleton, Lord Dorchester, returned home in the spring of 1786, disturbed that Whitehall was not as adamant about the Treaty of Fort Stanwix as the Indians, but partially appeased by the "curious weapons" bestowed on him and fellow chiefs of the Six Nations.[20] Soon after his return a twenty-man delegation from the Six Nations visited the southern Indians. Presumably Brant sent them to report the results of his London trip, encourage unity, and maintain traditional Iroquois leadership.[21]

Brant had been the first important spokesman for Indians living in the United States who appeared at Whitehall after the Revolution hoping to influence British policy. He was not the last. Delegates from the Shawnees, Cherokees, Creeks, and others regularly arrived in London, and even more frequently in Quebec and Nassau, until 1815 and later. There was nothing unique about this. Pocahontas and her contemporaries had set the precedent, and Brant himself had previously visited London in 1776. The United States after 1783, however, expected the Indians to visit their white father in Philadelphia, not London.

From London's standpoint Indian affairs were intertwined with the development of autonomous frontier settlements such as Vermont. That state's political and commercial bonds with Canada increased in proportion to the internal strife within the United States. The rapids at St. Jean on the Richelieu River impeded water communications between upper Vermont and the St. Lawrence, and there were many advocates of a canal. Silas Deane, an energetic patriot early in the Revolution though he later changed sides, was in the forefront. He lived in England after the war and, along with other loyalists, won over key officials: Sydney; Dorchester; John Baker Holroyd, Lord Sheffield; and John Graves Simcoe, future governor of Upper Canada.[22]

The Allens (Ethan in Vermont, Ira in Montreal, and Levi in London) urged in the strongest terms during the later half of the 1780s adoption of a formal commercial treaty. They avowed they had Thomas Chittenden's authorization to negotiate.[23] When this treaty became public—and it could not have remained secret for long—it meant that Britain considered Vermont completely independent. This is exactly what the Allen coterie, which could not find anyone else to recognize Vermont's independence, wanted. Concern for their land titles, coupled with the fact that Vermont's post-Revolutionary immigrants tended to vote for political opponents, made the Allens, especially Ethan, anxious for a Canadian union. Ethan could play a dominant role in a Vermont annexed to Canada. Without union the political future of the hero of Ticonderoga was uncertain.[24]

Vermont's request for a treaty more than any single thing jarred Sydney and forced him to reappraise his conduct toward the entire frontier. By the late 1780s an inchoate British policy was apparent: cautiously encourage Vermonters and other frontier separatists, retain the forts and support the Indians, and do not forget that the Floridas once had been British and that the 1783 peace treaty had not unalterably fixed the Mississippi Valley's status; but take no rash step that might reopen the war of the Revolution. A formal treaty with Vermont, the effect of which was to sever this state from the Confederation and to restore her to the British empire, was a bold measure.

Sydney realized that the current issue was whether to abandon the policy of caution and to actively work for American disintegration. In the past Sydney had sanctioned limited commercial privileges for Vermont, and he was willing to assume responsibility for this cautious policy. A full-fledged treaty, however, required the king's ratification and the ministry's consideration. Sydney refused to accept responsibility for a policy which, though it might restore part of the colonies to British control, at the same time increased the risks of another American war.[25]

Vermont and the Indians were issues that Britain had faced even before the peace treaty's signing. Kentucky and the growing western settlements presented new problems, because the great spurt in western population occurred in the 1780s. This is not to imply that diplomats had not fought over the West at Paris, but it was a West without many whites. Not only officials at Richmond who claimed jurisdiction over Kentucky but also those in Quebec, Nassau, and London studied this new sectional cleavage. When Simcoe talked about canals and sluices connecting part of the American frontier to Canada, he was as concerned with the West as Vermont.[26] Britain observed the rift over the Jay-Gardoqui negotiations, pondered the "Letter from a Gentleman at the Falls of the Ohio" suggesting Canadian-Kentucky cooperation, listened to proposals of loyalists in the Indian country and frontier towns about restoring the frontier to the British empire, and wondered if Canadians should become "hearty and zealous patrons of [western] *Independence.*"[27]

Nowhere was sectional controversy more pronounced than in Kentucky. Failure of the national government at Philadelphia to obtain free navigation of the Mississippi River from Spain and a general Eastern disinterest inspired several Kentucky conventions to assert that state's autonomy.[28] Kentucky might look to Britain, and even in 1785 Canadian Lt. Gov. Gen. Henry Hope had urged a formal alliance.[29] Lafayette, partisan of the republic he had fought to create, cautioned that Britain's "new system" was to encourage the Indians and to take the rising western states under her wing.[30] Even Americans visiting in London warned of mounting British influence in the West.[31] James Madison, dismayed by the Confederation's impotence, feared that Kentucky's conduct allowed Britain "to play the part of Vermont on a larger scale."[32]

London simultaneously had to contend with western separatism, the forts' disposition, the Indian problem, and Vermont. Overshadowing every consideration was whether critics were correct about the United States' future. If the republic failed, the autonomous western settlements' future must come to the forefront. Free navigation of the Mississippi was vital to them whether independent or part of the United States. If the westerners separated, they had to come to terms with Spain or Britain. Spain, controlling New Orleans, the Floridas, and the Mississippi's western bank, had the advantage. Sydney, his successor William Wyndham Grenville, and the affable Scotsman Henry Dundas—Pitt's colleagues most concerned with colonial affairs —worried about Spanish ascendancy on both banks of the Mississippi.[33]

Most disturbing was that this might presage France's return to the Mississippi Valley. Frenchmen, reminding Louis XVI that Louisiana had been named for his predecessor, argued that the end of the decade was the "golden moment" for France to regain this colony.[34] The danger of restoring Louisiana to France and the impact on French Canadians gave Dorchester and his London superiors sleepless nights.

Knowledge about the extent of western discontent was essential. This is why Dorchester sent Col. John Connolly to Detroit early in 1788.[35] Connolly, a loyalist, was a speculator with business and family contacts among westerners, Tories and patriots, red and white.[36] He sent his agents into the West. Their favorable reports encouraged the colonel to visit Pennsylvania and Kentucky, supposedly for business and personal reasons but secretly to gauge the strength of western separatism and to encourage frontiersmen to look to Canada rather than New Orleans.

The true purpose of Connolly's visit deceived few people. He met or corresponded with numerous western leaders in Pennsylvania and Kentucky.[37] The colonel encouraged western independence, an attack on New Orleans, and a Canadian rapprochement. Exactly how much aid he promised or the nature of the handsome offer he made to James Wilkinson may never be known.[38] Critics said he offered thousands of redcoats to help take New Orleans; but if he did, it was without Dorchester's knowledge. Something else that can never be known is the innermost thoughts of those western leaders he contacted. Thomas Marshall of Kentucky denounced Connolly to President-elect Washington and the merchant-speculator George Morgan reported his activities to the Spaniards.[39] But it was odd that Connolly, whose wartime reputation was slightly below that of Simon Girty and the "hair buyer," Col. Henry Hamilton, freely roamed throughout the West and conferred with political leaders unmolested. That the war had been over five years had something to do with it; that a Canadian alliance appealed even to some of his critics may have been equally important.

Connolly's reports and those of others who had special knowledge forced Whitehall to reconsider the West and appreciate the complexity of dealing with the Indians and whites living there. Newspapers flailed anew that "miserable tool" the earl of Shelburne for having abandoned the West in the peace treaty.[40] Canadians complained that friends "to humanity cannot but regret that steps weren't taken to secure the Indians their country."[41] Consul Phineas Bond reported from Philadelphia that "Nature, my Lord, seems to have pointed out a plain line of division between the Eastern and Western parts of this continent:—that wonderful range of mountains."[42] And Dorchester reminded Whitehall that New Orleans must soon become "the great emporium of North America" and is worthy of Britain's greatest attention.[43] The imperious Grenville, Pitt's cousin and one of his closest advisors for the next decade, became home secretary in 1789 and studied the frontier. For the time being he continued Sydney's policy of winning frontiersmen's goodwill but promising no open military assistance, encouraging the Indians to safeguard their independence, heeding advice about the importance of New Orleans and the Floridas, and watching developments in the United States which apparently were favoring British interests.

Britain and Spain had divided the Mississippi Valley (the old French province of Louisiana) at the end of the French and Indian War. Britain acquired the territory east of the river and Spain the region to the west. In some respects this division was illogical because the Mississippi River seemed ordained to be the commercial heart of North America, not a boundary. Different nations after 1763 aspired to reunite the Mississippi Valley. Whether France, Spain, Britain, or the United States would superintend the new arrangement was yet undetermined.

The Mississippi Valley's future had been a lively issue since the 1782–83 peace negotiations. Shelburne had ceded the Old West to the United States but wanted British merchants in Canada and on the Gulf Coast still to dominate the Mississippi Valley's commerce. Those associated with John Murray, fourth earl of Dunmore had expected Britain, in the wake of a successful campaign against Spanish Gulf Coast colonies, to command the Mississippi Valley politically as well as economically. Shelburne's plan envisioned postwar Anglo-American collaboration. Dunmore, once entrenched in the West, gladly would have let the Atlantic states go to the devil.

Neither Dunmore's nor Shelburne's plans were carried out at the end of the Revolution. But during the 1780s, as dissension increased in the United States, the ministry began taking a closer look at the West, and more from Dunmore's than Shelburne's point of view. Authorities in Quebec and Montreal did not forget that Canada's recent boundary had been the Ohio River. Dorchester, wondering if "Great Britain might be placed in the room of France," gave unidentified American men of property who approached him reason to hope for British aid in taking New Orleans; Grenville in London, helping to revise the Canadian constitution, deemed it sound policy not to specify the southern limits of Upper Canada.[44]

The United States alone—not Britain, Spain, or France—assumed that the 1783 Treaty had conferred the Old West on the new republic in perpetuity. It was the Mississippi Valley's final disposition that made the Floridas so important. Whoever had these provinces was likely to have New Orleans and command of the lower Mississippi, and whoever controlled the Mississippi's mouth had the key to North America's interior. Spain held this key after the Revolution, and, if Spanish intrigues in Kentucky and Tennessee succeeded, she would control most of the old province of French Louisiana. But Spain was at a disadvantage because her economy, though reviving, was not robust enough to exploit effectively the Mississippi Valley's resources. Rumors abounded during the 1780s that the Floridas and Louisiana must soon pass from Spanish hands. "Southward Ho! [was] the watchword" in the United States, and the danger of incipient American "manifest destiny" was obvious.[45] France approached Spain in the mid-1780s about Louisiana's and Florida's retrocession, and Versailles imperialists hoped French Louisiana's regeneration was imminent. British observers, following these negotiations, wondered why hundreds of French Acadian exiles, Evangeline's lover possibly among them, began flocking to Louisiana and West Florida. Bahamian loyalists were furious: it was a splendid idea for Louisiana and the Floridas to become havens for refugees—so long as they were British.[46]

The disturbing French involvement, internal strife in the United States, entreaties from Canadian authorities and fur traders, and the prospect of a Spanish American revolt forced Britain to take a second look at the Floridas and the Mississippi Valley. The London Daily Universal Register reported in 1786 that the project of giving Spain Gibraltar, the "grave of our soldiers . . . a mine of gold to contractors, an harbor for Jews, extortioners, and renegadoes," was again in the air.[47] Gibraltar's cession was synonymous with British acquisition of the Floridas or other Spanish colonial territory.

Ex-Floridians determined to regain Florida by negotiation or armed force and appealed to the sympathetic Charles Jenkinson, baron Hawkesbury, now head of the Board of Trade. John Miller, fresh from the Bahamas, advised the Board about the Floridas' importance.[48] John Cruden, who had not abandoned his "mad scheme," apprised Hawkesbury of an impending Spanish American revolt and its impact on the Floridas and Louisiana: "a crisis is approaching."[49] Gen. Archibald McArthur, military commander in the Bahamas who had helped evacuate East Florida, with the ministry's approval distributed the usual presents in 1787 to a Creek delegation visiting Nassau "on account of [their] strong attachment . . . to His Majesty's interest."[50] The question of reimbursing Georgia loyalists claiming land in the Creek country came up in the House of Commons. Pitt refused to discuss this publicly. He may have believed these loyalists soon would regain their lands since Florida could claim them as well as Georgia.[51]

Loyalists renewed their requests to settle in Spanish Louisiana and become a buffer between the Americans and Mexico. William Knox, Georgia loyalist and wartime colonial under-secretary of state, urged an Anglo-Spanish alliance whereby Britain assumed defense of Louisiana and the Floridas.[52] Assorted loyalists who had advocated seizing the Floridas and Louisiana at the end of the Revolution insisted that now was the time for Britain to reconsider this scheme.[53] Spaniards had reason to fear when Whitehall demanded free navigation of the Mississippi and when George III reportedly planned to provide for two of his sons, one in Canada, the other in Louisiana.[54]

The concept of a unified Mississippi Valley, economically and politically dominated by Britain, linked to Canada and a refuge for loyalists, reemerged in the latter part of the 1780s. This is what made the booming of cannon in 1787 that announced Lord Dunmore's arrival in Nassau as the new Bahamian governor so significant. Financially pressed, Dunmore had come to the Bahamas where he expected to provide for his large family and for at least some of the loyalists whom he had represented in London. Sheffield was delighted that the government had finally recognized the importance of the Bahamas and that the "strenuous, active" Dunmore was governor.[55] Ensconced in Nassau's Government House, the Scottish lord's dream of conducting loyalists to the Floridas and Louisiana had not faded, and he had not forgotten that Fort Pitt formerly had been called Fort Dunmore.

Thomas Dalton, a destitute loyalist who had knocked about Nova Scotia, the Bahamas, and the southern Indian country, in 1789 appeared in London. Dressed as an Indian, he brought a message from the Creeks and Cherokees to George III, petitioning him to take them under his wing and to establish a fort and trading post in their country.[56] His visit did not attract much attention, and in a sense he was pathetic as he froze in his skimpy Indian attire waiting an interview with Sydney or anyone in the home office. Dalton himself was of little consequence. But to that small group versed in American developments Dalton's visit was not ludicrous. More than any single individual, Dunmore was responsible for his coming to London. Dalton wanted the Indians to exist as an independent state under British protection. Alexander McGillivray, whose supplies of arms had been curtailed by the Spaniards in 1788, apparently had aided Dalton. Dalton's "independent" Indian state was part of Dunmore's larger plan for the Mississippi Valley.

Francisco de Miranda had returned to London from the continent and, whether conferring with ministers or dining with Gen. Frederick Haldimand, he included the Floridas and the Mississippi Valley in his plans for a Spanish American revolt.[57] The peripatetic Levi Allen was also in London urging a commercial treaty with Vermont, promising a regiment of Green Mountain Boys to help defend British-occupied posts, and reminding Whitehall that the "good intentions of Vermonters have not been attended to."[58] Dorchester wrote from Canada that the private views of Kentuckians were to declare independence, seize New Orleans, and align themselves with Britain. Home Secretary Grenville agreed that every means possible should be taken to win the friendship of all restless westerners.[59] Those who snickered at Dalton did so at their peril.

He was but a small part of schemes that involved much of North America and symbolized the continuing influence of loyalists at Whitehall. Exaggerated reports announced that the Creeks and Cherokees, some 35,000 strong, were threatening Georgia and South Carolina

not with predatory raids but with conquest, and that from Canada to
the Gulf the "Indian confederacy begins now to take effect, as most of
the tribes on the frontiers . . . are in motion."[60] Not only estranged
loyalists but American Secretary of War Henry Knox recognized that a
protracted Indian war would probably destroy the republic.[61] Loyalists advised the government that "nothing can prevent the five
northern colonies from returning to their allegiance," and regularly reported to William Pitt about American dissension.[62] Dalton, Dunmore,
the Allens, Sheffield, Simcoe, and Dorchester urged the ministry to
adopt a more aggressive frontier policy. During the 1780s there was
reason to fear for the future of "the High and Mighty States of America."[63]

4 • Nootka Crisis

BRITAIN was as unsure about the United States in 1789 as the fledgling republic was about itself. George III still had not dispatched a minister to the American capital, and no one knew what adoption of the new constitution portended. It might vitalize the nation or, as critics charged, make the republic's collapse inevitable. Discontented frontier districts threatened to spin off. Assorted British subjects, including a substantial group at Whitehall, felt this was probable, and their reaction was the main reason why Britain retained the forts, traded with and managed the Indians on American soil, and closely observed the Floridas and New Orleans. From the British standpoint it was just as logical for new states like Kentucky, retaining their autonomy, to align themselves with Canada as with the United States. William Wyndham Grenville's policy in 1789 was to let events take their course, allowing the Appalachian Mountains to become the new boundary without serious risk of war.

There were noteworthy developments in 1789 other than adoption of the United States' Constitution. An angry mob stormed the Bastille in Paris, and peasants terrorized nobles in the French countryside, forcing some of them to flee. The captain of a Spanish warship seized four British merchant vessels half way around the globe at obscure Nootka Sound on Vancouver Island, alleging that Nootka was part of New Spain, not Canada.[1] Rival Anglo-Spanish claims over Pacific Coast territory and the outbreak of the French Revolution had an immediate impact on the frontier. Grenville, observing the tumult across the channel and studying details of the Nootka affair as they trickled in, was among the first to realize that a policy of waiting to see if the United States were going to disintegrate was outdated.

One thing was certain: the main theater of action in any Anglo-Spanish conflict was not going to be at remote Nootka. With Britain in Canada and Spain in Louisiana and the Floridas, any hostilities inevitably would spread to the Mississippi Valley. Though it was unlikely that Spain could move against Canada, there was an excellent chance that

British troops in Canada, cooperating with a British expedition in the Gulf of Mexico, might attack Louisiana and the Floridas. The responses of France and the United States were crucial. Would France, Spain's traditional eighteenth-century ally, come to the rescue, or was the French Revolution so serious as to prevent Louis XVI from honoring the Bourbon family compact? If British troops in Detroit crossed the Old Northwest, would the United States fight, remain neutral, or join Britain in wresting Louisiana and the Floridas from Spain?

One British option was to form an alliance with the United States. During the American Revolution France, Spain, and the United States had combined against Britain, and as a result she had lost the thirteen American colonies and ceded the two Floridas to Spain. With France torn by internal strife and the United States won as a British ally, Spain, standing alone like Britain earlier, would be lucky if she lost no more than the Floridas. A British accommodation with the United States had its attractions.

As the Nootka crisis deepened, the question of whether the United States and Britain might reconcile their differences came to the forefront. It was at this point that Britain realized the disadvantages of not having an American minister. George III, out of spite and a conviction that the thirteen states would not long remain united, had opposed appointing a minister. British consuls in major American seaports were unsatisfactory for serious diplomatic negotiation. The closest thing Britain had to a resident minister was George Beckwith, Gen. Sir Henry Clinton's wartime secret service agent in New York. Sir Guy Carleton, Lord Dorchester had sent Beckwith back to New York in the late 1780s to report on developments in the United States and to ingratiate himself with principal men of influence.[2]

Beckwith, on his fifth postwar mission in 1790, arrived in New York. As the Nootka crisis worsened, he became more interested in the Mississippi Valley and Anglo-American cooperation. The Nootka dispute, threatening the new government's survival, presented the United States its first serious diplomatic crisis since the Constitution's adoption. Beckwith used a cypher in his reports to Dorchester and Grenville. Philip Schuyler was number two and John Jay number twelve. Number seven, Alexander Hamilton, was the most influential. Though Hamilton was secretary of the treasury and Beckwith not an accredited minister, in their conversations these two explored the chances of an alliance. Hamilton avowed that westerners must have free navigation of the Mississippi River, and he was intrigued by the possibility of Britain and the United States encouraging a Spanish American revolution. Beckwith assumed that with Spain expelled from the Mississippi Valley the disputed Louisiana-Canadian boundary could be adjusted in Canada's favor. The matter of free navigation of the Mississippi was important to Britain as well as to the United States. Spain, unsupported by France and confronted by truculent Anglo-Americans, must make concessions to Britain in the Mississippi Valley and elsewhere.[3]

Both parties believed that Spain would not keep Louisiana and the Floridas forever. But there were obstructions to any alliance. Without mentioning 1783 treaty violations and Britain's refusal to concede a favorable commercial treaty, one has to look no farther than the frontier. Britain still occupied posts on American soil and hoped that in the wake of a successful joint expedition the Americans would allow Britain to retain the forts.[4] President George Washington opposed this. Belligerent Indians of the Old Northwest presented another problem. The United States, raising an army on the Ohio under Revolutionary War veteran Gen. Josiah Harmar, resolved to make the Indians comprehend that the Ohio was not the boundary. She wanted Britain to withdraw support from these Indians and encourage them to peace on American terms.[5] But both Britain's Indian agents and her "villainous traders"[6] remained in the Indian country. There were divergent views over the disposition of Louisiana and the Floridas. Thomas Jefferson avowed that if Britain tried to annex territory contiguous to the United States, the Americans must ally with Spain.[7] Whitehall, in contrast, wanted New Orleans to become a British emporium with American approval.

The southern Indians were as numerous and bellicose as those in the Old Northwest. Their cooperation or at least their neutrality was desirable in any Spanish campaign. This made the presence in New York of twenty-odd Creek chiefs, headed by Alexander McGillivray, so significant. He had come to negotiate a treaty and make the Americans surrender their extravagant claims to native lands. McGillivray, a loyallist, had served in the British Indian department during the Revolution. Britain had to find out if he and the thousands of Creeks were on her side. Beckwith lengthened his cypher, and McGillivray became number nineteen.

Though McGillivray was a loyalist and a former Indian agent, Beckwith wondered about the chief's attachment to Britain. He now was in Spanish pay with a Spanish commission, and the Spanish governors in the Floridas and Louisiana considered him their most important representative among the southern Indians. In the 1790 Treaty of New York McGillivray accepted an American commission and salary.[8] Simultaneously employed by two foreign nations, McGillivray made Beckwith skeptical about the Creek leader's fidelity to Britain. Beckwith conferred with McGillivray before he left New York and was as confused by the chief's true motives as were the Spaniards and Americans. Beckwith reported that he did not know whether the southern Indians under McGillivray's leadership would align themselves with Britain or remain loyal to Spain.[9]

Grenville expected a Spanish war in which France would remain neutral. Though there were advantages to an Anglo-American alliance, the home secretary recognized that the two countries had divergent policies. Britain was not willing to give up the forts, to insist that the Indians make a humiliating peace, and to let the United States acquire all the Floridas and Louisiana. Grenville had instructed Beckwith to be noncommittal in discussing these controversial issues with the Americans, and it was good he was.[10] Though the home secretary had not made a final decision, he realized that differences over the Mississippi Valley were likely to prevent Anglo-American cooperation.

The Nootka dispute forced Whitehall to consider how much it should encourage a Spanish American revolt that might emancipate not only fringe provinces of Louisiana and the Floridas but also Mexico and South America. This was not a new issue. From Sir Francis Drake's exploits in the sixteenth century to the American Revolution, Britain had fomented Spanish American uprisings. Grenville appreciated the difficulties of blending British support for liberating Spanish America with an Anglo-American alliance. He knew that Americans hoped to open the Mississippi for their exclusive use, to annex adjacent Spanish territory that Britain coveted, and to spread republicanism throughout the New World.

More than anyone, Francisco de Miranda encouraged Britain and the United States to combine in 1790. He had influential friends on both sides of the Atlantic; he expected both countries to help free Spanish America; he assumed the Nootka controversy presented the opportune moment. According to the Venezuelan Creole, all must benefit at Spain's expense. Spanish Americans, throwing off the mother country's traces, could set themselves up as independent states. Britain, no longer excluded by Spain's mercantilistic policy, would get preferential commercial treatment; the United States would get free navigation of the Mississippi River; perhaps the two could divide the Floridas and Louisiana. Throughout 1790 Miranda reminded William Pitt that Spain was without allies and that Britain should do unto Spain in her extremity as Spain had done unto Britain during the American Revolution. Miranda pointed out to the Americans that in addition to free navigation of the Mississippi and territorial conquest, they could spread liberty and republicanism throughout the western hemisphere.[11]

Miranda intended that the United States, Britain, and disaffected Spanish American colonists combine and make Spain rue the day she impounded British merchant ships in far-off Nootka. The problem was in bringing the United States and Britain together. He implored Secretary of War Henry Knox: "For God's sake let me hear from you . . . or have you forgot your friends and promises?"[12] Knox, Hamilton, and other Americans were interested in liberating Spanish America but had reservations about cooperating with Britain. There was always a considerable group in Britain at anytime anxious to free Spanish America. Some wanted to combine with the Americans and unleash Henry Knox against Spanish Louisiana.[13] Others, still hoping to wrest Spanish America from Spain but noting the first wave of French emigrés to arrive in England, were not so sure they wanted to see "this flame of equal liberty to blaze over the Spanish and Portuguese colonies . . . [or] that the emancipation of the human race is worth almost any price."[14] In these troubled times Britain might do well not to align herself with any power having exaggerated notions of liberty.

Though Miranda's concern during the Nootka crisis was a Spanish American revolution, this was not the United States' main problem. Washington and his cabinet, alarmed by a possible Anglo-Spanish war, debated the proper response: neutrality, cooperation with Britain and discontented Spanish Americans, or siding with Spain and, if necessary, fighting Britain. The government had to resolve these questions first. Liberating Spanish America was secondary, and Knox kept Miranda waiting. Though both Britons and Americans recommended an Anglo-American compact, as time passed it became clearer that there were serious obstructions: disposition of Louisiana and the Floridas, Britain's retention of the forts and her policy toward the western Indians, and British concern that the "flame of equal liberty" kindled in the New World might consume the Old. As the Nootka dispute intensified, a British war with Spain appeared inevitable, and an Anglo-American alliance seemed less likely.

Britain apparently would have to go it alone—and so would Spain. In the wake of an Anglo-Spanish war, the United States might break up and frontier districts make new alignments. This is what alarmed Washington.[15] Across the Atlantic Pitt, and especially his ministerial colleagues—Grenville; Charles Jenkinson, Lord Hawkesbury; and Henry Dundas—wondering if rumors of a United States' pact with Spain were true and if an Anglo-Spanish war would act as a catalyst in dismembering the United States, regarded such a dissolution as desirable, even a godsend. The Appalachian Mountains, "ordained by nature" as a boundary, could become the United States' western limit and restrict the territory of a termagant republic.

British soldiers, loyalists, mercantilists fearful of American competition, members of the government, and those who still resented the rebellion of ungrateful colonists used their influence against an American alliance and instead sought to bring the Mississippi Valley under British dominion. Among the loyalist-soldier faction, Sir Henry Clinton, Gen. William Howe's successor as commander in chief in 1778, stood out. Though the government had generally ignored him after the Revolution, he was a member of Parliament and had a following among professional officers. George III's devoted brother, the Duke of Gloucester, was Clinton's particular friend and at every opportunity recommended Clinton to the king and to the Prince of Wales, the future George IV.[16] In the early 1790s the ministry and George III once again paid attention to Clinton. Sir Henry did not like Americans who had rebelled. They had confiscated his New York lands and tarnished his military reputation. He departed New York in 1782 but followed American developments closely and retained correspondents in America, usually loyalists. Though Lord Dorchester was appointed governor of Canada, Clinton interested himself in this colony, knew that until 1783 Quebec's boundary had extended to the Ohio, and understood the relationship between the St. Lawrence and Mississippi river valleys.[17]

Such influence as he had he used in and out of Parliament in behalf of reinforcing the posts, encouraging the Indians and loyalists on the frontier, and expelling both Spain and the United States from the Mississippi Valley. He thought Britain should take over Louisiana and the Floridas and shatter Spain's dream of making the Gulf of Mexico a Spanish lake: fate might give Britain a chance to take revenge on the houses of Bourbon.[18] Britain must reinforce Detroit and Niagara. As a result, "There will not be a settlement to the *West* of the Allegheney Mountains which [she] will not *influence*."[19] By controlling the West, Clinton expected Britain to be better able to make the United States see reason. The government had appointed Charles Cornwallis governor-general of India, and Clinton may have been thinking of himself as a Mississippi Valley proconsul. It is difficult to ascertain the innermost motives of a complex person like Clinton. But one thing was certain. He was anxious for a Spanish war and was not opposed to giving the Americans a thrashing if they ventured too far into the Mississippi Valley.[20]

John Graves Simcoe shared Clinton's views. Clinton was Simcoe's friend and patron. Partly through Clinton's influence the high-spirited Simcoe in 1791 was appointed lieutenant governor of the newly created province of Upper Canada. Simcoe did not sail for America until the fall of 1791 and, like Clinton, sat in Parliament. At the Revolution's end Simcoe had advocated setting aside part of the Old Northwest as a loyalist refuge, and he still considered this a good plan. Strengthening Britain on the south side of the Great Lakes and annexing Vermont were the best ways to guarantee the St. Lawrence–Great Lakes lifeline.[21] Hawkesbury, Grenville, and Pitt agreed with Simcoe during the Nootka crisis that it was sound policy to seize New Orleans.[22] Clinton suggested that "it may be necessary . . . to hold the Floridas also."[23]

British control of the lower Mississippi Valley offered more than commercial opportunity. Exiled West Florida loyalists wanted land and a refuge. The government had given them little compensation (because West Florida, in contrast to the other provinces, had been captured rather than voluntarily ceded), and these loyalists thought that during the Nootka dispute the time was ripe to secure overdue compensation. Alexander Ross indulged "the hope of being again restored to my former situation in West Florida which would make me contented and happy."[24] Though Ross had left West Florida for the Bahamas, other loyalists still living on the Mississippi around Natchez under Spanish rule notified Pitt that they wanted to be liberated with the rest of Spanish America. They had fought for Britain during the American Revolution and were anxious to do so again.[25]

The plan to capture Spanish Gulf Coast territory and make it a loyalist asylum reemerged during the Nootka controversy. John Murray, earl of Dunmore, had been at the head of this project in 1782–83, and the leader in 1790 was this same Scottish lord. After coming to the Bahamas in 1787 he had backed several unsuccessful schemes to place the Floridas directly or indirectly under British control. The prospect of a Spanish war gave him a fresh opportunity. He was surrounded at Government House in Nassau by loyalists eager for a campaign against Spain, and there were restive loyalists still on the Mississippi.[26] As in the past, some of Dunmore's loyalist following was black.

The most striking figure working for Britain's return to the lower Mississippi Valley was William Augustus Bowles who, as a young Maryland loyalist, had come to Pensacola in 1779 with the British army. From this point his career was wedded to the Floridas and the southern Indians. He lived among the Creeks, Cherokees, and Seminoles, took Indian wives, and was elected chief. He began to style himself director general of the Creek Nation or Muskogee. If he was not living among the southern Indians, he usually resided in the Bahamas where, as a loyalist, he had received land. When Dunmore came to Nassau and tried to organize an independent pro-British Indian state, Bowles was the governor's instrument. With Dunmore's blessing Bowles led an unsuccessful filibustering expedition in 1788 to the Floridas. Thomas Dalton, who the following year appeared in Sydney's office in behalf of the southern Indians, was one of Bowles's captains. Though Bowles and Dunmore did not have much to show for their efforts except contraband trade with the southern Indians, anticipation of a Spanish war renewed their enthusiasm.[27]

Their main interest was the Floridas and New Orleans. Dunmore feared that the Canadians, preoccupied with the Old Northwest posts and security of the Great Lakes–St. Lawrence communication, might neglect New Orleans and the Floridas. This is why Bowles himself with a handful of Creek and Cherokee chiefs sailed for Canada. Their ultimate destination was London where they expected to consummate an Anglo-Muskogee alliance.

But they stopped by Canada first, and Dorchester was surprised when he learned in the summer of 1790 that southern Indian chiefs dressed in native attire had stepped ashore at Quebec. When he thought about the Indians, he usually considered those in Canada or the Old Northwest, and he did not know what to make of the Creek and Cherokee chiefs. Bowles argued, however, that both he and Dunmore regarded the southern Indians as invaluable allies in a Spanish war. Other Creeks and Cherokees, apparently on Bowles's behalf, were at the same time at Detroit urging western unity and corresponding with Sir John Johnson.[28] The military potential of the southern Indians appealed to Dorchester, and he paid the expenses of Bowles's delegation and provided their passage to England.[29]

The six Creek and Cherokee chiefs arrived in London in the fall as a recent "hot press" to secure sailors for British warships intensified war fever. The public enthusiastically received reports that thousands of Creeks and Cherokees were ready to descend on Spain's possessions. Grenville, expecting war at a moment's notice, impatiently awaited the delegation's arrival at Whitehall.[30] The Nootka dispute had forced the ministry to study carefully the Mississippi Valley and the conflicting ambitions of the four interested parties: the Indians, the United States, Spain, and Britain. (France, distracted by revolution, perhaps could be ignored.) Any decision Whitehall made affected all four.

Though there was going to be no formal cooperation with the United States, Grenville did not forget the westerners. Just because Washington's administration decided on neutrality, it did not necessarily follow that the individualistic frontiersmen were going to continue inactive. They demanded immediate free navigation of the Mississippi. John Connolly had recently explored the possibility of these westerners, supported by Britain, taking New Orleans and the Floridas. They considered themselves autonomous, and Connolly maintained that western communities, retaining local self government, might bind themselves in a federal union with Britain rather than the United States. Consul Phineas Bond was frantic because of Whitehall's indecision. He believed that the United States would not interfere when Britain and frontiersmen took New Orleans. "One British officer with me will be sufficient to carry any such scheme into execution."[31] We can bind the West to us "forever in spite of Congress and all the world."[32] Bowles, without going into details of boundaries, expected to include Muskogee in any pro-British western federation.

Whitehall, during the Nootka crisis, examined reports from the United States that "the old enemies of the federal happiness are at length reviving" and that they had not been sufficiently chilled by the adoption of the Constitution.[33] Grenville encouraged Levi Allen; there was renewed agitation to annex Vermont, and Clinton argued, apparently openly in the House of Commons, that "self preservation" required it.[34] As the months passed in 1790 developments indicated that Whitehall was going to have to make private arrangements with frontier components rather than deal with a central government perhaps no more effective than its predecessor. Sheffield in 1783 had predicted that the American frontier must soon divide into independent governments. It appeared in 1790 this was happening.[35]

For the first time since the American Revolution the fate of the Mississippi Valley (including the Floridas and Vermont) became a major issue at Whitehall. Lord Hawkesbury and his subordinates at the Board of Trade sifted through their data, held special sessions, and interviewed anyone with firsthand knowledge. One point that he emphasized—as the earl of Shelburne had done in 1782—was that the Mississippi Valley was capable of absorbing enormous quantities of manufactures which could stimulate the British merchant marine. The fur trade was significant, but potentially more valuable was the market offered by thousands of western pioneers.[36] From the moment that Bond had arrived in Philadelphia he had stressed the commercial importance of New Orleans.[37] Simcoe, soon to become lieutenant governor of Upper Canada, was delighted that Upper Canada's boundaries had been made purposely vague so that it was possible to consider

Detroit an integral part of this new British province.[38] He expected it to become a New World Calais from which Britain could disseminate wares over a large area.[39] Hawkesbury urged that Britain reinforce the Old Northwest forts, obtain a foothold on the lower Mississippi, and make alignments with autonomous frontier states from Vermont to Muskogee. He also made it clear that Britain needed a comprehensive policy: courting Vermont and ignoring Kentucky would not do.[40]

The head of the Board of Trade, advocating a militant policy against Spain, and, if necessary, the United States, maintained that he was making his recommendations from a commercial point of view. Pitt, Grenville, and presumably George III had to make the basic political-diplomatic decisions. But Hawkesbury knew as well as the rest of the government that it was impossible to divorce commercial from political issues. What he was recommending—and Grenville concurred—was that a successful Spanish war afforded a splendid opportunity to whittle the United States down to size, to throttle the growth of a commercial rival, and to stimulate British shipping.[41]

Hawkesbury, pondering Vermont's status since the Revolution, had been most interested when in 1789 Levi Allen arrived in London. Allen's insistence on a commercial treaty perplexed Hawkesbury. He knew that Britain already had made sweeping economic concessions and there was not much left to negotiate. Allen must be up to something else, as indeed he was, and it had as much to do with politics as commerce: he wanted Vermont's union with Canada. The ministry appreciated the risks of annexing "a people who inhabit a country which the said States may consider as a part of their territory."[42] But Hawkesbury had advocated union long before the Nootka dispute and agreed with Clinton: "We must join with Vermont cost what it may."[43] Pitt's ministry sent Levi Allen back to Vermont to inform the state's leaders that the British government was most sympathetic to their cause;[44] meanwhile, loyalists reassured the government that Allen could manage affairs to Britain's complete satisfaction.[45]

What was good for Vermont was good for Kentucky. Grenville previously had ordered Dorchester to gain the Kentucky leaders' goodwill but to make no promises: Britain had to be in a position to act as events dictated.[46] As chances of an Anglo-American alliance faded in 1790, Grenville, who more than any single individual was responsible for foreign policy, assumed that the time was at hand to deal boldly with the Kentuckians, Vermonters, and other dissatisfied frontiersmen.[47]

It was paradoxical that the policies of Britain's and the United States' national governments toward Vermont and Kentucky were similar. Both powers encouraged these territories in their bid for independent statehood (within a British or American federation), and both countries feared that further delay might lose these regions altogether. The United States moved first, and in March 1791 Vermont and June 1792 Kentucky became the fourteenth and fifteenth states. Britain, after hesitating for years, in 1790 began to make positive overtures, though settlement of the Nootka affair and difficulty of communications allowed the United States to act more effectively. But for the first time in 1790 it became obvious to the cabinet as a whole that Vermont and Kentucky were part of a larger problem. There were similar frontier districts—six by Hawkesbury's reckoning—among which were western Pennsylvania, Kentucky, Tennessee, and the Wyoming Valley.[48] Bowles wanted Muskogee included, and Clinton threw in recalcitrant Rhode Island for good measure.[49]

For years Detroit authorities had taken the measure of western discontent. Simcoe was distressed that Samuel Holden Parsons, impecunious judge of the Northwest Territory, had recently died, though the lieutenant governor did not elaborate on why he was so dejected over the death of a former rebel general. But during the Revolution Clinton had tried to win over Parsons to the British cause, and Connolly had contacted him in 1788. Simcoe and Clinton doubtless expected Parsons to play a role in aligning western Pennsylvania and parts of the Old Northwest with Canada.[50]

The prospect that the United States might be restricted to the Appalachian Mountains alarmed Washington's cabinet. Jefferson feared that, in the event of an Anglo-Spanish war, the British "embraced from the St. Croix to the St. Mary's on one side by their possessions, on the other by their fleet . . . would soon find means to unite . . . all the territory covered by the ramifications of the Mississippi."[51]

An Anglo-Spanish war ensured political readjustments in the Mississippi Valley. Though whites probably outnumbered Indians in 1790, the natives controlled a majority of the Old West's territory and were concerned about any changes. The advantages of Indian allies in a war against Spain—and against the United States, too, if she made a fuss over neutral rights—were not lost on the British government. The Nootka dispute spurred on an Indian confederation under British protection. Reinforcing Detroit and the other posts, Britain distributed presents and courted the Indians' favor. This made them more determined than ever on the Ohio River boundary. Their confidence increased after defeating the American army under Gen. Josiah Harmar in the Maumee country. This and other victories over the whites and presents from Indian agents in the north and from Bowles and Dunmore in the south, encouraged Indians throughout the West. If Alexander McKee on the Maumee or Bowles among the Creeks were to be believed, the old alliance of the Revolution had been renewed and the British white father was seeing to it that the Americans took over no more native lands.

Publicity surrounded Bowles and his Creek-Cherokee delegation when in the fall of 1790 they arrived in London. A fellow loyalist prepared an account of Bowles's life for publication.[52] The contrast between Bowles's reception and that of Thomas Dalton, who had almost frozen the previous year awaiting an interview, reflected Whitehall's mounting interest in the Indians and the American frontier. George III prepared to receive Bowles at a royal levee.[53] Bowles was only one of many who expected Britain to return to the Mississippi Valley. Edmund Fanning, a loyalist who had served among the Creeks and Cherokees and whose considerable property in North Carolina had been confiscated, was cold and unhappy as lieutenant governor of Prince Edward Island. He saw Bowles in Canada, wanted to cooperate in making the Floridas and Louisiana loyalist refuges, and begged the crown to accept his offer of enlisting a loyalist regiment for service in the southern Indian country.[54]

Clinton presumed that a resolute stand against Spain, and if need be against the United States, would make the western Indians rally to the British standard,[55] and he expected white frontiersmen to cooperate. Though both white and red westerners had grievances against Spain and the eastern states and had reason to align themselves with Britain, it did not necessarily follow that Britain could get the two to embrace. Clinton, when he advocated turning Kentuckians and western Indians loose against Spain, for good reason did not dwell on this. Neither did Bowles when he promised Indian support for the Natchez loyalists. The conflicting interests of the Indians, for whom the fur trade was part of their way of life, and of the pioneers, who with few exceptions were farmers, could not be restrained for long. Clinton, Hawkesbury, Simcoe, and Bowles minimized this divergence during the Nootka controversy. As a result the Indian confederation grew tighter, McKee stepped up his distribution of presents, and loyalists in the southern Indian country awaited word and trading goods from Dunmore.[56]

The Nootka dispute illustrated the confusion in the Old Southwest where the southern Indians were only part of the picture. It seemed likely that Britain would employ Bowles's Muskogee in liberating Spanish America and acquire the Floridas in the process. Whoever had the Floridas had a boundary dispute. Depending on whose definition was consulted, most of the Old Southwest was either part of the United States or part of West Florida. Even before the Nootka controversy Britain had an important commercial stake in the Floridas. Manufactures disseminated among the Indians—and to an undetermined extent among the Spanish populace—were likely of British origin.

Rival merchant groups vied for the southern Indian trade and that of the Spanish Floridas. Both were based in the Bahamas and both were composed of loyalists, many of whom were Florida exiles. The only difference was that one firm enjoyed a monopoly from Spain and the other did not. Spain had granted Panton, Leslie, and Company in effect a monopoly of the southern fur trade and other commercial concessions. Alexander McGillivray was an important member of this firm, and Superintendent Thomas Brown, who had moved to the Bahamas, was associated with it.

During the Nootka dispute the Spanish government in East Florida made Brown an astounding offer; at least this is what Brown told Pitt and there is no reason to disbelieve him. The offer was for Brown, with a handsome salary and other perquisites, to become Spanish superintendent of the southern Indians.[57] With Brown as superintendent, Panton in Pensacola, Leslie at St. Augustine, and McGillivray in the Indian country at Little Tallassie, this company would be further entrenched and the management of the southern Indians even more in British hands. Panton, Leslie, and Company's position was enviable.

Though a Spanish war might lead to sweeping changes in the Old Southwest benefiting Britain, it is hard to imagine how this firm's position could improve. But it might deteriorate rapidly, and as a result Panton and Leslie steered a cautious course.

Miller, Bonnamy, and Company, with whom Bowles and Dunmore were associated, was the rival merchant firm. It had no compact with the Spaniards, little to lose, and much to gain by upsetting both the status quo in the south and Panton, Leslie, and Company's monopoly. One reason Dunmore advocated British return to the Floridas and the Mississippi Valley was that he expected to win a share of the trade. As long as Spain and Panton, Leslie, and Company were established in the Floridas and much of the Old Southwest, there was no room for Dunmore and his friends.

While Britain prepared to employ the southern Indians against Spain, Whitehall became aware of the cleavage between the rival factions of loyalist merchants. Beckwith in 1790 had talked to McGillivray in New York trying to determine the Indians' course in the event of a Spanish war. Beckwith never got an answer but formed the impression that, though McGillivray had served Britain during the Revolution and briefly in 1788 had cooperated with Dunmore, he was too bound to Spain and the United States to be of service to Britain. Beckwith's apprehension increased when Dalton, fresh from London, arrived in New York and asserted that McGillivray had turned away from Britain and in any case did not speak for a majority of the Creeks. Dalton insisted that he and his superior, Bowles, were the effective leaders of the Creek Nation.[58] Simcoe, pondering conditions in the south, hoped that McGillivray was "yet *not lost*" but had his doubts.[59]

The point that Dalton, Bowles, and Dunmore stressed during the Nootka dispute was that Panton, Leslie, and Company was tied closely to Spain and that these former loyalists were now "half Spanish." In the event of a Spanish war this firm would trade with Britain's enemy and manage the southern Indians in Spain's rather than Britain's behalf. Grenville wondered whether, if Spain paid Brown a handsome salary to superintend the southern Indians, Brown would remain loyal to Britain.

The rivalry of loyalist merchants in the southern Indian country was an extension of political divisions in the Bahamas. Dunmore,

Councilman John Miller, and numerous Dunmore appointees were in the Old Settler faction. Brown, Panton, and Thomas Forbes, some of whom were in the Bahamian assembly, were in the New Settler clique. Bahamian politics were so quarrelsome that Dunmore might have regarded his controversial Virginia governorship as tranquil by comparison. During the Nootka controversy Dunmore and Bowles called everyone associated with Panton, Leslie, and Company "traitor" or worse, but these factions had been exchanging epithets for years. Dissension reached a climax on the American mainland when early in 1792 Bowles seized Panton, Leslie, and Company's warehouse near Fort St. Marks in West Florida.[60]

As it turned out Whitehall never had to choose between the Dunmore faction and Panton, Leslie, and Company because there was no war. Spain without her French ally was no match for Britain who prepared to encourage a Spanish American revolt and unleash red and white Americans on Louisiana and the Floridas. Spain backed down and made peace.[61] Bowles, anxious for his reception at George III's levee and for an Anglo-Muskogee alliance, got neither. George Rogers Clark in the Mississippi Valley and Elijah Clarke in Georgia, eager to strike at New Orleans and the Floridas with British aid, were disappointed.[62] The Indians, anticipating presents as numerous as those distributed during the Revolution, were downcast. And Simcoe complained that Britain by delay was on the verge of losing Vermont and its one hundred thousand settlers.[63]

The Anglo-Spanish convention adjusted matters on the Pacific coast but settled nothing in the Mississippi Valley. The northern Indians, victorious over Gen. Harmar, were as resolute about the Ohio boundary as ever. In the south Dunmore and Bowles still tried to establish an independent Muskogee and expected a British alliance when they succeeded. Though Kentucky joined the union, neither that state nor any western settlement enjoyed free navigation of the Mississippi River. As Simcoe saw it, whenever Britain took New Orleans and opened the Mississippi, Kentucky must speedily make an accommodation with Britain.[64] The Nootka controversy betrayed the ministry's ambitions toward the American frontier. They abated in the Nootka convention's aftermath. But to assume that they had disappeared and would not reemerge in some new crisis was folly.

5 • Indian Impetuosity

THE SHAWNEES, Miamis, and other Old Northwest Indians after Josiah Harmar's defeat were more set than ever on the Ohio boundary, while the United States thought this claim as absurd in the 1790s as in 1783. Below the Ohio Tennesseans made inroads on Cherokee lands, and Georgians resolved to expand beyond the Oconee. From the Six Nations in the north to the Creek-Seminoles in the south Indians feared American expansion and realized that unity was essential. That the United States allocated five-sixths of the national budget to frontier defense illustrated the seriousness of the dispute.[1] Not only the Indians but also whites living in the Old West had complaints. George Rogers Clark, James Wilkinson, and similar frontier leaders, suspicious of seaboard rule whether at the national or state level, concluded that the East did not appreciate the West and was not sufficiently sympathetic to its demand for free navigation of the Mississippi.

Even if it had been possible to ignore the Indians and unruly white frontiersmen, the fact that both British and Spanish troops remained on soil claimed by the United States insured controversy. British ministers debated American designs on Detroit and the rest of "our posts" in the Old Northwest and at the same time encouraged Indians to defend their lands and began pressing for a neutral barrier state.[2] Spain, entrenched in Natchez and other posts above the thirty-first parallel, was reluctant to say what she considered West Florida's northern boundary, but, wherever it was, it encompassed much of the Old Southwest.

Spanish dominion over West Florida was far from absolute, and British subjects played an important role. Legally or not they managed West Florida's commerce and were sprinkled throughout this province. Probably a majority of the inhabitants in the Natchez district still considered themselves or would have liked to consider themselves British subjects.[3] Since Britain in the 1790s continued to dicker with Spain about Florida's cession, it was possible that the loyalists' wish might be gratified. When British ministers referred to "our posts" they might soon include Natchez, Pensacola, and St. Marks as well as Detroit, Michilimackinac, and Niagara. William Wyndham Grenville (created Baron Grenville in 1790) actively worked toward that end.[4]

Indian belligerence, restless pioneers, retention by Britain of the boundary posts and her designs on the Floridas, coupled with relentless American expansion, insured that the 1790s would not be tranquil. At the same time, revolutionary forces abroad threatened the frontier's peace. Even though the American Revolution was over and in 1791 Louis XVI proclaimed a new constitution for France, the "democratic" revolutions had not run their course. French republicans, not satisfied with their 1791 constitution, clamored to overthrow their monarch and to establish a republic. In doing so they embroiled France in civil war and rendered the powerful ally of Spain and the United States impotent. The effect of this on the frontier had been illustrated during the Nootka controversy. If French republicans were successful, westerners might take up the cause of liberty, equality, and fraternity with new enthusiasm. The alarmed Dorchester and Simcoe regarded the boundary forts important not only for the fur trade and the managing of the Indians but also as a barrier against the spread of republicanism among French Canadians.

The specter appeared of Spanish Americans embracing republican ideology and setting themselves up in independent states. Overthrowing the mother country's rule in Spanish Louisiana and the Floridas created a political vacuum. During the Nootka crisis both the British ministry and Washington's cabinet discussed how to fill this void, and that they held contrary viewpoints did not augur well for the Old West's concord.

British retention of the forts was the most dangerous threat to frontier peace. The overriding danger was that, when the United States sent an army into the Indian country, Indian hostilities easily could expand into an Anglo-American conflict. Canadians feared that the United States, as boastful frontiersmen advocated, might try to take the posts by force. Whenever the Americans raised an army—to go against Indians on the Maumee or to suppress Shays' Rebellion—Dorchester's first concern was for the forts' security.[5]

There was never doubt that Canadians furnished the muskets, powder, and knives used by the Indians to prey on flatboats floating down the Ohio or to smite General Harmar's men. Many were loyalists, and there were a few old French *coureurs de bois*. The Americans portrayed the typical fur trader as one like Simon Girty, a loyalist with an Indian family, allegedly cruel, grasping, unprincipled, who enjoyed watching Indians burn Americans at the stake, and whose passion was encouraging the natives to harry Americans. The facts were somewhat different. Some traders lived in Detroit or similar white communities, while others lived among the Indians. It was natural that these traders sympathized with the Indians' demand for the Ohio boundary and shared their hatred toward the Americans. But these merchants' livelihoods depended on the fur trade, and commercial considerations were paramount. Furs were the mainstay of commerce with the natives, and even the most illiterate white trader perceived that if the Indians used their powder and ball to kill Americans rather than to hunt, they would have no furs to trade. The natives themselves realized that though they might receive additional presents, ransom an occasional prisoner, or get a scalp bounty, constant fighting was not financially profitable.[6]

It was ironic that as hostilities intensified during the early 1790s in the Old Northwest, Canadian fur traders and western pioneers' pleas for peace mounted. Though one might wonder why, with such ardor for peace on both sides, there was no accommodation, the answer was not hard to find. Each was bent on peace on his own terms. The Americans demanded that the natives abandon nonsense about independence and an Ohio boundary and pay no heed to hostile counsels of British advisors. If Indians living in territory claimed by the United States did not listen to reason, the alternative was an expedition to raze Indian villages and crops and kill their braves until necessity forced them to capitulate. Gen. Arthur St. Clair in 1791 assembled and drilled a large army at Fort Washington (Cincinnati) preparing to march into the heart of the Indian country.[7]

Canadian fur traders petitioned their government to restore peace. Grenville, now foreign secretary, was sympathetic because protracted hostilities not only hurt the fur trade but kept alive the dispute over the forts. No less than the traders he wanted peace but insisted that "the terms not be inconsistent with the security of the Indians."[8] It was precisely this point that kept the Old Northwest in turmoil. To provide for Indian security Grenville hoped to become arbiter between the Indians and Americans and to establish a neutral buffer state in the Old Northwest. He preferred not even to discuss the matter of the posts with the United States because continued British occupation was important for the natives' protection. With Grenville advocating a buffer state and the posts' retention, and Washington and Secretary of War Henry Knox scraping up men for St. Clair's army, it was not surprising that, though both sides urged peace, there was no peace.

After innumerable delays testy General St. Clair moved his force northward in slow stages from Fort Washington. The Indians watched every move and informed Alexander McKee and the traders on the Maumee of the Americans' latest advance. The United States had insisted all along that St. Clair's army was directed at the Indians, not the British-occupied posts, but neither McKee nor Dorchester was convinced. The Shawnees, Kickapoos, Miamis, and other hostile tribes assembled on the Maumee, while McKee dispensed food and munitions. Despite St. Clair's precautions the Indians surprised his militia near the headwaters of the Wabash, forced them in confusion back on the main body of regulars, at which time the engagement turned into a rout. St. Clair's second-in-command and over six hundred men were killed, the artillery and stores lost, and the survivors sent fleeing back to Fort Washington. It was an amazing Indian victory, comparable to their defeat of Braddock during the French and Indian War, and both Washington and Dorchester were surprised by the decisive triumph. Only the Shawnee, Blue Jacket, who commanded the Indians, and possibly Simon and James Girty, Matthew Elliott, and loyalist merchants engaged in the battle anticipated the outcome.[9]

News of the American defeat spread throughout the Indian country almost as rapidly as St. Clair's survivors fled from the battlefield to Fort Washington. Americans feared that more "of us will be apt to lose our hair."[10] The Delawares and Wyandots, previously skeptical about defending the Ohio boundary, joined the confederacy. The advice of Joseph Brant, advocating a less militant policy, was ignored. The southern Indians were overjoyed and more committed than ever to a confederation defying American expansion everywhere, whether above the Ohio or beyond the Oconee.

St. Clair's defeat strengthened the hand of those like Gen. Sir Henry Clinton who urged a forceful policy against the United States, a nation that was weak, torn by dissension, and unable even to cope with the Indians. Sir Henry was coming back into official favor, and both the ministry and the king, prodded by the king's brother, paid more attention to his suggestions. Sir Henry believed that the moment Britain surrendered the forts and abandoned the Indians Canada was lost. This he determined to avoid at all costs, and when he thought of preserving Canada, he still tended to think of Canada with extended boundaries.

During the Nootka affair Clinton had wanted to establish a viable Canada at the expense of the United States and Spain. When Charles Stevenson, Simcoe's right-hand man, wrote from Philadelphia about St. Clair's rout, Clinton took new hope. He believed that if the Indians followed up their victory, the Americans must sue for peace, and he pondered what terms the Indians should exact from the Americans and how much aid Britain should give the natives. She might use her good offices in establishing an Indian buffer state. So as not to unduly antagonize the Americans, Clinton expected the Indians first to solicit British mediation—but McKee could easily arrange that. Clinton pressed his views on the ministry which in its wisdom now concurred with him.[11]

One of Grenville's major objectives was to create a buffer state.[12] He indicated that when the Americans made concessions in the Old Northwest, Britain might reciprocate elsewhere. The youthful George Hammond, recently appointed minister to the United States, engaged in far-ranging discussions with Jefferson and Hamilton. Sir Henry, though unenthusiastic about making concessions, considered Britain's proffer of mediation a realistic solution to tensions in the Old Northwest which might spare "the blushes of America."[13] He was sure there must be dusty treaties in the Home Office proving that Britain never had the right to give away Indian lands, thereby justifying intervention.[14]

Sir Henry felt the alternative to a buffer state was to ignore the Philadelphia government and take necessary steps to protect the forts, retain the Indians' good will, and provide for Canada's security. This meant that Britain had to do more for the Indians than rummage through Whitehall's cubbyholes searching for ancient documents justifying the Ohio boundary. As a last resort Clinton suggested again

committing British troops in America—but only in the West. With
Simcoe commanding in the Old Northwest, the spirited cavalry leader,
Banastre Tarleton, dispatched to the lower Mississippi, western Indians unleashed against the Americans, and a cooperating naval force
in the Gulf of Mexico, Clinton dreamed of bringing the Americans to
heel in one or two short campaigns. At the same time he expected
Britain to woo disaffected frontier districts—Kentucky, western
Pennsylvania, western New York, Vermont, anywhere. If they proved
recalcitrant, Sir Henry was prepared to turn the Indians loose against
them also.

During the Revolution he had learned the futility of trying to subdue the eastern states by force and resolved to restrict hostilities to the
frontier. If Americans opposed British designs, they had to send forces
into the Indian country and in a sense would be the invaders. In en-
gaging the Americans Clinton did not envision either the United
States' destruction or its restoration to the British empire. He
merely assumed that the Appalachian Mountains were a natural line of
division and that Vermont and bits of New England properly belonged
to Canada.[15]

As the months passed after St. Clair's defeat Clinton believed that
Grenville and Hammond were not going to get far with their buffer
state. America had lost all reason, and the radical philosophy of
Thomas Paine, which had already caused Sir Henry his share of grief,
had a lot to do with it. He was horrified as republican extremists in the
National Convention, one of whom was that damn Paine, gained control of France. There seemed to be an international republican design
bent on subverting the British constitution. Clinton insisted that Britain do everything possible in both the Old World and the New to frustrate republican expansion, and constricting the United States'
boundaries was one way. Force was necessary, and Clinton knew the
Indians could not shoulder the burden alone; but Simcoe in the north,
Tarleton in the south, and a fleet in the Gulf of Mexico, all cooperating
with the Indians, could do the job.

Sir Henry, speculating about the "zealous, cooperating head
chief,"[16] regarded the veteran Dorchester, already on the scene in Canada, as the logical choice. Dorchester, however, was old and somewhat
infirm. "Honest pride" prevented Clinton from "offering [his] services

which have been marked with slight." He would accept service but not solicit it.[17] Though Clinton doubted the government would appoint him overall commander, he hoped so. He never had understood why Dorchester had gotten a peerage for losing Fort Ticonderoga while the government had done nothing for Sir Henry. The United States showed little interest in a buffer state, and Clinton assumed that only a show of force on the frontier offered a solution. He presented a double-barreled gun to Joseph Brant. New York had confiscated the property of both Brant and Clinton. Aiming this new weapon at Americans expanding into the Mohawk Valley, Brant could pull one trigger for himself, the other for Sir Henry.[18]

Although Clinton, other than being a member of Parliament, had no official voice, he advised ministers and the king. Some who completely shared his views, like Lieutenant Governor Simcoe of Upper Canada, held responsible posts. Even more than did Clinton, Simcoe believed Canada's security depended on the forts' retention and Indian goodwill. A buffer state, in effect moving the province of Upper Canada's boundary southward, helped, but Simcoe wanted nothing better than to restrict the United States to the Appalachian Mountains. The Old West must be preserved for the Indians, loyalists, and disaffected frontiersmen not addicted to Paine's *Age of Reason*. Discharged Revolutionary War veterans of Simcoe's Queen's Rangers were already established at Niagara and Detroit, and Simcoe enlisted a new regiment of Queen's Rangers in England and stationed them at key positions in Upper Canada. He envisioned his province of Upper Canada as a quasi-military colony peopled by active and retired soldiers and their families on the order of the *coloniae* Romans had established in England.[19] Simcoe had set out for Upper Canada in 1791 determined to make it a thriving colony instrumental in the *"Re-union of Empire."*[20] He knew that Upper Canada's boundaries were vague—deliberately so because of the forts—and he intended to make the most of it.

Charles Stevenson was Simcoe's subordinate and personal agent. As Simcoe's unofficial representative, Stevenson had much in common with George Beckwith. Both had served in New York during the Revolution and had been in Clinton's confidence; both were acquainted with men of influence; after the Revolution both simultaneously served Canadian governors. Stevenson loyally defended Simcoe until the general's death years later. When not in Upper Canada, Stevenson hopped about to New York, Philadelphia, Vermont, even London, conferring with political leaders and members of the royal family and keeping abreast of conditions on both sides of the Atlantic.

John Connolly, employed by Sir John Johnson in the Indian department at Cataraqui, wanted to move to Upper Canada, to serve under Simcoe and augment his contacts with dissatisfied westerners, and to continue his land speculations.[21] Simcoe, distrusting Connolly's dealings with the prince of speculators, Robert Morris, corresponded directly with frontier leaders sympathetic to a British connection.[22] Dorchester's loyalist advisors at Quebec assumed that the decisive Indian victories must lead to an extension of Canada's limits.[23] The Duke of Kent, George III's son and regimental commander at Quebec who aspired to succeed Dorchester, visited Simcoe at Niagara in the fall of 1792, watching Indians from both sides of the boundary enthusiastically renew their allegiance to the king. The Duke asked his father for permission to visit the United States, and it would be interesting to know where he expected to go and whom he planned to contact.[24] Authorities in both Upper and Lower Canada, members of the royal family, Hawkesbury and Grenville, key members of the ministry, all agreed that retention of the forts, maintaining Indian friendship, and, at the minimum, establishing a buffer state were indispensable for Canada's security.

The ministry thought more of a satellite buffer state than of unleashing Simcoe and Banastre Tarleton. In view of St. Clair's defeat, Indian determination on the Ohio boundary, and British occupation of the posts for a decade, Whitehall regarded the buffer state a reasonable compromise, one that could reconcile all parties. Clinton thought the United States should appreciate Britain's efforts to restore peace on the frontier. But, as Hammond and Grenville quickly found out in their negotiations, it was going to take more than an Indian defeat to make the United States surrender territory for a buffer state.

Britain wanted a buffer state to obtain free navigation of the Mississippi River. Treaties with both the United States and Spain guaranteed this but to no effect. At the time of the 1783 Anglo-American peace treaty it was incorrectly assumed that the Mississippi's headwaters were in Canada. There was in fact a gap, and Canadian traders had to cross

United States territory to get to the Mississippi. A buffer state naturally included portages linking the Great Lakes with the Mississippi. Simcoe was adamant that he have access to the Maumee-Wabash river route, the best means of communicating with Kentucky.[25]

The United States agreed in principle that Britain no less than the United States should have free navigation of the Mississippi River because the 1783 peace treaty so stipulated.[26] Britain's first hurdle was to secure the Great Lakes–Mississippi portages through the establishment of a buffer state or by outright conquest. In contrast the United States' initial goal was to obtain Spanish permission for unrestricted use of the port of New Orleans and the lower Mississippi River. Americans readily agreed that both Britain and the United States should have free navigation of the Mississippi River and that both should work together to obtain it. But what the United States meant was that Britain should back to the Americans in pressing Spain to throw open New Orleans.

A free New Orleans was of immediate value to the United States but of limited utility to Canada without access to the upper Mississippi. Although Hamilton flirted with ceding a small strip in the Old Northwest to link Canada with the upper Mississippi, Washington's administration opposed any territorial cession as strongly as they opposed an Indian buffer state.[27] Britain's insistence on free navigation of the Mississippi was inseparable from the buffer state project or outright cession. American demands for free navigation had nothing to do with relinquishing territory and reflected the disparate views of the two countries toward the Old Northwest and Mississippi navigation.

By 1793 it was obvious that a crisis was approaching. Gen. Anthony Wayne was raising and drilling a large American army on the Ohio to march against the Indians. The western Indians, more united than at any time since the Revolution, resolved to fight for the Ohio boundary. McKee, Johnson, and their subordinates in the Indian department dispensed munitions, food, and black wampum for war belts and encouraged the Indians to defend their lands. Minister Hammond in Philadelphia, still advocating a neutral buffer state as a peaceful compromise, made no headway; no one could tell if the British government would listen to Clinton's recommendation to turn Simcoe and Tarleton loose in the West.

The United States made a final attempt at peace by proposing to meet the Indians at Lower Sandusky near Lake Erie's south shore, site of a British Revolutionary War fort and rendezvous of Canadian fur traders. Timothy Pickering, Benjamin Lincoln, and Beverly Randolph were authorized to grant limited concessions and to make a liberal financial settlement. The Indians held mixed views. Brant thought that a statesmanlike policy in the wake of St. Clair's defeat was to retreat slightly from the upper Ohio to the Muskingum River as a boundary while making it clear that the remainder of the Old Northwest belonged to the independent Indians.[28] This was Hammond's buffer state. The western Indians, intoxicated by their recent victories, opposed concessions. As they told Brant, we will go to Sandusky, but "the Ohio must be the boundary line, as we long ago agreed upon."[29] Because of divisions in native councils, the Indians decided—and McKee helped make the decision—to have a preliminary meeting at the Rapids of the Maumee, McKee's headquarters sixty-five miles below Detroit.

As the Indians assembled at the Rapids of the Maumee, the American commissioners began their journey. The first stage brought them to Upper Canada's temporary capital at Navy Hall (Niagara-on-the-Lake) where Simcoe resided. The ever-suspicious Pickering, astonished by Simcoe's hospitality, was further encouraged when an Iroquois delegation announced that the Indians were not unalterably set on the Ohio boundary.[30] But presumably Pickering knew that the Iroquois had a tradition of giving up lands belonging to other tribes. Simcoe made arrangements to forward the American commissioners to Fort Erie, commanding Lake Erie's entrance into the Niagara River, and from there by boat to Detroit. It was indicative of the Old Northwest's status that Simcoe had to manage details about sending the commissioners safely into the heart of the Indian country. He told them exactly how long they had to stay at Niagara and that they next would have to go to Detroit even though it was out of the way.[31]

From Detroit the American commissioners were anxious to get on to Lower Sandusky and begin negotiations. But Detroit was as far as they got. The contentious Indians, still at the Rapids of the Maumee, refused to budge until they saw the commissioners' instructions, instructions which stated that at the outset the Americans agreed to the Ohio boundary. The more militant western Indians had won out over Brant. Pickering, optimistic at Niagara, became discouraged after reaching Detroit when it appeared more likely each day the Lower Sandusky council would never begin. Even worse, British authorities did not permit the Americans to go to the Rapids of the Maumee and directly confront the Indians. This was partly for the commissioners' safety—many Indians thought the Americans were luring them to Lower Sandusky under false pretenses—and partly because Simcoe did not want Americans on the spot where they might exploit native divisions. The proposed council at Lower Sandusky never began, and the dejected American commissioners, after a frustrating period at Detroit, returned home.[32]

General Wayne, following negotiations as best he could from the Ohio, assumed that Britain, emboldened by France's domestic strife, was deliberately procrastinating and had resolved to restrict the United States to the Ohio at least.[33] Wayne's viewpoint was not surprising but at this particular time he was unfair to Simcoe. Like Brant, Simcoe was willing to retreat from the Ohio line if he could get a buffer state. He thought this possible and he expected to establish a fixed boundary between the Indians and Kentucky, restore peace to the frontier, and later attach Kentucky to Upper Canada. Both Indians and whites, according to the Canadian governor, could then live in peace and prosper under Britain's liberal rule. Simcoe, though he was not thinking about the same kind of concessions that the American commissioners were, was annoyed by the western Indians' intransigence.[34]

Wayne's appraisal was a military one, based on the concept of balance of power, and similar to that of his Revolutionary adversary, General Clinton. Sir Henry, across the channel from France, could almost hear the tumbrels bouncing over Parisian cobblestones bearing the latest victims to the guillotine. Like most Britishers he was alarmed by Louis XVI's execution and the radical turn of the French Revolution, and he heard about French developments months before Simcoe learned about them in Upper Canada. By 1793 Clinton essentially agreed with Wayne. France was in turmoil, and any measure to contain republicanism, whether supporting French monarchists, or allying with France's continental enemies, or backing the Indians' demand for the Ohio, was justified.[35]

So far the Old Northwest has been treated as a unit, as in fact it was. Before the American Revolution Britain had divided the West and had installed one Indian superintendent above the Ohio and another below. After the Revolution the United States had organized the Old Northwest as a territory through the Northwest Ordinance. But the Ohio was a tributary of the Mississippi, and geographically the Mississippi united the Old West far more effectively than the Ohio separated it. It is not realistic to discuss the abortive council at Lower Sandusky, an Indian buffer state, and Britain's Indian policy, and to ignore the Old Southwest. During the Nootka crisis William Augustus Bowles, with good reason, had expected overt British support for his state of Muskogee. The Nootka Convention dashed these hopes. But all was not lost. Bowles argued that there would inevitably be future crises and that Britain must court the southern Indians' friendship. They wanted "to learn from your Majesty's own mouth whether it is your gracious intention to maintain the old alliance" and whether they should keep the silver medals British officers had given them in 1764.[36] What Bowles really wanted was a liberal interpretation of the 1787 Free Port Act to allow merchant vessels flying Muskogee's pennant to trade freely in Nassau or other West Indian ports.

Grenville presumed Bowles exaggerated, "though perhaps not much," about how the Indians and westerners could annoy Spain, and after the Nootka settlement he opposed open assistance. But commerce via the free port of Nassau was another matter: "Nothing will tend more to establish a connection with them."[37] Grenville was thinking of more than commerce. His objective was to attach all North American Indians to Britain. That was the way to protect "our posts." Grenville, giving Bowles indirect official recognition and all possible commercial encouragement, asked Hawkesbury and the Board of Trade to work out details.[38] Under the circumstances Bowles obtained everything he could expect. He took leave of Grenville and promised to send him copies of Muskogee's correspondence with Spain and the United States.[39]

Bowles returned to Nassau in June 1791, conferred with Dunmore before sailing for the Indian country, and soon vessels flying Muskogee's banner, laden with cargoes of deerskins, arrived in Nassau. On the mainland Bowles did what he could to breathe life into Muskogee, whose capital at the time was Coweta (near Columbus) on the Chatta-hoochee River. The Indian state's boundaries were vague but included much of the Old Southwest and the Floridas. Denouncing the policies of Panton, Leslie, and Company and heading a party of Lower Creek–Seminoles, he captured that firm's St. Mark's warehouse early in 1792.

Soon afterwards he went to New Orleans and negotiated with the Spaniards. He assumed they had had enough of Panton and McGilli-vray and were ready to deal with Bowles and Dunmore. Bowles con-sidered a robust Muskogee a buffer between the United States and Spanish colonies. The Spaniards, always distrusting McGillivray and Panton, appreciated the logic of Bowles's arguments. But they were never sure that Spanish colonies would be better off with bumptious Muskogee as a neighbor. They sent Bowles to Spain where they debated whether to return him to head Muskogee or to keep him im-prisoned forever. After vacillating for three years, they banished him in 1795 to permanent exile in the Philippines—so they thought.[40]

But while Bowles had been on the mainland in 1791–92 and had un-furled Muskogee's ensign at Coweta, while his army had captured Pan-ton, Leslie, and Company's warehouse and his navy had plied the Gulf of Mexico, impetuous Muskogee had created a stir. Both Beckwith, as Dorchester's representative, and Stevenson, as Simcoe's agent, were in the American capital and informed their superiors that Bowles had re-turned, was posing as a British agent, and had prevented surveying the 1790 Treaty of New York boundary line.[41] When the United States complained to Hammond about this, the British minister reassured Jefferson that since Britain was not inciting the northern Indians, she certainly would not encourage them in a more remote quarter.

Hammond was not telling the truth, because in a variety of ways Britain was rousing the northern Indians, and Minister Hammond had done his share.[42] Even before Grenville wrote about Bowles, Ham-mond must have known that Britain probably was giving the same sort of support to the southern as to the northern Indians, i.e., trading with them and encouraging them to defend their lands. Dorchester, at least in 1791–92, wondered if the risks of patronizing Bowles were worth it. Simcoe, having few qualms, was delighted that the director general had defeated the Treaty of New York and that the southern Indians were more united and committed to defending their hunting lands than ever.[43]

Though Bowles left the Indian country in 1792, his presence was still felt. He had exploited native opposition to Alexander McGillivray's Treaty of New York, and this mixed-blooded chieftain eventually repudiated his New York concessions. It was still undetermined whether Bowles's associates, Dunmore and John Miller, would wrest control of commerce in the southern Indian country. But Panton, Leslie, and Company enjoyed Spanish backing and had the advantage. Bowles's supporters still lived among the Cherokees and Chickamaugas. Though they continued to correspond with McKee, they were forced in order to secure a stock of trading goods to do business with Panton.[44] But Bowles's picture still hung in a Chickamauga cabin, and Spaniards, who held him prisoner in Spain, still had not decided whether to return him to Muskogee. George Wellbank, Bowles's chief lieutenant, continued among the Creeks and Cherokees and remained true to the cause. With some success he maintained an open commerce with Nassau. Dunmore still occupied Government House where he received southern Indians, gave them commissions and ordered them to train their warriors and hold them in readiness for George III, and at the same time he informed Whitehall how eager they were to cede lands to British subjects.[45] The governor may have been on the verge of sending over one of his sons as Bowles's replacement.

Whether Bowles was on the scene or not, there was more enthusiasm during 1791–93 for an Indian confederation than ever. At any time it was difficult to unite the Indians who were scattered in numerous villages with different languages, customs, and ancient rivalries. But there were many, especially the Shawnees and the Chickamauga Cherokees, who worked to overcome these obstacles. Both tribes, in the immediate path of American expansion, had suffered and had the best reasons to advocate unity and no land cessions. They had the advantage of a central location and widespread personal contacts through kinship. Hundreds of loyalists, from McKee, whose wife was a Shawnee, to Bowles, whose first wife had been a Cherokee, pled for unity.

During the early 1790s Shawnee emissaries, one of whom was the young Tecumseh, visited the principal Cherokee and Creek towns.

The Cherokees, in conjunction with the northern Indians, preyed on flatboats floating down the Ohio River. Both Johnson and McKee corresponded with Indians below the Ohio. The aged Chickamauga war chief, Dragging Canoe, symbol of Chickamauga defiance since before the Revolution, in the early 1790s lived in the vicinity of Lookout Mountain, Tennessee. McKee sent him munitions and a variety of presents, but said he was "sorry I could not send you a French horn nor a fife."[46] Creeks and Cherokees fought against St. Clair, and in the wake of his rout Simcoe was anxious to turn "our friends the *United Indian Americans* against our friends the United States."[47]

St. Clair's defeat gave new hope to the western Indians, and they called a general council in 1792 to meet at the Glaize (where the Auglaize River joins the Maumee). Bowles had expected to attend but unfortunately was in Spanish hands. The southern Indians, however, were represented: "You see there, the Creeks, sitting by us who have come in consequence of our speeches."[48] The western Indians, agreeing to go to Lower Sandusky the following year and parley with the Americans, informed Brant that the Ohio had to be the boundary. As has been discussed, the Indians held a preliminary council at the Rapids of the Maumee before going to Lower Sandusky. The southern Indians, perhaps three hundred or more, were represented.

One of the southern "Indians" who arrived at the Rapids of the Maumee was loyalist George Wellbank, Bowles's second-in-command. After Bowles's departure Wellbank lived in the Creek-Cherokee country and spent part of his time at his warehouses near the Ochlockonee River's mouth trying to maintain a Muskogee-Bahama commerce. He wrote Dunmore in the Bahamas and McKee on the Maumee urging British support for the western Indians in general and for himself in particular. When northern delegations arrived among the Creeks and Cherokees, Wellbank did the best he could for them in the way of presents and munitions.[49] Accompanied by twenty-six Indians, he left the Lower Creek–Seminole country, made a three-month overland journey, and arrived at the Rapids of the Maumee early in the summer of 1793. He met with McKee and other Indian agents and interrogated captured American soldiers who had information about Wayne's army at Fort Jefferson.[50]

He went on to Detroit, consulted with the British commander, and dined with the recently arrived American commissioners. From here he set out for Niagara to see Simcoe. The American commissioners, anxious to begin the council at Sandusky, were dejected when the British vessel reserved to take them to Lower Sandusky instead sailed away to Niagara with Wellbank aboard. Wellbank, who had served under Simcoe during the Revolution, was no stranger. He reported on affairs in the south: that Georgians trespassed on the Oconee lands, that Gov. William Blount and the Tennesseans had cheated the Cherokees and were encroaching on their lands, and that the latest reports indicated that Spain was returning Bowles to Muskogee. Wellbank avowed that the Georgians and Blount were as bad as those Americans appropriating lands above the Ohio River.[51]

The general council at Lower Sandusky never began, and both the American commissioners and, as has been presented earlier, even Simcoe were provoked. But the northwestern Indians were adamant and refused to make concessions. Recent Indian victories had much to do with native intransigence. The southern Indians, supporting a western confederacy and determined on no territorial cessions, were also influential. At the Rapids of the Maumee, they made it clear that they would never go to Lower Sandusky unless it was understood that not only was the Ohio the boundary but also that the southern Indians had to be included in any settlement. Both Brant and Simcoe blamed the southern Indians for the western Indians' militancy, and they criticized the Shawnees, who had invited the southern Indians, for promising more British aid than Simcoe at the time wanted to deliver. But it is hard to decide whether to blame the Shawnee delegation that visited the southern villages or McKee and his subordinates who met with this delegation before it departed.[52]

Only the previous year Simcoe had been enthusiastic about turning the united Indians against the Americans. But native resentment had gotten out of hand. This spelled the downfall of Simcoe's barrier state which was to have been the first step in dislodging the United States from the Old West. Even though British merchants controlled the western Indian trade, the Indians considered themselves independent. While Simcoe was telling the Americans that he was not concerned about the Cherokees' dispute with Blount, the Cherokees and other southern Indians were exchanging war belts and pieces of tobacco "died red" with the northwestern tribes.[53]

Simcoe had a nagging fear that if he crossed the Indians, the natives would turn on him.[54] As a result southern Indians at the Rapids of the Maumee got their share of the presents. McKee distributed to Wellbank and the party of chiefs accompanying him rifles, munitions, gorgets, and tobacco before their return. Simcoe himself gave Wellbank a small sum to sustain Britain's influence among the southern Indians. Simcoe traditionally looked after those who had served under him during the Revolution.[55]

The lieutenant governor recognized that there were forces at work affecting the Old West's destiny over which he had little control. One was the western Indians' impatience for unity and their determination to stop the American advance. Another of great import was the progress of the French Revolution. When Simcoe sailed for Canada in the fall of 1791 it appeared that the Revolution might have run its course. But this was not to be. Republicans assumed control of the government in 1792. Francisco de Miranda rushed to France and became a general in the French army. Though he was engrossed in the campaign in the Low Countries, the radical turn of the French Revolution again raised the issue of a Spanish-American revolt. This portended political change in much of the Mississippi Valley, and Simcoe expected Britain to fill any void. But Simcoe, no friend to republicanism and democracy, feared that if these doctrines took root in the Mississippi Valley they might spread to Canada. He wanted to replace Spain in Louisiana and the Floridas, but not at the cost of unleashing liberty throughout the Mississippi Valley.

Britain could not wait forever to decide what to do. Citizen Edmond Charles Genêt, tempestuous French minister to the United States, landed in Charleston early in 1793 and proceeded to organize two revolutionary legions, one aimed at Spanish Florida, the other at Spanish Louisiana. He enlisted the services of influential frontiersmen: George Rogers Clark, James O'Fallon, and Elijah Clarke (the same ones Britain had contacted during the Nootka dispute), while Genêt's agents among the Indians announced the imminent return of their French father. Wellbank and others warned of a resurgence of French activity in the West.[56] Simcoe at Navy Hall felt the reverberations from the impact of the blade that severed Louis XVI's head.

Britain and Spain drew together in 1793 and declared war on the regicidal French republic. This Anglo-Spanish alliance, unique in the eighteenth century, worked to keep the tricolor away from the American frontier. Stevenson returned to England in 1793 and consulted with Clinton, John Baker Holroyd, baron Sheffield, and William Henry, first Duke of Gloucester. They recommended that Britain take a more active role in the Mississippi Valley. As they saw it, Spain alone could not protect the Floridas and Louisiana. Spain needed Britain's help and in return should grant free navigation of the Mississippi River and cede West Florida, a prospect that appalled the Americans. Stevenson suggested two buffers: an Indian barrier state in the Old Northwest to protect Canada and British occupation of West Florida (the Old Southwest) to keep Americans at arm's length from the remaining Spanish colonies. William Pitt's closest advisors, Henry Dundas and Grenville, along with Hawkesbury, thought it a good idea, though the prime minister had not made up his mind.[57]

The western Indians were unconcerned about republican ideology and the vagaries of European diplomacy. But with the advent of an Anglo-French war and Genêt's arrival in America, the Indians hoped to inspire George III to "reach out his long sword against America once more."[58] So long as Britain did not remain inactive, the Indians were likely to support her rather than Genêt. But it never occurred to Simcoe to remain passive. He expected Spain, as junior partner in the new alliance, to join Britain in consummating a western Indian confederation. Ceding Pensacola or all of West Florida to Britain and, as Simcoe suggested to the Louisiana governor, returning Bowles to Muskogee contributed to the good cause of keeping the tricolor out of the Mississippi Valley, restraining ambitious Americans, and protecting remaining Spanish colonies.[59]

It was impossible to ignore the American frontiersmen in any restructuring of the Old West. Numerous British authorities presumed that the United States, even with a new constitution, would fail and that the republic could not long endure with its present boundaries. These same Britons determined to hasten disintegration. Simcoe had not abandoned Kentucky or any other frontier region. After arriving in

Canada he corresponded with westerners, attempting to keep them in the British interest. Simcoe maintained that once he had opened the Mississippi, with or without Spanish approval, and had arranged an Indian peace, Kentucky and other frontier areas must become reconciled with Upper Canada.[60] There were two interrelated issues: restructuring the Old West and Canadian security. Simcoe assumed that if the Old West were not under British influence, Canada was lost. Beckwith, back in the American capital early in 1793, agreed and warned that if Wayne's army marched into the Indian country and defeated the natives, the Americans would not slow down until they reached the Maritime Provinces.[61]

The reason Simcoe had been so angry with Indian obstinacy at the abortive Lower Sandusky council was that he expected when the Indians retreated slightly from the Ohio boundary, sufficient territory would remain for a huge buffer state, and, more important, an agreement would bring peace to the frontier and become the first step in a reconciliation between Kentucky and Upper Canada. Kentucky was not the only area involved. Simcoe listened to the rumblings in western Pennsylvania that led to the Whiskey Rebellion, and his agents reported how anxious the whites in the Illinois country were for a union with Canada.[62]

Vermont was not necessarily lost. Simcoe, before he took office in Upper Canada, hoped to stop by Vermont on some pretext and meet with that state's leaders.[63] During the Revolution he had been involved in the plot to restore the Hudson River Valley, including Vermont, to British control. Disclosure of Benedict Arnold's treason and Maj. John André's execution frustrated this scheme. But when Simcoe offered to go to Vermont, in effect he suggested resumption of his wartime intrigues.[64] Though he did not return, his aide Stevenson did in 1792 where he consulted with the Allens and reviewed advantages of a Richelieu River canal.[65] At the same time the British government, prodded by Simcoe, considered extending the new Anglican bishopric of Canada's authority into Vermont as a means of binding that state to Canada.[66] New England Anglicans, as opposed to those in Virginia, were typically loyalists. Though the Americans had recently recognized Vermont, neither British authorities nor the surviving Allens abandoned the idea of reunion.

Simcoe, Dorchester, and the fur traders in America, along with Grenville, Dundas, and Hawkesbury, the ministers at Whitehall most concerned with America, did not forget that upper Vermont, the Old Northwest, Kentucky, and most of West Florida had been part of France's American empire. Simcoe, the surging waters of the Niagara River at his feet, appreciated the importance of the St. Lawrence–Great Lakes–Mississippi communications system: "[Remember] what the French did."[67] France had failed to guard her river-interlaced empire properly and had lost all. Simcoe, as he corresponded with McKee, Brant, Wellbank, and frontier leaders in Vermont and Kentucky and urged that Spain turn over Pensacola and open the Mississippi,[68] resolved that Britain would not repeat France's folly. With Wayne's army on the Ohio steadily growing in numbers and the western Indians obdurate, a new confrontation was in prospect.

6 • Encounter on the Maumee

BRITAIN encouraged the natives in their demand for the Ohio boundary and, with Spanish approval, anticipated playing a larger role in the Old Southwest. If Britain, the Indians, Spain, and disgruntled American frontiersmen had their way, the United States' boundary would be the Appalachian Mountains, not the Mississippi River. Washington and his cabinet, though they squabbled over other issues, considered the Mississippi boundary inviolable and charged that alien flags flew illegally over Detroit in the north and Natchez in the south.

It was not surprising that the United States ignored the 1768 Treaty of Fort Stanwix and the Ohio boundary: her citizens were bent on expansion. Anthony Wayne drilled his army, preparing to march into the Indian country and clear the way for the Old Northwest's settlement. American pioneers were already trekking into western New York on lands that John Graves Simcoe argued belonged to the Indians and Canada's sphere of influence. That one of the leading promoters was Capt. Charles Williamson, a half-pay officer in the British army who should have known better, made this new settlement even more reprehensible. Simcoe caustically demanded "by what authority Williamson's establishment is ordered," insisted that his actions endangered frontier peace, and lectured to the captain about his "natural allegiance to Britain."[1] In the province of New Brunswick, forty miles above the newly founded capital of Fredericton, American "strangers," liberally interpreting the northern limit of Maine's boundary, "came in from the wilderness and planted a land-mark."[2] Yazoo River land speculators and Edmond Genêt's followers expected to carve up the Old Southwest and the Floridas and Louisiana. American expansion confronted by a mounting resolve of Britain, the Indians, and Spain to restrict the United States to the mountains created many tensions.

Anglo-American disputes were not confined to the frontier. Failure of Britain to negotiate a commercial treaty and violations by both parties of the 1783 treaty were long-standing irritations. Virulent republicanism of the 1790s threatened the peace. Though Britain realized there were Americans dismayed by the radical turn of the French Revolution (one of whom fortunately was President Washington), she also knew about Citizen Genêt's enthusiastic reception in the southern states, about the liberty poles erected in his honor, and about the eagerness with which Americans enlisted in his revolutionary legions.

Britain no more than Americans themselves comprehended whether the United States would side with or denounce French extremism. After the outbreak of the European war in 1793, Washington proclaimed American neutrality, but Genêt's attempts to enlist French soldiers on American soil and his sending out French privateers from American ports, acts enthusiastically supported by many Americans, were anything but neutral. The crisis on the frontier and Genêt's favorable reception in southern states endangered Anglo-American harmony. British seizure without warning in the winter of 1793–94 of more than 250 American merchant vessels trading with the French West Indies removed all doubt about a possible break.[3] Although the Americans suffered most, this action was aimed primarily at France. French republicans through desperate measures not only had saved the Revolution but also had initiated wars of expansion in Europe and America.

Many elements contributed to the Anglo-American war scare—capture of American ships, nonpayment of pre-Revolutionary war debts, and the like—but frontier problems were as important as any. More was at stake than just British-occupied posts on American soil. The disputed Maine–New Brunswick boundary and American "strangers" settled near Fredericton were issues. The fact that Britain and Spain were allies brought the imbroglio of the Old Southwest, the Floridas, and Louisiana to the forefront. If the United States went to war with Britain, would not she declare war on Britain's Spanish ally? Would Britain help defend—and in the process take over—the Spanish Floridas and Louisiana? Britain was involved along the entire frontier from New Brunswick to the Floridas.

No one appreciated this more than the veteran Sir Guy Carleton, Lord Dorchester. When he heard of Britain's arbitrary seizure of American ships, he needed no formal warning from Whitehall or from the British minister in Philadelphia to realize that war was likely. He had been the Canadian governor in 1775–76 when Americans had invaded Canada and attacked Quebec, and after hearing of the capture of American vessels, his first thought was of Canada's security. Though the Americans had been turned back at Quebec's walls during the Revolution, it was as true then as in 1794 that numerically the Canadians were outnumbered and Canada's French population was of dubious loyalty. When French republicans in the 1790s began tempting "leurs frères les Canadiens,"[4] Dorchester was alarmed. During the early years of the American Revolution he had been responsible for keeping the Union Jack flying over Quebec. Again he was in the Canadian capital confronted with defending an extensive boundary with limited forces and little prospect of reinforcements. In 1794 as in 1775 he was alone and had to rely on his own wits.

Despite the small body of regulars and an uncertain militia, Dorchester had certain advantages. One was the pro-British Indians. Like many soldiers he questioned their capabilities in a regular campaign, though he revised his opinion after St. Clair's rout. The Indians, although not comparable to regulars, had a military potential and were natural allies. By invitation a delegation of northwestern Indians arrived at Quebec early in 1794. Dorchester addressed them on February 10 and circulated copies of his speech in the Indian country. Inevitably the Americans learned of its contents and denounced this "speech . . . to the Indians to excite them to hostility."[5] His speech became more controversial than Dorchester envisioned. He contended that the United States had not honored the 1783 treaty—which was true—and therefore the present Canadian boundary was not sacrosanct. He upheld the validity of the Treaty of Fort Stanwix, the concept of usufruct, and the Ohio boundary. Dorchester argued that United States' land purchases from the Indians after 1783 were invalid because the United States had broken that peace treaty and the chiefs involved did not speak for a majority of the Indians: American settlements after 1783 were "an infringement on the King's rights." And he insisted that war with the United States was imminent and urged the whole Indian confederacy from Canada to Florida to join Britain in breaking up frontier settlements and fixing a new boundary.[6]

This speech was widely publicized in American newspapers, and ministerial critics denounced it in Parliament. To doubters about Brit-

ain's responsibility for Indian atrocities, this address was proof
enough. The Americans protested, and after five months Whitehall
disavowed Dorchester's conduct.[7] But to assert that Whitehall immediately agreed with the Americans and that Dorchester exceeded
his authority misrepresents conditions as they existed between November 1793 and late spring of 1794. The most controversial part of Dorchester's speech was the announcement that Britain's aggressive policy
toward France would probably lead to war with the United States. But
when he communicated this to the Indians, he was not letting the
aborigines in on a state secret. In an attempt to weaken France and in a
move not paying much attention to effects on Canada, Whitehall resolved in November to seize American vessels trading with the French
West Indies.

An American war did seem probable, and the decision to risk hostilities was made in London, not Quebec. When Dorchester told the Indians that post-Revolutionary American settlements on the frontier
were illegal, this was not some notion he conceived in 1794. Since 1783,
which was before Dorchester arrived in Canada, Canadian officials had
reassured the Indians that they retained their rights to the use of the
soil of the Old Northwest and that the Americans had no authority to
expand without Indian permission. Despite the Whitehall visits of
Joseph Brant, William Augustus Bowles, and others after 1783, the
ministry may not have been as clear about these assurances as was the
Canadian Indian Department. But with the prospect of war, it was not
surprising that Dorchester reaffirmed that Americans were illegally
established in much of the frontier; it would have been astounding if
he had not. Dorchester's Indian speech and his subsequent conduct
reflected the ministry's belligerence when it ordered capture of American merchantmen. If there was blame, it belonged at Whitehall. Simcoe assumed that Dorchester had been notified privately that the cabinet, alarmed by the successes of French arms, had determined to risk
an American war, and there is every indication that Simcoe was right.[8]

The Canadian governor had closely observed negotiations that cul-
minated in the failure of the Lower Sandusky council. Western Indian
militancy then had gotten out of hand, causing negotiations to break
down, and in 1793 Dorchester, like Simcoe, had been annoyed. But
that was in 1793. In 1794, assuming war was inevitable, he was no

longer vexed by native fervor and he urged Indian unity. Dorchester gave the Indians the same assurances that Alexander McKee, Simcoe, Dunmore, and Bowles had given in the past. Whitehall, aroused by the French terror and realizing that the United States could not rely on her former allies, France and Spain, had decided to risk war. The Canadian governor resolved that Whitehall's policy should not result in Canada's loss.

Though Dorchester by nature was not reckless, he assumed that circumstances forced him to adopt extreme measures. What he was doing in 1794 was agreeing with the more aggressive Simcoe, something that pained the Canadian governor. The two, both strong-willed, identified with different political factions in Britain, had been rivals after Canada had been divided into Upper and Lower provinces. When Dorchester had criticized Simcoe it was hard to tell whether this opposition was based on principle or pique. But when Dorchester harangued the Indians in February 1794 he was admitting that Simcoe's more aggressive policy toward the Indians and the Mississippi Valley was correct. Dorchester sent a copy of his Indian speech to Simcoe who could not have been more pleased: maybe there was a larger measure of wisdom in the Chateau St. Louis than he had suspected.

Dorchester's speech and Britain's capture of American vessels made Simcoe confident that the ministry had come around to his point of view. Capt. Charles Stevenson had been in England for some months urging the ministry and members of the royal family to support the Indians, to work for dismemberment of the United States, and to pressure Spain to hand over the Floridas and Louisiana. When Stevenson had consulted with Henry Dundas and other cabinet members in the summer of 1793, Simcoe notified the government that he had given Stevenson no formal commission: he was making informal suggestions as a private citizen and if the ministry was opposed there was no need to reprimand Simcoe.[9] After the ministry resolved to seize American ships and risk war, Stevenson renewed his proposals: "Tell Simcoe that I have not committed him but without the advice of his best friends," i.e., Gen. Henry Clinton; George Nugent-Temple-Grenville, marquis of Buckingham; William Henry, Duke of Gloucester; and John Baker Holroyd, Lord Sheffield.[10]

Simcoe viewed the present crisis as an opportunity and confidently looked to an alteration of the North American balance of power: "I hold war to be inevitable . . . Wayne must be driven back."[11] Timothy Pickering, soon to join Washington's cabinet, was neither a clairvoyant nor an intellect of the first order, but he had firsthand knowledge of the Indians and frontier conditions. After Britain's capture of American ships he assumed London's strategy was to carve up North America while Britain's allies divided Poland.[12] This was precisely what Simcoe, Dorchester, William Pitt's closest advisors in the ministry, George III's brother, and presumably the king, had in mind. Enhancing Britain's position in the New World helped maintain the balance in the Old.

As Wayne advanced into the Indian country, Simcoe worried about the security of Detroit and the other Upper Canada posts. During the Revolution and earlier, Britain had placed garrisons on the Maumee River and near the mouth of the Sandusky River. From time to time British troops had been at these posts after the Revolution. Simcoe was overjoyed when Dorchester agreed to rebuild one on the Maumee River near McKee's residence.[13] Detroit merchants were anxious to throw up stockades on the Sandusky and farther up the Maumee at the Glaize.[14] For years Superintendent McKee had been urging building a fort at the Maumee rapids, and even in 1791 Dorchester had thought such a fortification a judicious idea.[15] Little wonder, as McKee examined Fort Miamis' new stockade, that he reflected, "Affairs in this country [have been] considerably altered for the better."[16] The veteran McKee had fought to kick France out of the Ohio country in the Seven Years War and expected the Americans to be no more successful than the French.

Rebuilding Fort Miamis and possibly others in the Indian country, calling out the Upper Canada militia who were mostly loyalists, and promoting Indian unity were measures to protect Detroit. But Simcoe believed the best way to protect Detroit was to assume the offensive. First Wayne had to abandon his chain of forts stretching northward from the Ohio. The Indians needed help from Canadian regulars and militia and especially from their cannon. Simcoe planned to send his forces down the Ohio River and to take Fort Washington, thereby cutting Wayne's supply line and forcing him to withdraw.[17] Britain could then rearrange the frontier to her liking.

Captain Williamson must abandon the Genesee country or place his

New York settlement under British protection. Britain could reoccupy Forts Le Boeuf and Oswego to better protect the Great Lakes communication and to help reunite the Iroquois in Canada and western New York.[18] Mohawks from the Grand River in Canada appeared among the Onondagas in New York proclaiming the good news. Even Cornplanter, a Seneca and perhaps the most influential Six Nations' chieftain in New York, though previously in the American interest, declared that Simcoe now was his *"best"* friend and that he was anxious to serve him.[19]

Simcoe had not given up on Vermont. Though the Allen-Chittenden faction had been losing strength over the years, it still was a potent force in Vermont politics. Dorchester wondered whether Vermonters had adopted French principles and whether annexing upper Vermont and opening the Richelieu–Lake Champlain route might allow Jacobin propaganda to spew over Lower Canada. Simcoe, discounting this risk, was anxious to join Vermont to Canada. So were the surviving Allens and Gov. Thomas Chittenden.[20]

Simcoe's underlying assumption in 1794—and Dorchester's too—was that the United States was about to crumble. Only this feeling allowed him realistically to hope for Vermont's annexation. Much more was involved than Vermont and feuds between the Allen-Chittenden faction and their political rivals. Similar tensions existed all along the frontier. The whiskey tax fell heavily on frontier Pennsylvania and Kentucky bringing western distrust of the East to the breaking point. Wayne charged that Kentuckians wanted to see the British flag raised at the Ohio, though it is hard to tell in this specific instance whether he was telling the truth or maligning critics.[21] But because of the whiskey tax, the problem of free navigation of the Mississippi, and distrust of Federalist policies, there was no doubt about western dissatisfaction and the possibility that frontiersmen might proclaim their independence and combine with Britain or Spain. Factionalism was rampant in the United States, and there were Federalists and Republicans alike contemplating disunion.

In addition to profiting from United States dissension, Dorchester, as has been discussed, relied on the Indians. The northwestern Indians could not have been more buoyant as Britain rebuilt and garrisoned Fort Miamis and as McKee dispensed presents in a handsome manner.

There was the prospect of a reunited Six Nations joining the western Indians.[22] In the province of New Brunswick the governor sent French Catholic priests among the Maine Indians to deter American "strangers" from settling on the upper St. John River and to prepare for incorporating part of Maine (by United States' definition) into New Brunswick.[23]

Reports of rebuilding Fort Miamis and of the probable war with the United States circulated among the southern Indians. Confident Cherokees promptly arrived at Fort Miamis and informed McKee of the "general cry of the southern Indians in wishing the return of the British" to the Old Southwest.[24] George Wellbank redoubled his efforts toward strengthening the confederation. Already some seven hundred southern Indians were above the Ohio watching Wayne's advance.[25] After rousing the southern Indians Wellbank expected to go to Nassau and consult with Lord Dunmore. Wellbank offered to deliver Simcoe's letters to the Bahamian governor and do everything possible to strengthen a pro-British confederation.[26]

Not only Britain but also Spain might encourage native unity. Simcoe expected Spain, even though as a junior partner, to cooperate. He still wanted Spain to cede Pensacola and possibly New Orleans, allowing Britons to become a shield protecting Mexico. Simcoe wrote Gov. François Hector Carondelet in New Orleans, lamenting the "unfortunate situation of Mr. Bowles whose influence with the Creek and Cherokee nations was directed to the establishment of a boundary between those nations of Indians, and the people of Georgia and Carolina, and who was by no means hostile either to the interests of Spain or of Great Britain."[27] Spain debated whether to encourage a British-dominated confederation. Officials, still pondering whether to return him to Muskogee or to keep him in prison, renewed negotiations with Bowles in Spain.[28]

If Spain sanctioned merging the southern Indians into a pro-British confederacy, there was the problem of which Britons—the Dunmore-Bowles faction or Panton, Leslie, and Company—Spain should utilize. In the summer of 1794 former superintendent Col. Thomas Brown arrived in Pensacola.[29] Panton approved a pro-British confederation only if Spain employed Brown, not Bowles.

Spain, not trusting either Bowles or Panton, feared that Britain would manipulate the natives and end up with the Floridas and Louisiana. The reason Spain considered collaborating with Britain in 1794 was that she was Britain's ally and the alternatives were worse. Jacobinism alarmed both Britain and Spain, whether it was the appearance of French republican armies in the Low Countries and northern Spain in the Old World or Genêt's exertions in the New. Spanish galleys patrolled the Mississippi River, and their crews stopped foreign vessels, impounding the incendiary writings of Rousseau and other *philosophes*.[30] Dorchester, surrounded by French-speaking subjects, never had an easy moment because of his fear that French Canadians might turn Jacobin. Spain, like Britain, determined to contain aggressive French republicanism. Britain was her natural ally, and without British support republicanism might sweep over the Iberian peninsula and Genêt's legions overrun the Floridas, Louisiana, and much more. Allowing Britain to assume part or all of Spain's role in the Mississippi Valley was less undesirable than losing Britain as an ally against France.

Hostilities, part of a larger European conflict, pitting Britain and Spain against France and the United States seemed inevitable early in 1794. Despite a long tradition of distrust, there was surprising Anglo-Spanish cooperation in the Mississippi Valley. The spirited Carondelet, ever suspicious of Britain, but fearing for Louisiana's safety, asked Simcoe for five hundred men to protect St. Louis from Genêt's legions.[31] Simcoe, with Wayne advancing toward Detroit, had no force to spare. But he held out hope of aid after Britain had declared war on the United States and disposed of Wayne.[32]

In the meantime Simcoe played on Spanish fears by insinuating that Frenchmen scattered throughout the Mississippi Valley had succumbed to Jacobinism, and Spain therefore should support Britain. She could send her galleys, the most effective naval force on the western waters, to the mouth of the Wabash River. These gunboats had the power to deny American access to the Maumee-Wabash route and help keep open communications between Canada and Louisiana.[33] Moreover, Simcoe argued, Spain ought to allow British fur trading posts on the upper Mississippi and Missouri rivers.[34] Carondelet had misgivings but realized that in upper Louisiana as in the Floridas British merchants were likely to control the fur trade. The basic question was whether Spain would reach an understanding with these foreign traders like the arrangement with Panton, Leslie, and Company in the Floridas.

As governor of Louisiana and West Florida, Carondelet tried to organize all the tribes in the Old Southwest into a confederation under Spanish direction. In letters to his superiors and to Simcoe, he stressed the advantages of cooperation between the Spanish Indians of the Old Southwest and the British Indians in the Old Northwest, and he wanted to station native runners in the Illinois country to improve communications. What Carondelet overlooked in his letters—though he was well aware of it—was that, with few exceptions white agents among the southern Indians spoke English, not Spanish, and presents and trade items came from Britain, not Spain. Solemn treaties with the natives aside, Carondelet exaggerated in claiming to have unified the southern Indians.[35] It really was not necessary for him to post messengers in the Illinois region. McKee had been corresponding with loyalist Indian traders below the Ohio for years, and in 1794 he dispatched still another wampum belt to the southern Indians—all without reference to Spain.[36]

An invigorated Indian alliance under Anglo-Spanish patronage and a constriction of United States western lands never occurred for two reasons: Britain, to the surprise of many, settled her dispute with the United States; and Wayne defeated the northern Indians. Jay's Treaty, which the United States and Britain signed on November 19, 1794, prevented war. Washington, realizing the seriousness of the threat to the United States, dispatched John Jay, envoy extraordinary, to England in May 1794. From the British point of view Jay was inclined to be reasonable, though the ministry during the summer and fall of 1794 did not know whether or not hostilities could be avoided.

If Britain declared war on her, the United States would be less able to ship foodstuffs to France, and America might be divided. But if Britain went to war, she would have another enemy; with inspired French troops overrunning the Low Countries, northern Spain, and elsewhere, Britain did not need more enemies. The United States, though a republic, apparently had not turned Jacobin. British leaders praised Washington, Hamilton, and the Federalists when they opposed French extremism and demanded Genêt's recall early in 1794. Though Britain cavalierly had risked war with the United States by seizing American ships in 1793, the mounting French threat and Washington's opposition to the Paris regime forced Pitt and his ministers in 1794 to have second thoughts about plunging into hostilities.[37]

Instructions to Dorchester and Simcoe in the late spring and summer of 1794 reflected the ministry's uncertainty. They asserted that Jay's mission might succeed and that in the meantime Canadians should take no aggressive action upsetting the status quo.[38] But if Jay failed, Dorchester, Simcoe, Hawkesbury, Grenville, and Dundas expected with the aid of Spain and the Indians to rearrange matters in the Mississippi Valley. Whitehall first ordered the Canadians to restrain themselves and then, with misgivings, concluded a treaty with the United States. Reasons for reaching this agreement were found not on the frontier but had to do with the overriding French menace and Federalist moderation. The marquis of Buckingham professed to his younger brother, Foreign Secretary Grenville, that he was "glad your American treaty goes on to your liking. We had indeed enough upon our hands."[39]

The treaty's effect on the frontier was substantial and had much to do with Wayne's victory at Fallen Timbers. Wayne methodically moved from Fort Washington into the Indian country building forts along his line of march. The Indians, assisted by Indian agent Matthew Elliott and loyalist traders, captured supplies moving between the forts but injudiciously attacked Fort Recovery where they were repulsed.[40] Wayne reached the Glaize in August 1794, advanced down the Maumee, attacked and defeated the Indians and a detachment of Detroit militia barricaded behind fallen trees. The Battle of Fallen Timbers was easily won and over in forty-five minutes. When the Indians withdrew to the nearby British fort at the Maumee rapids the commander refused to let them enter. This could have led to British regulars' firing at Americans. Whitehall's instructions had been not to upset the balance in the Old Northwest, and as the fort's door closed in their faces, the dismayed Indian survivors of Fallen Timbers realized what this meant. The Indians continued their retreat, while Wayne's soldiers and the British at Fort Miamis glared at each other almost within rifle shot.[41]

As a military engagement the Battle of Fallen Timbers was in no wise comparable to Arthur St. Clair's rout or to Andrew Jackson's later victory at Horseshoe Bend. Merely four hundred Indian warriors were directly involved, only a fraction of the some two thousand that McKee had recently assembled. In a sense there had been no real confrontation between Wayne and the Indians. Gen. James Wilkinson was amazed how the United States had "prospered beyond calculation, and the wreath is prepared for the brow of the Blockhead [Wayne]."[42]

There had been a decided shift in Britain's policy between the late fall of 1793 and the summer of 1794. Britain, thinking primarily of the French menace, at first had willingly risked an American war. This is why Dorchester had given his speech to the Indians, why he had ordered Simcoe to rebuild Fort Miamis, and it is why Britain had collaborated with Spain in creating an Indian confederation and in dislodging the American flag from the Mississippi Valley. But by the summer of 1794 the ministry, aware of the astonishing French military victories, hoped to avoid an American war and warned Dorchester and Simcoe that Jay might succeed in negotiating peace.

The assumption of an inevitable Anglo-American war was no longer valid and partly explained why Wilkinson's "blockhead" general succeeded so easily. If there had been no doubt of a conflct, it is hard to imagine that Simcoe and the Indian Department could not have found food and munitions for the hundreds of Indians not present at Fallen Timbers and more effectively encouraged them to join their brethren in confronting Wayne. Confident of an American war, Simcoe would never have allowed his lieutenant to slam Fort Miamis' door shut in the Indians' faces, and Canadian regulars and militia would have taken a far more active role than they did.

This is not to minimize the effects of the Battle of Fallen Timbers because this defeat, coupled with Britain's decision to conclude a treaty with the United States and other circumstances, shattered hopes for an Indian confederation under British protection. It was not realistic for Britain to reach an agreement with the United States and at the same time work for American dismemberment. Britain had to put aside plans for annexing Vermont, Pennsylvania, and Kentucky. What made the Battle of Fallen Timbers significant was not so much the triumph of Wayne's infantry and the killing of perhaps twenty warriors but the fact that this battle occurred at the time when Britain, for reasons having more to do with France than the frontier, decided to reconcile herself with the United States. Spain in 1795 broke away from her British alliance, terminating Anglo-Spanish cooperation in the Mississippi Valley and ending the possibility that West Florida might peacefully come under British control.

The Indians, though losing few warriors at the Battle of Fallen Timbers, saw dreams of unity shattered. As the months passed and they realized that the Americans were going to occupy Detroit and the other disputed posts, they became despondent and disorganized. Carondelet, recently urging union of all western Indians under Anglo-Spanish supervision, now opposed collaboration with the British. Discouraged northwestern Indians met with Wayne in August 1795 and signed the Treaty of Greenville, ceding most of the modern state of Ohio and enclaves deep in Indian territory.[43] The Treaty of Fort Stanwix was dead.

It was almost a year after Fallen Timbers before the Indians met Wayne at Fort Greenville, and it was not until 1796 that the British evacuated Detroit. There was an interval after the battle before it became clear that Britain's hopes for Indian unity and American dismemberment were overturned. Keeping alive hopes for an Indian confederation, Simcoe convened a grand council near Detroit after the Battle of Fallen Timbers, including representatives from the Mohawks and southern Indians.[44] Home Secretary William Henry Cavendish, third duke of Portland wanted Britain to continue directing the western Indians and considered mediation to secure a favorable Indian boundary; Dundas still assumed the time would come when it would be necessary to collaborate with alienated Americans.[45]

Describing the battle in his letter to Clinton, Simcoe depreciated its military significance; he still thought there might be an American war.[46] One reason was the hostile reaction of Jefferson's Republicans to Jay's Treaty and the question whether the Senate would give its approval. Another was the Whiskey Rebellion that broke out in western Pennsylvania while Wayne was advancing toward Fort Miamis. Simcoe maintained that the timing was not accidental;[47] reportedly British agents joined the insurgents. Some leaders were frank in admitting that they expected to reach an understanding with Britain or Spain, while a hostile press cited conclusive evidence that the rebels planned to hand the Old Northwest over to Britain.[48] The basic causes of the Whiskey Rebellion, however, were local, and Simcoe merely planned to take advantage of a fortuitous uprising. But since 1783 there had been a long list of exiled loyalists who had been working for Pennsylvania's separation, and there were those in frontier Pennsylvania who had collaborated with them.

The ease with which the United States quelled the Whiskey Rebellion, eventual ratification of Jay's Treaty, Spain's parting company with Britain and subsequently making concessions to the United States in the 1795 Pinckney Treaty—along with the Battle of Fallen Timbers and the Treaty of Greenville—were disastrous for Simcoe's expectations. The British ministry, however, did not abandon interest in the Mississippi Valley. Half of it was still under Spanish dominion, and American frontiersmen still distrusted eastern Federalists. Some of the discontented corresponded with the Spaniards and the British: Wilkinson apparently still retained his illicit correspondence with not only New Orleans but also Detroit.[49]

Hawkesbury, in the Jay negotiations, had demanded that Britain be allowed to mediate for the Indians on United States' soil and that Canadian traders be permitted to traffic freely with them. The commercial provision was the only one that the United States allowed. Some historians claim that this was another instance of Britain's predominant interest in the Old Northwest fur trade and that it reflected Britain's ancient fear that the Indians might massacre her subjects should she abandon the natives. But what Hawkesbury was thinking about—and Dundas and other ministers generally agreed—was that, despite any treaty with Jay, the Mississippi Valley eventually was destined to come under British political and commercial domination: "Nothing should be conceded which will embarrass us in this business in the future."[50] It was the fur traders themselves, not the ministry, who were so fearful of losing their profits and scalps.

But in the winter of 1794 and on into 1795 the Indians became disorganized and dismayed. The schism between the Six Nations and the northwestern Indians intensified. Iroquois living in western New York became debilitated or drifted away to join their brethren on the Grand River. Despite native protests, the Americans refused to allow the half-blood William Johnson, Sir William's Mohawk son, to take part in any negotiations. They rightly considered him a British agent.[51]

Northwestern Indians who had come for miles to confront Wayne returned home discouraged with bitter memories of the British closing Fort Miamis' door.

Dorchester defended his conduct and vowed that under similar circumstances he would do exactly the same thing. But because of age, poor health, and controversy surrounding his recent actions, the veteran governor thought it appropriate to offer his resignation.[52] Simcoe, suddenly discovering that all along it had been Dorchester's idea to build Fort Miamis, considered the resignation long overdue.[53] Though Whitehall, because "national interests . . . require[d]," disavowed Dorchester's Indian speech, in all fairness it could not reproach him too severely for telling the Indians in 1794 essentially what Britain had been saying since 1783.[54] Such blame as there was belonged to Hawkesbury, Dundas, and Grenville in the ministry and probably to the king.

The southern Indians were as downcast as any. William Blount, governor of the Southwest Territory, met the Cherokees at Tellico Block House and offered to give details of the Battle of Fallen Timbers and explain its effect on the southern Indians. Chief John Watts needed no description of the conflict ("Some of my people were in the action, who have already informed me") any more than he needed Blount to discuss its impact on the southern Indians.[55] He knew that hopes for a confederation backed by Britain were fading and that he might be forced to make concessions to the Americans. Warlike Cherokees who had been fighting Americans above the Ohio returned home disillusioned, while Shawnees living among the militant southern Cherokees moved above the Ohio.[56]

John McDonald, veteran loyalist merchant among the Cherokees with a Cherokee family, had corresponded and traded with the British in Canada and Panton in Pensacola. Blount thought it an opportune moment to ask him to become the American Cherokee agent.[57] Wellbank was dead. Creek Indians had killed him. Whether Indians Panton paid to murder him succeeded or whether Indians Wellbank accused of stealing his chest of silver turned on him is unclear. Whatever the reason, drunken Indians put him to death "in a manner too shocking to relate," so the loyalist who had been the most active in bringing the southern Indians into the confederation during 1793 and 1794 was no more.[58]

Wellbank's mentors were not faring much better. The Spaniards, who had been undecided whether to return Bowles to Muskogee or to keep him in prison, exiled him in 1795 to the Philippines.[59] At about the same time Whitehall recalled Dunmore because his old political enemy, the duke of Portland, had joined the ministry and because George III was incensed that Dunmore's daughter had married the king's son without permission.[60] The removal of these key figures, all of whom had been working since the Revolution to make the Old Southwest a loyalist asylum and to bring it under British control, was another setback. Panton, Leslie, and Company and Spain, not Bowles and Dunmore, were managing Indian affairs in the south.

The Canadian Indian department in the north was in turmoil. Wayne destroyed McKee's house and the store near Fort Miamis, and the aged superintendent moved to the Thames River in Upper Canada. His deputy, Elliott, whose headquarters had been at the Glaize and who had dressed as an Indian and accompanied the natives in raids on Wayne's army, relocated at Amherstburg on the Canadian side of the Detroit River. Soon the government dismissed Elliott, charging him with peculation.[61] John Connolly was caught appropriating Indian stores. Though he maintained concern for his wife and six children had forced him to steal, there was no question about his dismissal, and he pleaded for a pardon or a light sentence.[62] Simcoe, endeavoring to transfer traditional native council fires with great pomp from Detroit and Niagara onto Canadian soil, dispelled little of the Indian Department's gloom.[63] Detroit merchants and fur traders with dubious claims to Indian lands south of the boundary began a corrupt intrigue in Philadelphia to get Congress to recognize their validity.[64] Regardless of where one looked—at Detroit, Fort Miamis, and Michilimackinac where the British prepared to evacuate, in Indian villages in the Old Southwest, or in Nassau as Lord Dunmore departed in high dudgeon—it was apparent that British influence on the frontier had diminished.

American land speculators knew this. Governor Blount had not come to Tellico Block House to ruminate with the Cherokees over the

Battle of Fallen Timbers: he wanted their land. Robert Morris wrote to a prospective British investor: "The sure road to fortune is to do what Williamson is doing."[65] Charles Williamson was Sir William Pulteney's agent in developing a large tract in western New York. A retired British officer, Williamson operated under American laws. After Fallen Timbers and the Jay Treaty, Simcoe stopped lecturing to the half-pay captain about his obligations as a British officer to His Majesty's subjects in Canada.

Niagara's evacuation and diminished British influence in western New York offered possibilities for gain. Early 1795 seemed the most opportune time since the Revolution to open up large segments of the frontier for settlement. Morris was optimistic about his contested lands in western New York, and his North American Land Company claimed millions of acres of frontier lands stretching from New York to Georgia. His land dealings were on such a huge scale, so complex and clouded with secrecy, that they have defied comprehension. But the diminution of British ascendancy in the north and Anglo-Spanish influence in the south made him sanguine about opportunities in western New York and frontier Georgia alike.[66]

Some twelve years after the Revolution the frontier was about to be adjusted to American liking: Britain was preparing to evacuate the northern posts; the hostile Indian confederation was fragmented; the Spaniards in 1795 conceded free navigation of the Mississippi River and the thirty-first parallel as West Florida's northern boundary. Both President Washington and speculator Morris viewed the frontier with satisfaction and assumed that obstacles to American expansion were largely removed. America in 1795 could begin to exploit what had been rightfully hers since 1783. What had brought about these favorable occurrences was not so much the Battle of Fallen Timbers as European fluctuations which induced first Britain in 1794 and then Spain in 1795 to yield to the United States. Few Americans acknowledged the real concessions Britain made in the Jay Treaty regarding the frontier posts and much of the Mississippi Valley.

7 • Liberté, Egalité, Fraternité

EUROPEAN developments in 1794–95 that had favored America could change—and in the latter part of 1795 they did. Overnight Britain again became deeply involved in the frontier, and Robert Morris, rather than reaping profits from his lands, spent most of his remaining years as a bankrupt in Philadelphia's Prune Street prison. Responsible for these changes was the collapse of the French Terror. The Jacobins were overthrown in 1794, and France established a more conservative government, the Directory. Spain made peace with this new regime in 1795, renewed her traditional eighteenth-century French alliance, and the following year declared war on Britain.

France again threatened to take over the Mississippi Valley. Spain in the 1795 Treaty of Basel almost ceded Louisiana and Florida to France,[1] and Frenchmen were active in the Mississippi Valley. Gen. Victor Collot mapped it and urged Louisiana's restoration.[2] The Directory commissioned George Rogers Clark in 1797 general in the French army a second time to court frontiersmen's support.[3] Leclerc de Milfort, a Frenchman who had married Alexander McGillivray's sister, also commissioned general by the Directory, expected the southern Indians to play their part.[4]

The spread of Jacobinism alarmed Britain. In British eyes the Directory was hardly less radical than its predecessor, and Spain's new alliance meant that French extremism was spreading not only to the Iberian peninsula but also to Spanish America. Republicans in the United States, like the followers of George Rogers Clark, wanted to see the tricolor waving throughout the Mississippi Valley. The United States experienced its first contested election in 1796. The surprisingly anti-French Washington was retiring, and the Republican Jefferson might succeed him. It was one thing for Britain to reach an understanding with Washington's Federalist administration; with Jefferson as chief executive it might be another story.

The danger of both the Mississippi Valley and the United States coming under Jacobin influence made Britain reconsider her North

American policies. If France, as reports indicated, were going to resume control of Louisiana, Britain might have to take it first. Jefferson's Republicans at the helm might force Britain to revert to her earlier policy of American dismemberment. The duke of Portland ordered John Graves Simcoe and Sir Guy Carleton, Lord Dorchester to continue cultivating influential westerners and New Englanders and to remind the Indians that the Jay Treaty allowed Canadian merchants to traffic below the boundary and that Britain had not really deserted her former allies.[5] Britain announced that she, no less than the United States, was entitled to free navigation of the Mississippi River.[6] The ministry began reverting to its previous frontier policy, the Jay Treaty notwithstanding.

French Minister Pierre A. Adet in Philadelphia, and Collot and Milfort in the West wanted to enlist soldiers (both white and Indian) on United States soil to liberate the Mississippi Valley and Canada and to restore France's empire. Britain thought in these exact same terms, except that Canada and the Mississippi Valley should come under British, not French, dominion. If France could raise troops on United States' soil, so could Britain. Simcoe asserted that he could easily enlist a regiment in upper Vermont,[7] while ministers studied Col. Charles Stevenson's proposal to raise a Negro regiment from the American eastern coast.[8] Britain, desperate in 1776, had been driven to extremes to combat republicanism. History might repeat itself in 1796.

It is hard to determine the extent to which Britain tried to win over individual frontiersmen. Ira Allen was in London, and Simcoe again urged the ministry to make definite arrangements for annexing northern Vermont.[9] George Morgan, veteran Pennsylvania land speculator, offered to move near Detroit, to take his old friend Alexander McKee once more by the hand, and to become a British subject—that is, he promised that at least some of his family would.[10] James Wilkinson apparently still was in treasonable correspondence with McKee. John Connolly, attempting to rehabilitate his reputation, surveyed the Ohio River in 1796, though there is no record of with whom he corresponded.[11] William Tatham, a former frontiersman himself, was in London explaining to the ministry how it was inevitable that the West was going to separate, all the while insisting that, though he was in British pay, his case was not exactly like Benedict Arnold's.[12] Dr.

Nicholas Romayne, of New York, more of a land speculator than a physician, apprised Sir William Pulteney and Henry Dundas about the unfortunate spread of radicalism in the United States.[13] Though John Murray, Lord Dunmore no longer occupied Government House in Nassau, Bahamians counseled Whitehall that in the event of a Spanish war, "the *Cumberland* and *Kentucky* men [should] be attended to" and let loose on Louisiana and the Floridas.[14]

Britain knew about the discontent in the United States and about the exasperation that inspired Oliver Wolcott, Connecticut's governor, to write his son (Hamilton's successor as secretary of the treasury) that if "French arms continue to preponderate, and a governing influence of this nation shall continue in the southern and western countries, I am confident, and indeed hope, that a separation will soon take place."[15] Or as William Knox, former under-secretary of state for the American colonies, angry with the southerners for not paying their debts, put it, "The division . . . will be between the honest and dishonest."[16] Charles Jenkinson, Lord Hawkesbury, while lavishing praise on President Washington, knew the Virginian was retiring and believed that the United States was far too big for a democracy and without Washington would soon fragment.[17] Britain might ally with those sections directed by politicians who thought like the High Federalist Timothy Dwight. During the controversy preceding the Jay Treaty, Dwight avowed ninety-nine out of one hundred New Englanders would separate rather than fight Britain.[18] It was this sectional vehemence that made Stevenson's proposal to enlist a Negro regiment from Jefferson's Virginia not so preposterous.

A small detachment of American soldiers arrived at Detroit in July 1796. The American flag was raised in a simple ceremony, and the British garrison marched out. Similar transfers occurred at Michilimackinac and Niagara, and, though Spain had not yet evacuated Chickasaw Bluffs (Memphis) and Natchez, she had agreed to give them up. The great paradox was, that as the American flag began to fly over Detroit, this represented not a consolidation of American authority in the West but one of the more serious threats to the American frontier since the Revolution. One has to look at Europe as much as the frontier to discover the reason why.

Despite Edmond Genêt's dismissal and his failure to capture the

Floridas and Louisiana, there still was a danger that the tricolor might wave over the American frontier, including both Floridas and both Canadas. Spain renewed her French alliance in 1795 and possibly would agree with the French traveler, the Duc de La Rouchefoucauld Liancourt, that it was even in Spanish interest to surrender Louisiana and the Floridas to her ally.[19] Minister Adet reportedly was at Pointe au Fer on upper Lake Champlain attempting to revolutionize Canada.[20] Terrified Canadian authorities captured the more impetuous foreign and domestic republican firebrands and executed one, all on flimsy evidence.[21] A revived French empire in America could strengthen France economically, reinvigorate her navy, and force the United States back into the orbit of French diplomacy.

This prospect, distasteful enough under the *ancien régime*, doubly alarmed Britain with republicans in the Tuileries. Dependent on her navy and commerce for security and prosperity, Britain could not allow France to return to North America. Since 1795 there had been rumors that Spain had ceded Louisiana to France and French troops had actually landed at New Orleans and Pensacola.[22] These ports in themselves were not too important. But if French forces debarked there it signified that France was beginning to recover her American empire and usurp British New World commerce. Britain resolved to avoid this at all costs and as a result reevaluated her frontier policy.

With the danger of pro-French Republicans winning supremacy from the Floridas to Vermont, John Graves Simcoe continued to prod the ministry to complete arrangements with Ira Allen and brother Levi to combat Adet's machinations.[23] But the government again put the Allens off, and Ira set off for France. There he procured twenty thousand stands of arms supposedly for the Vermont militia and loaded them aboard the *Olive Branch*.

The commander of a British warship, warned by a sympathetic Vermonter, stopped the *Olive Branch*, impounded the arms, and imprisoned Allen, charging that these arms were to help Adet liberate Canada. What had interested Ira was a canal and commerce, and geography more than ideology had made him turn to France.[24] But the lesson to the British ministry was clear: friendly relations with the United States were not enough to protect Canada.

Britain intended to keep the tricolor off the mainland. It had the options of building on the unsteady foundations of the Jay Treaty and cooperating with the United States or acting unilaterally. Unfortunately, British ministers did not know any more than Americans who wielded political power in Philadelphia. Parties—Federalists and Republicans—had developed in the 1790s, and one of the major issues dividing them was whether they were pro-British or pro-French. The first disputed presidential election occurred in 1796. The electors balloted in December, and John Adams, a moderate Federalist, narrowly defeated Jefferson, his allegedly Francophile opponent. This victory pleased the American Federalists and the British ministry alike, and both regarded it as a defeat for international radicalism and the doctrines of itinerant philosophers.

But both realized that Adams' margin of victory had been close and that Republicanism in the United States was potent. Though the Federalist Adams was president, the Republican Jefferson was vice-president and Adams' successor in the event of death. The president and his cabinet were Federalists, and Federalists predominated in the Senate, but there were vocal Republican partisans throughout the country. They had a majority in the House of Representatives and by controlling appropriations, they defied the Federalists. Though Washington signed the Jay Treaty and the Senate gave its approval, Republicans in the House, by refusing until April 1796 to vote money to implement this treaty, almost wrecked it. Whitehall, by the end of 1796, no longer doubted the good intentions of Washington, Adams, Hamilton, John Jay, Timothy Pickering and other leading Federalists and that they desired close economic and political ties with Britain, possibly even war with France, to suppress republicanism at home and abroad. What worried Whitehall was whether the Federalists had power to execute their well-meaning policies.[25]

American Federalists and the British ministry both wanted to stamp out democratic republicanism along the American frontier, though neither was sure of the proper method. It made little difference to Anglo-American conservatives whether republican enthusiasts spoke English or French and whether they were on United States or Canadian soil. Strengthening the Anglo-American alliance and possibly bringing the United States openly into the war against France and Spain appealed to extreme Federalists and their British counterparts.

This permitted the British navy and the American army to cooperate, restrain the Vermonters, and capture the Floridas and Louisiana. The American army, commanded by determined Federalists, while denying Spanish colonies to France, at the same time could impress on Jefferson's western followers the majesty and determination of the Federalist administration. Hamilton, retired since 1795 but whose influence was enormous, was the most conspicuous advocate of this policy.[26]

High Federalists, even those who basked in the light of Hamilton's halo, had reservations about western expansion. The new states of Kentucky and Tennessee were Republican strongholds, and presumably future states would have Republican administrations. American conquest of the Floridas and Louisiana, though it kept French troops out, facilitated western settlement. Federalists such as Jay, Pickering, and Gouverneur Morris distrusted creation of additional states with Republican regimes and looked upon their admission to statehood as allowing the Goths into the empire. They worried about migration of solid citizens from the seaboard to the frontier, undermining "the good old thirteen states."[27]

One Federalist faction was tempted to abandon the Mississippi Valley to republicanism, thereby allowing eastern conservatives to retain their purity, strength, and ability to defend the United States from social upheaval. Though this involved separation, republicanism in the Mississippi Valley would not necessarily run amuck. The Appalachian Mountains were still a formidable barrier.

Whitehall recognized that one way to curb unrestrained frontier republicanism was for Britain rather than the United States to take the Floridas and Louisiana. British command of Gulf Coast ports placed western commerce at her mercy. This was an effective cudgel to intimidate unruly westerners. Even High Federalists were tempted to let Britain overawe Jefferson's western republicans since the Federalists themselves were unable to do so. Contradictory dispatches to Canadians reflected the ministry's indecision: court the favor of westerners and both northern and southern Indians, but do not antagonize the government in Philadelphia.[28]

Whitehall's confusion was manifest in her response to the so-called Blount Conspiracy. Sen. William Blount, recently elected to the Senate from the state of Tennessee, was the most conspicuous, though not necessarily the central figure, in the scheme to detach the Old Southwest from the United States with British aid. Many people were involved—Blount and alienated Americans, Indian traders, the British minister in Philadelphia, British naval captains of the North American squadron, ministers at Whitehall, loyalists settled on the frontier and exiles hoping to return, Canadians, and apparently Spanish officials in the Floridas—and none necessarily knew what the other was doing. All assumed that an upheaval was inevitable. Either France would secure Louisiana and the Floridas or Britain and the United States must take them to forestall France and satisfy ambitions of land-hungry subjects.

Speculator Blount was on the verge of bankruptcy. European hostilities deterred men of fortune from investing in western lands and European immigrants from settling on the frontier. Blount assumed that once Britain acquired the Floridas and Louisiana and the British navy protected communications with the Gulf Coast, men of wealth would resume purchases of western lands, especially Blount's, and pioneers in large numbers would invade the frontier. Having recently broken with the Federalist administration, Blount found it easier to consider separation and independent cooperation with Britain.[29] He concurred with his associate, Nicholas Romayne: "With respect to the United States [government] we are to be pissed upon and degraded."[30]

Blount, a Prune Street prison staring him in the face, was desperate in 1797. He knew British assistance was indispensable and encouraged Romayne to visit England again. Romayne, a friend of the wealthy real estate promotor Sir William Pulteney, and of Secretary of War Dundas, was Blount's liaison. Romayne urged Whitehall to provide ships, provisions, and possibly Canadian forces to help westerners capture the Floridas and Louisiana. Britain's main contribution would be naval, while Blount would organize the Indians and frontiersmen to descend on the Spaniards by land.[31] Romayne, arguing that the British navy's sturdy wooden walls were indispensable in keeping France off the North American mainland, at the same time spread rumors that French troops had already landed in the Floridas and Louisiana and were encouraging the southern Negroes to grasp *liberté* by massacring their white masters.[32]

Western Indians and loyalists living among them figured in Blount's scheme. Indians unalterably opposed American expansion and cooperated with anyone—Britain, Spain, France—in defense of their lands. Loyalist Indian traders told the natives that despite Britain's setbacks in the Old Northwest and Spain's conceding the thirty-first parallel boundary, hope of outside aid was not dead. Semiliterate traders needed no private advice from Whitehall. They merely had to be aware of newspaper accounts reporting that France was on the verge of returning to the lower Mississippi Valley or had actually taken possession. It was no state secret that Britain would use force to keep France out of North America. From the Shawnees and Hurons in the north to the Creeks and Cherokees in the south the pro-British Indian confederation began reviving around 1797.[33]

Loyalist traders like John Chisholm helped stimulate this renewed interest. He had come to Pensacola during the American Revolution and, after the city's capture in 1781, had retired to the Indian country. Living among the Cherokees and marrying a native, in time he became a deputy Indian agent for the United States. He accompanied an angry Cherokee delegation to Philadelphia in 1796 which felt that the United States had unjustly taken Cherokee land. They sought redress but got none.[34]

It was at this point early in 1797 that Chisholm sought out the British minister, Robert Liston. The unpolished frontiersman knew that France wanted Louisiana and the Floridas. Chisholm asserted he knew how to check the French: let the British navy, Indians, and loyalists take the Floridas and New Orleans. Once in possession Britain could force westerners, despite French sympathies, to come to terms with Britain. An impecunious trader and minor Indian agent, Chisholm felt rejected by the United States. He expected to help Britain manage the western Indians and to become a man of consequence.[35]

Despite later denials to his Federalist friends, Liston was intrigued by the unlettered frontiersman's proposals. The vision of French republicanism sweeping over North America's heartland obsessed him. French predominance in the Mississippi Valley endangered Canada and portended a revival of the Franco-American alliance that had brought about Cornwallis's downfall. Federalists were as alarmed as Liston by the prospect of France's return to the American mainland

and the possibility of her inciting Canadians to revolt. But Liston recognized that probably a majority of Americans opposed the Federalists. Political divisions might allow French troops to land unmolested in the Floridas and New Orleans and permit the intrigues of Vermont revolutionaries to go unchecked. Utilizing false papers and diverse subterfuges, Liston paid Chisholm's passage to London, authorized him to approach the government directly, and hoped Grenville would be won over.[36] At the same time the minister encouraged Canadians to cooperate in any campaign against the Floridas and Louisiana.[37]

The hardened frontiersman Chisholm and the urbane New York physician Romayne during the winter and spring of 1797 simultaneously urged the ministry to adopt the same policy. The question immediately arises whether these two were part of Blount's design. Romayne was definitely Blount's representative. Chisholm had served as an Indian agent under Blount and counted Blount his friend.[38] Nevertheless, it is possible that Blount and Chisholm, both understanding conditions in the Indian country and watching international developments, independently initiated essentially the same scheme and only later discovered that each had either an unsuspected collaborator or a rival.

In unraveling the intricacies of the so-called Blount Conspiracy one cannot stop with the intrigues of Blount, Romayne, Liston, and Chisholm. At stake were Spain's Gulf Coast colonies, Britain's direct or indirect control of the Mississippi Valley, and Canada's security. An enormous territory was involved, including the two Floridas.

West Florida, with settlements at Pensacola, Mobile, St. Marks, and Natchez, was inextricably bound to the destiny of the Mississippi Valley. East Florida, whose population centered on the Atlantic Coast around St. Augustine and the mouths of the St. Johns and St. Marys rivers, though in no wise part of the Mississippi Valley, played a part in the Blount Conspiracy. Whether Blount concerned himself with East Florida or knew exactly what was going on is another matter.

The overriding peril from the standpoint of the British admiralty was the danger of East Florida's cession to France. French privateers would gain bases close by the Gulf Stream and be advantageously located to harry British commerce. Genêt's privateers were fresh in mind. Once France established herself in East Florida, she could intrigue with Jefferson's followers and undermine the Federalists. Spanish East Florida had only a small, poorly equipped garrison and a few thousand inhabitants, but the colony's importance was greater than the narrow interests of the underpaid Spanish garrison and the local planters and artisans.

Loyalists, who for years had been urging British return to Florida, comprised part of the population. But Whitehall concerned itself with East Florida not so much because of loyalists' pleas but because of the French threat. Debating how to forestall France, the government was not sure whether or not to cooperate with the United States. Considering the volatile framework of American politics in 1796–97 and France's resolve to acquire East Florida, the ministry was not inclined to depend on the United States.

This is why early in 1797 as Chisholm sounded out Minister Liston in Philadelphia, the admiralty contacted John McIntosh and laid the groundwork for recovering East Florida. The veteran American soldier who had fought against the British now agreed to enlist Georgians for service under the Union Jack. After they conquered East Florida, Britain promised to reward them with lands. McIntosh began raising Georgia volunteers. At the same time English-speaking prisoners jailed in St. Augustine's Castillo de San Marcos tried to break out, presumably expecting to swell the ranks of McIntosh's army.[39] The British navy contrived private signals to communicate with McIntosh at his plantation on St. Simons Island—"a French ensign at the main topgallant masthead and a Spanish one at the fore," to be acknowledged by "two smokes on shore."[40]

As British naval officers conspired with McIntosh and the Georgians, an obscure Irish priest in Wexford made an unusual disclosure to the local mayor. The priest revealed that his friend, Enrique White, Irish-born governor of Pensacola, was dissatisfied with Spanish service and willing to hand over Pensacola to Britain. The plan was simple: the governor would foment an Indian disturbance in the interior, dispatch the garrison to deal with it, and when the Spanish troops returned to Pensacola the British flag would greet them. The priest, who recently had served four years in the Floridas under the Spanish regime, swore that White could be depended upon.[41]

Taking the larger view in 1797 it is hard to escape the conclusion that Governor White's alleged treason was but one manifestation of the resurrection of a venerable land speculation—the Muscle Shoals project. For years speculators had tried to make a settlement at the lower bend of the Tennessee River (Muscle Shoals) and to link it by road and canal with Pensacola and Mobile. This opened millions of acres of fertile lands for immediate settlement. Since the mid-1780s an influential coterie had advocated this scheme and had solicited support from the United States national government, the state of Georgia, Spain, and Britain. North Carolina, Tennessee, and Georgia politicians played a leading role in this undertaking.[42] Whitehall, however, was concerned not about real estate promotion but the danger of France's return to the American mainland. The ministry was willing to employ land speculators but was not foolish enough to rely on them exclusively.

Fortunately, from the ministry's standpoint, there was a way to forestall France without reference to land jobbers. In 1797 it appeared that the European belligerents might conclude peace. Representatives of Britain, Spain, and France in Lille discussed possible terms. Spain still craved Gibraltar and hoped to induce Britain to swap this fortress for the Floridas and Louisiana or other Spanish American colonies. During the hard times of the American Revolution and immediately thereafter George III had questioned the expense of retaining Gibraltar and recommended exchanging it for Spanish colonies. The importance of British sea power in the Mediterranean during the wars of the French Revolution, however, made it less probable that Britain would relinquish this base.

But it was possible, indeed justice demanded, according to James Harris, Lord Malmesbury, the astute British representative at Lille, that Spain still cede Britain the Floridas, Louisiana, or other Spanish American territory. To maintain the balance of power he insisted that Spain surrender colonial territory to compensate for her recent cession of Santo Domingo to France. A peace settlement was possible at Lille, but in the end negotiations failed, the European war continued, and Malmesbury failed to attain either peace or the Floridas and Louisiana.[43]

Force rather than diplomacy was necessary for Britain to recover these colonies. Blount and his associates knew this and assumed that the frontiersmen and Indians, aided by the British navy, would have no trouble. But his plans were prematurely disclosed. Blount had written an incriminating letter to James Carey, Indian agent among the Cherokees: "I believe . . . the plan then talked of [to the British minister last winter] will be attempted . . . in a much larger way than then talked of. . . . I shall . . . probably be at the head of the business on the part of the British."[44] Blount was betrayed, and political enemies obtained his indiscreet letter. The Federalist administration was torn between prosecuting the apostate Blount and withholding the letter so as not to embarrass Britain.

In the end the administration exposed Blount while playing down British complicity. The Carey letter was sent to the Senate, which after an investigation expelled the senator. He was charged with serving a foreign power and enlisting forces on American territory to attack a peaceful neighbor. These points were of more import to the eastern Federalists than to frontiersmen. Tennessee authorities refused to arrest Blount, and Tennessee voters showed their contempt for both the Senate and easterners by electing Blount to the state senate.[45]

Publicity surrounding Blount's machinations seemingly caused the collapse of the undertaking. Blount had been expelled from the United States Senate and forced to flee westward to escape arrest by federal officers. Chisholm fared no better. Liston had paid his passage to London and arranged interviews with key ministers. But after the Carey letter exposé Liston advised Whitehall to dismiss Chisholm and return him discreetly to the Indian country.[46] The government complied, though from Chisholm's standpoint there was an unwarranted delay while he was shamefully neglected. He ran out of money and was thrown into London's unhealthy debtors' prison, where his diet was abominable and he was severely bitten by a vicious Newgate cat. The ministry eventually reimbursed Chisholm, but he was furious.[47] As a result he visited Rufus King, American minister in London, and presumably for a consideration, disclosed the names of his accomplices.[48] Romayne was in New York at the time of the Carey disclosure. United States officers descended on his house, impounded his correspondence, and asked the mercurial doctor to explain his conduct and demonstrate how it was in the best interests of the United States.[49]

All the while Liston in Philadelphia avowed that the British government was only peripherally involved. The minister readily admitted that he had sent Chisholm to London, but merely because the matter was so important that only Whitehall could deal with it. As soon as William Wyndham Grenville heard about Chisholm's plans, however, the foreign secretary disavowed them because of the difficulty of obtaining supplies, the danger of employing the Indians, "and the impropriety of originating within the United States any hostile expedition against a nation with which they are at peace."[50] Liston showed the Americans Grenville's original dispatch containing the disavowal. Secretary of State Pickering thanked Liston, delighted and relieved over conclusive proof that Britain was not implicated. Pickering charged that Blount, Chisholm, and the rest were adventurers and speculators whom Whitehall judiciously had spurned.[51]

These explanations were too simple, the British ministry's motives too honorable, and Pickering's naïveté too complete. Pickering only four years before had avowed that Whitehall's fixed policy was to carve up the United States. Yet Pickering in 1797 announced to his Federalist friends and the country at large that Britain's disavowal of Chisholm was sincere and that she would not think of encouraging western separation. Rufus King in London, like Pickering, was delighted that Britain had apparently turned down Chisholm's and Romayne's overtures. But King could not help wondering why, since Liston had taken Pickering into his confidence, Liston had not given earlier warning of Chisholm's designs.[52]

Liston readily acknowledged sending Chisholm to London; the minister asserted that he was not otherwise implicated. He was not telling the truth. For a time he thought the plan an excellent one, the best way to keep the Mississippi Valley out of French hands and to protect Canada. He recommended not only Chisholm but also Romayne to the ministry, and at the same time he asked Canadian authorities how they could best cooperate.[53] Even after Blount's expulsion, Liston searched for a discreet person to replace Chisholm, perhaps a Canadian Indian trader who legally could traffic south of the boundary.[54]

The Carey letter and Grenville's dispatch denying British complicity do not satisfactorily explain the downfall of the Blount conspiracy. The threat that France might return to North America had given rise to the project. With Jefferson's possible election and divisions between the Republicans and Federalists during the winter of 1796–97, it seemed best at first for Britain to take the initiative and employ Chisholm or someone like him. Even after John Adams' narrow victory, the ministry wondered if pro-British Federalists controlled their own house.

But popular support for the Federalists increased, and France was more responsible than John Adams. France was furious with the Jay Treaty and maintained that the United States, by permitting Britain to detain American ships trading with the French West Indies, had abandoned both the 1778 Franco-American treaty of alliance and her own independence. France, resolving to imitate Britain, intercepted scores of American merchant ships trading with the British West Indies. An aroused public, increasingly anti-French and pro-Federalist, demanded war if there was no satisfaction.[55] A Franco-American conflict was anticipated as Chisholm, Romayne, and Tatham sounded out the British ministry during the first part of 1797. This, not the Carey letter, was why Grenville declined their overtures and the admiralty never gave McIntosh orders to unleash the Georgians. Whitehall, in order to keep France off the American mainland, again reversed itself and decided to cooperate with the United States.

This basic shift in Britain's policy was responsible for the failure of the Blount Conspiracy and related schemes that Blount may or may not have been aware of. Britain and the United States during 1797–98 worked more closely together than at any time since the Revolution, and the reason was a common fear of France and international republicanism. Both countries passed harsh sedition laws to restrain domestic Jacobins. Canadians suspended the writ of habeas corpus, and sentenced one radical, David McLane, on flimsy evidence to be hanged by the neck, cut down alive, and his bowels to be taken out and burnt before his face. The entire execution before a large crowd was drawn out for two hours.[56]

Conservatism no more than fanatic republicanism respected national boundaries. In a sense extreme American Federalists had more in common with Edmund Burke's British admirers than with domestic Republicans. Pickering did not flinch when Liston explained away British complicity in the Blount affair, and the secretary of state acclaimed Liston for revealing Grenville's private dispatches which, to Pickering's apparent satisfaction, proved British innocence. Soon the ultra-Federalist Pickering maintained that the Carey letter was but a Republican stratagem: Blount was a French rather than a British agent deviously working to implant French extremism and the tricolor in the Mississippi Valley. In numerous letters to his High Federalist friends Pickering convinced some of them and possibly himself that French, not British, influence was behind Blount.[57]

Tory exiles in Canada and conservative American patriots of '76, alarmed by radical republicanism on both sides of the boundary, put aside their differences and banded together in face of a common peril. Edward Winslow, Jr., an active Massachusetts loyalist who achieved high rank in Britain's provincial forces during the Revolution, had moved to New Brunswick after 1783. The American Revolution was a thing of the past, but French extremism menaced established authority everywhere. He corresponded with Massachusetts Federalists, expressing relief that "party animosities have subsided and [youthful] affections have returned to their proper channels . . . remember me . . . to the whole circle of my friends."[58]

The ultra-conservative Gouverneur Morris, Washington's friend and framer of the Constitution, traveled throughout Europe, regularly reported to Grenville about the status of republicanism, and possibly was in the British minister's pay.[59] At the same time Morris urged Washington to curb the "hot speeches" of Kentuckians who openly proclaimed that Britain still harbored designs on the Mississippi Valley.[60] The aristocratic Morris and the haughty Grenville felt exactly the same way about the spread of republicanism, both in Europe and America.

Whitehall and American Federalists began to act in concert. The Federalists, because of hostility to France, roused the American public and were more popular than ever. France began seizing American merchant ships in 1797, and the following year witnessed the XYZ affair and an undeclared naval war. High Federalists clamored for a complete break. Whenever the United States declared war on France she automatically became Britain's ally. The ministry in 1797–98 decided to work with the United States in keeping French interest off the American mainland rather than intriguing individually with Blount, Chisholm, and other westerners.

Alexander Hamilton represented the faction urging Anglo-American collaboration. Though he was in retirement, some thought that he rather than President Adams directed the administration. Hamilton wanted war with France. This ensured effective cooperation with Britain and paved the way for Americans, supported by the British navy, to take the Floridas and Louisiana. Hamilton expected the United States to keep these Spanish colonies and reasoned that Britain should be content with preventing France from returning to North America. Besides, there were other Spanish colonies for Britain. Hamilton wanted Britain and the United States to assist Francisco de Miranda.[61] The Venezuelan Creole, in London soliciting aid to liberate Spanish America, was conferring with British ministers.

Some Federalists believed that it was unwise for the United States to add territory to her southern and western frontiers. The danger in 1798 was that if Anglo-American conservatives did not join in seizing the Floridas and Louisiana, then French or English-speaking republicans would grab them first. This consideration prompted these Federalists to agree with Hamilton and appear more expansionist than in fact they were.[62]

It was uncertain during 1798 whether there would be a formal Anglo-American alliance. The British press announced that one actually had been concluded.[63] Though newspapers exaggerated, Gen. Thomas Maitland arrived in Philadelphia to negotiate an understanding concerning rebellious Saint Domingue. Pickering wanted an unofficial arrangement because a formal treaty laid his party open to Republican charges that the Federalists had become British lackeys who had forgotten the "Spirit of '76."[64]

The two countries cooperated while negotiating. Britain returned cannon she had carried away in 1782 from Charleston to help Americans keep the French out of that port.[65] Alert British diplomats reminded sympathetic Federalists that French *philosophes* hoped to settle in the upper Mississippi Valley and that the United States' new alien law was aimed at just such firebrands.[66] The two countries considered Britain's lending men-of-war and American volunteers' serving in the British navy. If Britain assisted the United States in the Floridas then the United States could help Britain subdue French Saint Domingue.[67]

Britain expected the United States, if she got the Floridas, to recognize previous British land grants there.[68]

The anti-French frenzy touched off by the XYZ affair and the undeclared naval war with France pulled the United States and Britain together. But Whitehall delayed reaching any definite understanding. Britain was not as sure as Hamilton that the Floridas and Louisiana were reserved for the United States. American merchants had misgivings about incorporating French Saint Domingue into the British empire, because at some future date Britain might exclude Americans from trading with this important sugar colony.

In the summer of 1798 William Augustus Bowles, director general of the Creek Nation, supposedly safely confined in a Manila prison, arrived in London. He had escaped, made his way first to British Sierra Leone and then to England. Publicity attended his remarkable deliverance, and the director general conferred with Pitt, Grenville, and lesser members of the administration. Assorted loyalists and merchants from Nova Scotia to the Bahamas spoke to ministers in Bowles's behalf.[69]

Bowles knew that Spain was on the verge of losing the Floridas and Louisiana and, like Chisholm, expected the southern Indians to render Britain valuable service. He did not want the United States in the Floridas and, in contrast to Edward Winslow, Jr. had not forgotten what the rebels had done to his loyalist family in 1776. The only sure way to keep American or French republicans out of Spain's Gulf Coast colonies, Bowles argued, was for Britain to take them. A half-pay British officer, he was anxious to lead the southern Indians. Chances seemed good in the fall of 1798 for an Anglo-American alliance, and even inveterate Tory Bowles considered how Britain, the United States, and the southern Indians could best cooperate against the Floridas and Louisiana. But his heart was not in it because he wanted to see the Union Jack or the banner of a pro-British Muskogee flying over these Spanish colonies.[70]

Whitehall procrastinated during 1798 and on into 1799, and delay proved fatal for an American alliance. Contrary to expectations the United States did not declare war on France. When President Adams dispatched commissioners to Paris in November 1799, Federalists began fighting among themselves over Adams' conduct. To High

Federalists the president's course smacked of parleying with Lucifer. At the same time, Britain, emboldened by successes of the Second Coalition against France, became more aggressive in impressing American seamen and capturing American merchant ships. Whitehall could not tell who in the United States wielded power—the moderate pro-Adams Federalists, the High Federalists of the Hamilton, Pickering, Gouverneur Morris stripe, or the Republicans. With Republicans gaining strength at High Federalists' expense, the British ministry had misgivings about allying with bickering Federalists perhaps about to be turned out of office.

Whatever the vagaries of American politics, there was the immediate possibility that France might revolutionize the Mississippi Valley and tamper with Canada. Joseph Brant was discontented, and reportedly French influence had reasserted itself among the Six Nations and other tribes. Fearing that France might win back the Indians, Whitehall took another look at Brant's claim to contested lands and agreed that, if necessary, he should revisit London.[71]

Canadian security and a commitment to keep France off the American mainland were fixed policies at Whitehall. Cooperation with the United States was a variable, and as 1799 wore on American cooperation seemed less desirable. Whitehall sent Bowles back to the southern Indians aboard a British warship; Canadians reassured the Shawnees and northern Indians that Britain had not abandoned them; there were attempts to revive the Blount affair. The British threat to the entire American frontier, dormant during the era of Federalist ascendancy, reappeared.

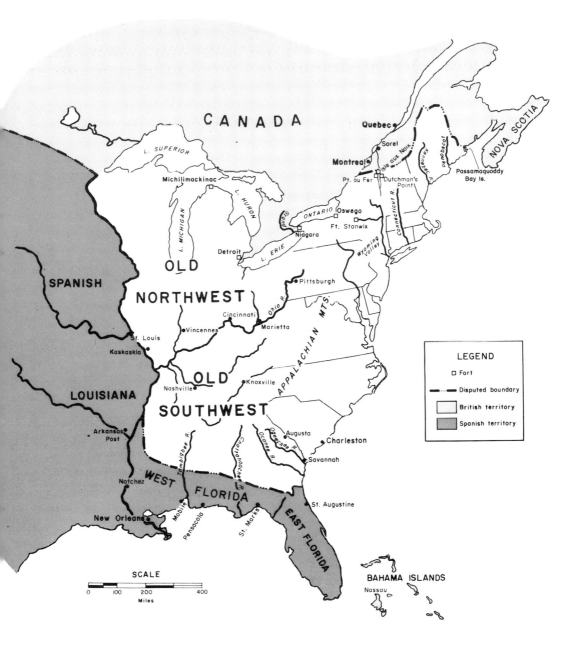

North America after 1783

Prepared by Albert Gregory

Tecumseh

Joseph Brant

John Graves Simcoe

Scottish National Portrait Gallery

John Murray, fourth earl of Dunmore

Right Hon^{le}
Henry Dundas.
Lord Advocate
1783.

Reynolds. ft

Scottish National Portrait Gallery

Henry Dundas, Lord Melville

University College, Oxford

Charles Jenkinson, Lord Hawkesbury

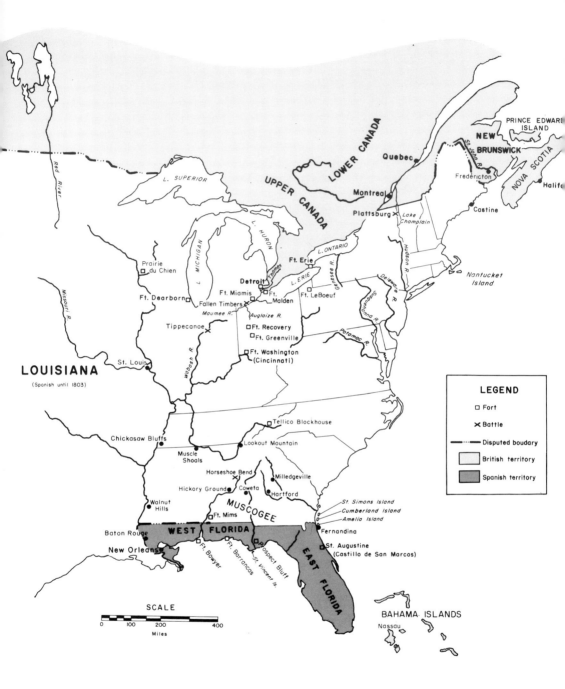

LEGEND

□ Fort
✕ Battle
······ Disputed boudary
British territory
Spanish territory

North America before 1815

Prepared by Albert Gregory

8 • Louisiana

AFTER the Federalist Party split in the latter part of Adams' administration after Jefferson's election and the decisive Republican victory in 1800, there was still talk of an Anglo-American community of interests. But in the United States those who advocated cooperation with Britain were usually Federalists who did not wield power rather than Republicans who did. Chances for Anglo-American harmony would improve if the Federalists regained control of the national government, or as a last resort, discouraged Federalists in the northern states could secede and form a close connection with Britain. Except for a resurgence in the War of 1812 era, Federalists steadily lost power after 1799, and many Britons and Americans alike who warmly advocated Anglo-American collaboration sanctioned, consciously or not, separation of the northern states. With some difficulty one can make a case that the accommodation of the late 1790s carried over into the next decade after the Federalists' fall from power, but a respectable number of people on both sides of the Atlantic advocating cooperation were not thinking of the United States as "one nation indivisible."[1]

The considerations that motivated New England Federalists to contemplate separation after Jefferson's election were more than chagrin on account of losing political power. To diehard Federalists Jefferson's Jacobinic, atheistic Republican Party threatened to undermine the gains won by the bloodshed at Lexington and Bunker Hill. If secession were necessary to protect the precious fruits of '76, then so be it: they adjudged it God's will.[2] Canadian loyalist exiles closely followed New England political developments. Nova Scotia's lieutenant governor, John Wentworth, a Harvard graduate, reminisced about his classmate and "old and intimate friend," John Adams,[3] while fellow exile, Edward Winslow, assumed Jefferson's election forecast the union's dissolution.[4] The idea gained currency both above and below the St. Croix boundary that the United States was about to divide. In the aftermath either New Brunswick would be added to New England or vice versa, the point of view depending on whether one was a Canadian or a New

Englander. In any case men of good will and sound principles in America would be reunited directly or indirectly under British protection.[5]

Disunionist sentiment was not confined to New England nor necessarily motivated by ideology. Ira Allen would as soon work with Britain as France, and the Georgian John McIntosh was not particular which foreign power helped him capture Florida. The West was a distinct geographical region, and the Appalachian Mountains remained a formidable barrier. James Wilkinson, recognizing geographical dictates, was willing to cooperate with Spain, Britain, anyone to open the Mississippi. Even with Jefferson in the executive mansion, western particularism was merely muted, not extinguished.

Though the possibility of the American republic's dissolution still existed after the turn of the century, British ministers did not overly concern themselves with the import of such a dismemberment unless there was a crisis. In 1800 there was. For over a decade France had tried to reestablish her North American empire, but all attempts, notably the Edmond Genêt episode, had failed. In October 1800 she concluded the secret treaty of San Ildefonso with Spain whereby Spain ceded Louisiana to France and in exchange the Spanish king's nephew received Italian territory.[6] Though this treaty was not immediately published and it took Britain time to ascertain all its provisions, there was little doubt after 1800 about the retrocession of Louisiana. Well-meaning Frenchmen had advocated reforms during the decade of the 1790s, many of which because of confusion and a lack of direction were not enacted. But after Bonaparte seized power in 1799 his organizational genius and iron will produced results. Whitehall feared that his enterprise would place French troops in New Orleans. With Bonaparte in the Tuileries there was a heightened awareness in the British ministry over implications of France's controlling the Mississippi Valley.

This French menace especially alarmed British statesmen responsible for military and naval affairs and for foreign commerce, including Secretary of War Henry Dundas, Secretary at War William Windham, Earl Spencer or the Earl of St. Vincent at the admiralty, and Charles Jenkinson, Lord Hawkesbury (earl of Liverpool since 1796) at the board of trade. Dundas, Windham, and senior generals realized that as a result of past failures and the first consul's remarkable continental victories, it was absurd to think of invading France. But Dundas, who after 1800 was probably William Pitt's closest advisor, intended to prevent France from again becoming a major colonial power. The British army and navy by 1799 had defeated Bonaparte in Egypt and had saved the eastern Mediterranean and India from French influence.

Defeated in the east, the first consul looked westward, and Dundas proposed to take the initiative and thwart French New World designs. He opposed any part of Spanish America, from Louisiana and the Floridas in the north to Argentina in the south, coming under French dominion. Dundas wanted to occupy Spanish American ports to keep France out and permit Britain to expand her New World commerce. In North America Dundas recommended taking New Orleans, and possibly Mobile and Pensacola, to protect Canada and make westerners turn to Britain and perhaps become British protectorates.[7]

The point that bothered the wealthy Windham, who was Edmund Burke's protégé, and British conservatives—which included every member of the ministry—was whether it were wise to revolutionize America to prevent France from republicanizing it.[8] The ministry applauded those Spanish Americans and Kentuckians and Tennesseans who asserted their independence, but these rebels must achieve freedom without overt British aid. Dundas refused support for either Francisco de Miranda in South America or revolutionaries on either bank of the Mississippi in North America. A member of Parliament during the American Revolution, Dundas had no desire to see British forces again roaming about the interior of North or South America. The secretary of war remembered Saratoga and Central American disasters. But during the American Revolution, usually without much difficulty, Britain had occupied every important North American port. Acquisition of key ports was what Dundas advocated.[9]

A variety of British subjects, frequently loyalists, urged Britain to take New Orleans and other Gulf Coast ports, and many of them had few qualms about British involvement in the interior. John Graves Simcoe, after leaving Upper Canada in 1796, commanded forces in the Caribbean that unsuccessfully tried to implant British control over revolution-ridden Saint Domingue. Though recalled to England in 1797 for consultation, he followed French ambitions in America and understood the dangers of French imperialists. A capable professional soldier and administrator not yet fifty, he had no interest in early retirement. He wanted another command and set his hopes on one of the Canadas. In his memorial to Pitt soliciting another appointment, Simcoe defended building the controversial fort on the Maumee River and declared that it alone had kept Wayne's forces away from Detroit, thereby preventing Anglo-American hostilities in spite of Jay's negotiations.[10]

Simcoe merely asked Pitt for any appropriate appointment. But Charles Stevenson wanted his chief to return to Canada. With Louisiana about to come under French control, with hordes of Francophile frontiersmen in Kentucky and Tennessee, and with roughly half of the Canadian populace speaking French, the danger to Canada was serious. Dismemberment of the United States, Stevenson avowed, was the best way to protect outnumbered Canadians. The ministry knew about the rift between Federalists and Republicans and that embittered New Englanders threatened secession. Stevenson argued that it was imperative to return the experienced Simcoe to America. During and since the American Revolution he had negotiated with disaffected Americans and encouraged them to align themselves with Canada. No one was better versed in this business than Simcoe, Stevenson asserted, and only prompt British action could keep the Mississippi Valley— Spanish Louisiana and Kentucky alike—out of Bonaparte's clutches.[11]

John Connolly, like Simcoe, wanted to return to Canada. Both had commanded loyalist regiments during the Revolution, and their views toward Britain's role in the Mississippi Valley and stimulating American disunion were similar. But they were rivals and did not like each other. Simcoe thought Connolly "a low man," untrustworthy, and a land jobber.[12] But Connolly enjoyed the confidence of the Duke of Kent, commander of British North American forces. Though Connolly's military record during the American Revolution was less distinguished than Simcoe's, Connolly had suffered more at rebel hands and had a strong claim on the government for his wartime exploits. Through Kent's influence the government overlooked Connolly's post-revolutionary indiscretions and appointed him deputy Indian superintendent for Upper Canada, the deceased Alexander McKee's old post.

Entrusted with dispatches from Whitehall, Connolly sailed for Cana-

da in 1799 determined to play a decisive role on the frontier and to
ensure that the Mississippi Valley came under British rather than
French influence. After arriving in Canada he discovered that he
would not be in a position to shape events in the Mississippi Valley: he
had been removed from office. Opposition from Sir William Johnson's
descendents in Canada, who assumed that Indian superintendencies
were their prerogative, and from the civil government, which argued
that the military had no authority to appoint Connolly, resulted in Connolly's downfall. The dispute dragged out for several years and
pitted the Duke of Kent, commander in chief of British forces in North
America, against his royal brother, the Duke of York, overall commander in chief of the army, who sided with those who contended that
Indian department patronage should not be controlled by the military.
Eventually Prime Minister Henry Addington stepped in, and Connolly
never got his appointment. Capt. William Claus, Sir William Johnson's
grandson, did.[13]

Britain considered occupying New Orleans and probably all the Gulf
Coast to frustrate the Corsican's New World ambitions.[14] What worried Secretary of War Dundas some, and his critics more, was that British troops might become committed in the interior. Director general
William Augustus Bowles, returned to the southern Indian country by
the Royal Navy, had the solution. He maintained that New World
sepoys were as effective as those in India and that his native army and
fledgling navy, reinforced by whites, could easily take all ports on the
Gulf of Mexico. Properly supported by Britain his "independent" Indian state of Muskogee, embracing much of the Old Southwest, would
have no difficulty maintaining its autonomy.

Already Muskogee's army had besieged and captured the Spanish
fort at St. Marks, and, if the director general were to be believed, the
Spaniards had fled from the town of Pensacola into the adjoining forts.
Prizes captured by Bowles's small navy were regularly condemned by
Muskogee's admiralty courts in harbors on the Apalachicola River and
elsewhere. With limited British aid, Bowles declared that Pensacola
and New Orleans must soon capitulate, and even the distant Spanish
garrison at isolated Arkansas Post across the Mississippi River fretted
about resurgent Muskogee.[15] British loyalists and French royalist
exiles who administered the state of Muskogee had no sympathy for re-

publican extremism and, in cooperation with the Indians, expected to keep out Jacobins of either the French or American persuasion.[16]

Bowles urged Britain to appropriate the Gulf Coast and make it a British protectorate. This was little more than a revival of the project for making this region a refuge for loyalists. Bowles was a loyalist, the handful of whites and half-bloods who were with him were usually loyalists, and he was not exaggerating when he asserted hundreds of loyalists would rally to a Muskogee propped up by Britain. Reportedly "all the Old Torys" on either side of the St. Marys River were "preparing to meet" Bowles,[17] and the "Old Torys" at Natchez and on the Tensaw and Tombigbee observed Bowles's activities closely.[18] Bowles also encouraged French emigrés of sound conservative principles to come to Muskogee, and a few had already arrived.[19]

Both Lord Liverpool (formerly Charles Jenkinson, Lord Hawkesbury) and his son, young Robert Banks Jenkinson, members of Addington's new ministry, were disturbed by the prospect of France's return to Louisiana. Rufus King, American minister in London, at first asserted that Robert Jenkinson was not sure of New Orleans' precise location.[20] But the foreign secretary's father, a continuous member of the government since before the American Revolution, knew all about New Orleans. For years he had tried to bring the transmontane region under British control and had long appreciated New Orleans' importance. When the inexperienced Robert Jenkinson had problems with New World geography, his proficient father set him straight, and it was only a short time before Secretary Robert Jenkinson hinted to Rufus King that Britain might have to preempt New Orleans to keep France out.[21] Bowles knew about the government's interest in the Floridas and Louisiana, and the exploits of Muskogee's minuscule army and navy were of more consequence than at first appeared.

Possible French occupation of Louisiana evoked different reactions. Canadians feared for Canada. Spanish Americans considered the possibility of New Orleans' changing hands inextricably bound up with revolution throughout Spanish America. British subjects agreed, and those who advocated seizing New Orleans and the Floridas looked to much more of Spanish America. Bowles claimed that Muskogee's forces, properly reinforced, could not only seize New Orleans but also liberate Mexico.[22]

Occupying New Orleans was but part of a comprehensive policy for all Spanish America. John Smyth Stuart, when not sulking over how shabbily the Americans had treated him in 1775 and projecting a loyalist colony on the Gulf Coast and a liberal marking of Canada's southern boundary, focused his attention on the isthmus of Panama. Britons since Sir Francis Drake's time had hoped to command this strategic spot, and at the turn of the eighteenth century Smyth Stuart was one of the more vocal advocates.[23] Miranda agreed that the fate of Louisiana and the Floridas was inseparable from the destiny of all Spanish America. Opinions of British authorities differed. The ultraconservative future Duke of Wellington opposed revolutions everywhere and by force of arms wanted to substitute British for Spanish dominion.[24] Other British statesmen opposed any involvement on the mainland outside Canada. If Whitehall had a comprehensive policy for Spanish America, including Louisiana and the Floridas, it tended toward Dundas' position: occupy New Orleans and other Spanish American ports but do not actively promote revolutions or commit British troops in the interior.

It appeared around 1800 that either France or Britain was on the verge of returning to the Mississippi Valley. Reports announcing a British return heartened the Indians who had to secure munitions and assurances from someone other than the Americans if they hoped to retain their lands. Necessity forced them to follow international developments closely. The Shawnee chief, Blue Jacket, Arthur St. Clair's nemesis, journeyed to Amherstburg on the Canadian side of the Detroit River and then, accompanied by other Shawnees, visited major Indian villages throughout the Old Northwest. He encouraged unity and implied that Britain was going to assume a more active role in the West.[25] The Indian council in 1801 at Brownstown below Detroit contained delegates from Indians of the Old Northwest, a few from the Cherokees and Chickasaws to the south, and Joseph Brant expected to represent the Mohawks. The Indian confederation was reviving.[26]

In the south Bowles breathed life into Muskogee. Though its boundaries were vague, this Indian state included most of the Floridas and considerable territory above the thirty-first parallel. The director general, as he lashed out first at President Adams and then Jefferson, asserted that the Indians had not signed the Pinckney Treaty and that neither the United States nor Spain had the right to bisect independent Muskogee at the thirty-first parallel. Bowles took credit when Creek-Seminole Indians ran off the joint United States–Spanish surveying party marking the boundary.[27] Minister Robert Liston was in a quandary because he did not understand Bowles's relationship with Whitehall. He informed Timothy Pickering that though he had received no communication from London, he presumed Bowles's mission was unauthorized. Privately he assumed, as the Americans charged, that Bowles was a British agent.[28] The truth lay somewhere in the middle. Whitehall had not decided what to do with Bowles because it had not resolved what to do with the Floridas and Louisiana.

Congress in January 1800 passed an act for the Preservation of Peace with the Indian Tribes to provide a legal basis for apprehending Bowles deep in the Indian country.[29] American sovereignty there, however, was different from that in the settled areas in the East. Indians living on both sides of the Florida boundary, along with whites in the St. Marys region and elsewhere, joined or promised to serve the director general.

Having captured Fort St. Marks in 1800 from the Spaniards, holding promises of support from Indians and whites both in the Floridas and above the boundary, and with part of the ministry anxious to seize the Gulf Coast, Bowles was confident that Muskogee soon must come under British protection. A new ministry, headed by Addington, assumed office in February 1801 and the following October signed a preliminary treaty with France. This treaty dashed Bowles's hopes in the south and whatever expectations Blue Jacket had of Britain's intervening on behalf of the northern Indians. The Addington administration, willing to make concessions and trusting Bonaparte to honor his commitments, in 1802 concluded a definitive peace settlement.

For the first time since 1792 there were no European hostilities. Pitt, no longer prime minister but friendly with Addington and wielding great influence, defended the settlement: "I find Windham (as might be expected) in agonies, but the rest of the world, as far as one can yet judge, very much delighted with the peace."[30] Pitt exaggerated. Others were unhappy, including William Wyndham Grenville, foreign secretary until early 1801 and influential in devising foreign policy during the past decade.[31] Another was Bowles's kinsman, the English pamphleteer, John Bowles, who proclaimed at length how it was impossible to trust Bonaparte and how Britain was the last bastion of civilization.[32]

They were among a sizable vocal minority that maintained Britain had made too many concessions at Amiens and that France was not likely to carry out her part of the bargain. Nevertheless, more agreed with Pitt than with Grenville, Windham, and John Bowles, and they hoped that rival ambitions in Europe and in the colonies had been put to rest, at least for awhile. There was no mention of Louisiana in the negotiations leading to the preliminary treaty. After signing the preliminaries the Addington ministry assumed or hoped that France would not try to upset the balance of power in either Europe or America. If the peace were to be durable, naturally she should not occupy Louisiana. Britain in turn would not occupy any Gulf Coast territory to forestall France. This was what discouraged Bowles and his followers in the south and the Shawnees and neighboring Indians in the north.

William Cobbett, "Peter Porcupine," was also dismayed by the Treaty of Amiens. Largely self-educated, widely read, opinionated, and contentious, he had turned to journalism after serving a term in the ranks of the British army. Excesses of the French Revolution provoked the fanatically anti-Jacobin phase of his career. He had established a press in the United States during Adams' administration and leveled blasts from *Porcupine's Gazette* at the Republicans. Jefferson's election signified to Cobbett that the tricolor and liberty cap reigned at Washington. Scarred by partisan attacks and convicted for libel, he returned to England where he hoped to be more effective in combatting international republicanism. He was Windham's friend and in many respects after 1800 became his spokesman. Even though his base was England, Cobbett still worked to curb republicanism in America. After Jefferson's election he felt the best policy was to encourage New England secession. Cobbett's contacts with northern conservatives led him to believe there was a good possibility of disunion.[33]

His stay in America had made him aware of Louisiana's importance and of the boost to international republicanism that French possession entailed: "From New Orleans, as from Abijah's *little cloud no bigger than a man's hand*, will come the living waters that are to cherish, or the streams of fire that are to destroy, the British monarchy."[34] Cobbett was furious when he found out about the preliminary Anglo-French settlement that Britain signed on October 1, 1801, and he assumed that Bonaparte had duped Addington. Restraining his passions as best as he could, the journalist tried to convince Foreign Secretary Robert Jenkinson of his errors and of his foolishness in depending on French good faith.[35]

Louisiana exemplified French duplicity. France had deliberately withheld news of the Treaty of San Ildefonso and of Louisiana's retrocession during the recent negotiations. Yet within a matter of two and one-half months after the preliminary Anglo-French treaty had been concluded, the Treaty of San Ildefonso was published. France, Cobbett argued, intended to occupy this colony and much more in America, and Britain was stupid to permit it. He urged George III not to ratify the Treaty of Amiens because, if Britain trusted France and sat idly by, the Mississippi Valley, Canada, Saint Domingue, and all Spanish America would come under French control—then "adieu to the British independence."[36] Robert Jenkinson, defending his treaty, joined others in persuading George III's government to sign the Treaty of Amiens on March 27, 1802. Jenkinson maintained that Louisiana was of little value. Cobbett was dumbfounded: "And all this of a country, the exports of which are nearly, if not quite, equal to those of Jamaica!"[37]

Cobbett, Windham, Grenville, and others of the conservative anti-Jacobin persuasion denounced the Treaty of Amiens and asserted that Bonaparte was using the peace merely to take advantage of Britain. The first consul strengthened his control over Italy and Switzerland, and there were ample indications that he expected to reestablish a colonial American empire, an important part of which lay in the Mississippi Valley. Louisiana's fate, Windham avowed, was crucial: "It is really a point on which may turn the fate of the world."[38] He admitted that British occupation of New Orleans might lead to a war with France, but hostilities seemed inevitable, and better New Orleans in British than French hands.

As it became obvious that Bonaparte had not satiated his ambitions when he concluded the preliminary Anglo-French treaty in October 1801, British opinion shifted toward Windham's point of view. Edward Cooke, soon to become undersecretary for war and the colonies, thought that concealing the Treaty of San Ildefonso and Louisiana's retrocession during the preliminary treaty negotiations was "fraudulent, insulting, and hostile."[39] Pitt, temporarily out of office during 1801–04, felt that Britain needed a breathing spell, defended the peace, and prevailed on George III to ratify the definitive Treaty of Amiens. But Pitt too, as he watched Bonaparte's designs on Louisiana unfold, became convinced that France was trying to take undue advantage of Britain, and in time his speeches began to "breathe war" as much as Windham's.[40] At first Prime Minister Addington in defending the peace settlement asserted that Louisiana was of little consequence. But it was not long before he recognized Louisiana's value, though he suggested it was not as great as Windham maintained.[41]

The preliminary Anglo-French treaty was concluded in early October 1801; France publicly announced the Treaty of San Ildefonso and Louisiana's retrocession in December 1801; and on March 27, 1802, British negotiators signed the definitive Treaty of Amiens. Though Louisiana was not mentioned in the Treaty of Amiens, the question arose whether George III's ratification, coming after publication of the Treaty of San Ildefonso, meant that Britain implicitly sanctioned French acquisition of Louisiana. Despite initial uncertainty, the Addington ministry within a few weeks made its position clear. Britain expected to remain at peace and honor the Treaty of Amiens as long as France did. But nothing had been said about Louisiana at Amiens. Addington reaffirmed Britain's policy of keeping France out of the Mississippi Valley and asserted that if necessary he would use force.[42]

But he did not want to resort to hostilities, and there were other measures to restrain at least partially French ambitions. John Baker Holroyd, Lord Sheffield looked into Louisiana's northern limits. It did not surprise him when he discovered there was no agreed upon boundary. He wanted to push Upper Canada's boundary as far southward as possible, perhaps to the Missouri River, thereby restricting French influence in the Mississippi Valley.[43] There was uncertainty whether part of the Floridas was included in Spain's retrocession of Louisiana. During 1802–3 British diplomats supported Spain and avowed that the Floridas were distinct from Louisiana and that France had no claim on them. British statesmen endeavored to prevent Spain from giving the Floridas to France in any subsequent treaty.[44]

With Bonaparte's troops in Holland in late fall 1802 and destined for Louisiana, with his agents and money tempting the western Indians, and with his minions inciting the French Canadians to revolt, Addington recognized he might have to use force despite the Amiens peace. He ordered the admiral commanding the British naval squadron off the Dutch coast in March 1803 to reason with the commander of the French expedition and to suggest it would not be wise for him to depart for Louisiana. If he persisted the British admiral was to capture the French transports and bring them into British harbors.[45]

In the winter the Dutch harbors froze, and early in 1803 a storm damaged French ships causing additional delay. All the while Adm. Edward Thornbrough in the North Sea did not know whether or not the French were inclined to accept British logic. During this period of uncertainty, the prospect that intimidated Addington was the same that alarmed Canadians: "It does not require the gift of prophecy to foresee what will be the consequent fate of the two Canadas and all the territory of the United States to the west of the Allegany Mountains" if France took Louisiana and the Floridas.[46]

British policy during 1802–3 was to keep French troops out of these Spanish colonies, and the only question was how. An American alliance was one possibility. Most historians treating events leading up to the Louisiana Purchase have emphasized that French occupation of New Orleans inevitably meant Anglo-American collaboration. As Jefferson put it: "We must marry ourselves to the British fleet."[47] Addington told Rufus King in London that before France attempted to take over Louisiana, Britain would promptly occupy New Orleans. But Addington implied, or King assumed the prime minister implied, that Britain had no long-term interest in New Orleans and would soon turn it over to the United States.[48] The American press expected the British ministry to be grateful for Americans seizing New Orleans and curbing French expansion.[49] After conclusion of the Louisiana Purchase Pickering asked Alexander Baring, the English banker whose firm helped the United States finance the fifteen-million-dollar purchase, if Britain were opposed to the United States' acquiring Louisiana. Baring replied certainly not, that Britain was pleased and, if necessary, would gladly have advanced the entire purchase price to have prevented this colony from going to France.[50]

Anglo-American cooperation as suggested by Baring and Jefferson was possible but not probable. Baring, not part of the British administration and having limited political influence, gave his personal opinion, not Whitehall's. And banker Baring was not a disinterested observer. The *Times* (London) more accurately reflected British ministerial and public thinking: "It is singular, however, that in the United States there should prevail a hope or an opinion of this country taking up arms again in their defense. How *America* has deserved this at our hands, we shall be glad to hear explained by the statesmen of Philadelphia or Washington."[51] James Harris, Lord Malmesbury, perhaps Britain's most experienced diplomat, did not think that the Americans, a "mean, shabby people," should have Louisiana.[52] Though circumstances forced Jefferson to consider an Anglo-American marriage, there are many indications that the eager American bride might have waited an inordinately long time at the altar.

A British alliance with only part of the United States was another matter. Britain and an exasperated Aaron Burr in 1802 tentatively contemplated cooperation between westerners and the British navy in taking New Orleans. Burr, even at this early date, apparently expected to become the independent ruler of a grandiose Mississippi Valley empire and Jefferson's political equal.[53] One of the reasons Simcoe was anxious to return to Canada was so that he could resume working for a northern separation. If New England did secede, as Pickering, Massachusetts Governor Caleb Strong, William Plumer, senator from New Hampshire, Congressman Roger Griswold of Connecticut, and other Federalists were considering, then there could be an Anglo-American alliance but it would be a far cry from Jefferson's "marriage."[54]

Despite British hostility to the Jefferson administration, Anglo-American collaboration of some type to keep France off the Gulf Coast was possible. In the aftermath the United States might win the Floridas and Britain Louisiana. But to assume that Britain, after taking New Orleans, would hand it over to the United States, represented more wishful thinking than reality. Thomas Douglas, earl of Selkirk, Sir Walter Scott's friend and future colonizer of the Red River in Manitoba, was in America in 1803 searching for likely spots to relocate impoverished Highlanders. Western Canada was one good possibility, lower Louisiana another. Selkirk, who had had his eye on Louisiana for some time, assumed that whenever Britain got Louisiana she should keep it.[55]

Director General Bowles concurred. Muskogee's fortunes had varied according to the relations between Britain, France, and Spain. Hopes for Muskogee had soared around 1800 when Dundas and Windham were on the verge of committing the ministry to dispatching an expedition to the Gulf of Mexico. Bowles prepared the way by capturing Fort St. Marks. The Treaty of Amiens depressed the director general, because it meant that no British force was coming to the Gulf. The Spaniards recaptured St. Marks, interrupted his trade with British merchants in the Bahamas, and Bowles wandered about, sometimes above but usually below the thirty-first parallel.

His hopes rose again in the winter of 1802-3, because it was evident that Bonaparte not only had acquired title to Louisiana but had troops poised in Holland ready to take possession. Whitehall, aware that the Amiens peace was breaking down, prepared if necessary to occupy New Orleans. This change in events reassured Bowles and inspired him to set out for the Hickory Ground, a Creek ceremonial site near present-day Montgomery, Alabama. It was far above the thirty-first parallel and, by American definition, well into United States territory. But it was in the heart of the Indian country, the nearest white settlement some 200 miles away. Bowles harangued the assembled Seminoles, Creeks, Cherokees, Chickasaws, and Choctaws, urging them to elect him leader of the southern Indians, promising British aid in defending their lands. A British expedition, he asserted, soon would arrive in the Gulf of Mexico.

Bowles came closer to speaking the truth than the Indians and handful of whites assembled at the Hickory Ground realized. But, deep in the Indian country, he could not convince most of the Indians that British support was forthcoming. As a result, Benjamin Hawkins, United States Indian agent, Esteban Folch, son of the Pensacola governor, and John Forbes, head of Forbes and Company (formerly Panton, Leslie, and Company), who were at the Hickory Ground and hostile to Bowles, engineered his downfall. Hawkins and some Indians captured Bowles, turned him over to Folch and the Spaniards, who without delay packed him off to a cell in Havana.[56]

Unknown to Bowles as he had prepared to set out for the Hickory

Ground in 1803, Louisiana's fate had already been decided. The determination was made in the Old World rather than the New. American representatives in May 1803 accepted Bonaparte's surprising offer to sell all of Louisiana, and they immediately apprised Britain of this purchase and claimed there was no need to send redcoats to New Orleans.[57] The British in time agreed, though not as readily and with as much enthusiasm as Americans assumed.

There was an interval before it was ascertained that the Americans and not the French were going to occupy New Orleans permanently. Both Jefferson's Republicans and New England Federalists for different reasons had misgivings about the Louisiana Purchase, and it was not until December 20, 1803, that the United States took possession of New Orleans. The prospect of the fifteen-million-dollar purchase price dropping into Bonaparte's war chest disturbed Whitehall and not a few Federalists. Unfounded rumors persisted that Britain still was going to take New Orleans to keep Bonaparte from getting the fifteen million.[58] Spain insisted the French sale was illegal because Bonaparte had not honored other provisions of the Treaty of San Ildefonso.[59]

Despite delay and with some qualms, the United States finally occupied Louisiana. To all appearances the Mississippi Valley's destiny was sealed. Between 1800 and 1803, and especially in the latter year, there had been an enormous interest in Louisiana. Frenchmen, publishing works extolling pre-1763 Louisiana, urged Bonaparte to reestablish French dominion. Englishmen, not to be outdone, dedicated tracts to Addington and other ministers imploring prompt British occupation of Louisiana.[60] Bowles's friends brought out a new edition of his life illustrating the importance of Muskogee and the Gulf Coast.[61] Both British and French authors stressed that it was folly to think exclusively of Louisiana. Ambitious Frenchmen regarded Louisiana's acquisition as the first step to regaining Canada, while their British counterparts maintained that the best way to safeguard Canada was to take New Orleans.

Foreign, that is, non-Spanish, occupation of New Orleans could have triggered United States dismemberment, a phenomenon not likely to have been confined to the West. But with the American, not the British or French ensign, waving over New Orleans, the threat to the republic's territorial integrity seemed to have passed. The deluge of pamphlets and newspaper articles acclaiming the advantages of a British colony in the Mississippi Valley and on the Gulf Coast ceased, and Director General Bowles, wasting away in his Havana cell, soon died. With Americans established on both banks of the Mississippi, there seemed to be little reason for Whitehall to concern itself with the heart of North America.

9 • Burr's Intrigues

AMERICAN occupation of New Orleans and St. Louis apparently symbolized the ultimate disposition of the Mississippi Valley. The United States, subjected to great stresses since independence, had endured, prospered, and now seemed the dominant New World power. Anglo-American frontier disputes still existed after the Louisiana Purchase, but statesmen did not regard them as critical.

The Floridas were a tangential region where rival British and American interests continued to clash. That Spain occupied both Floridas did not preclude an Anglo-American conflict. The United States, meaning to have these colonies, maintained that West Florida was an integral part of the Louisiana Purchase.[1] But at least for the time being Britain wanted the Floridas to remain under relatively weak Spanish control. There were various reasons why British subjects and at times the ministry paid so much attention to these colonies. British rather than Spanish merchants for years had superintended their commerce. Despite American competition, this was still true after 1803, and as always Forbes and Company was in the forefront. Though the skin trade was now less significant, there were increasing opportunities of trafficking in cotton and other agricultural produce grown in the southern United States.

The Floridas themselves had certain economic assets. Procuring lumber for the British navy was a centuries-old problem affecting national security. With hostilities breaking out afresh in 1804 and Napoleon threatening to send his army across the Channel, Britain relied on her fleet. Merchants associated with Forbes and Company and their British competitors reminded the ministry that the Floridas were one of the best sources in the world for live oak. They expected the navy to see that this timber reached British shipyards and to ensure that the Americans did not get the Floridas.[2]

As long as Britain controlled the Floridas' commerce she was content for these provinces to remain in Spain's possession. But the years after the American and French revolutions witnessed many upheavals, and change was the norm. The Floridas' status might be altered. The United States considered buying the Floridas, paying Napoleon an additional *douceur* to induce Spain to part with her colonies, or seizing them outright. In British eyes the outcome was the same. The United States gained Florida territory, and the money involved inflated Napoleon's war chest. If Spain passively allowed the Floridas to slip from her grasp, Whitehall intended either to prevent this by force or to demand a territorial equivalent.[3]

Unrest spread throughout Spanish America, part of which was manifest in the Floridas. Baton Rouge on the Mississippi in West Florida was the center of agitation. Most of the inhabitants spoke English and were either recent immigrants from the United States or former loyalists. They wanted to overturn Spanish rule and required outside support from the United States, Britain, or France. West Florida merchants had close ties with the Bahamas, and the insurgent Reuben Kemper looked to Nassau for encouragement. The Bahamian governor, like his predecessors in every year since 1783, wanted to strengthen ties with the Floridas.[4]

But Whitehall did not. The ministry on several occasions between 1800 and 1803 had been on the verge of taking Pensacola, Mobile, and New Orleans to counter the French menace. But after Napoleon sold Louisiana, Whitehall regarded West Florida as of little consequence. Kemper, unlike William Augustus Bowles and William Blount, received little encouragement from British ministers. Americans were skeptical. William C. C. Claiborne, vacillating governor of the Territory of Orleans, needlessly fretted whether he had authority to intercept any Bahamian expedition coming to aid West Florida rebels.[5]

The ministry gradually became conscious that West Florida, though relatively insignificant, represented but a small part of Spain's American empire and that if a foreign power acquired this colony it might be the first step toward winning all of Spanish America. The vital issue was commerce. When Napoleon instituted his continental system in 1806 and attempted to disrupt Britain's European trade, British overseas commerce became more important than ever. In one fashion or another she had a large share of not only the trade of the Floridas but all Spanish America. Commerce with Spanish America was indispensable if Britain were successfully to counter the continental system.

The United States and France endangered Britain's commercial role in Spanish America. Francisco de Miranda had friends in the United States, and Britain feared that the United States might help free Spanish America and exclude British merchants from the new independent states. William Pitt, though warned to anticipate the United States and capture Spanish America, did not think that Jefferson would aid Miranda or that the United States could take over Spanish American commerce in the foreseeable future.[6]

Napoleon, who might force Spain to give him the Floridas along with the rest of Spanish America, was more dangerous. Despite the naval setback at Trafalgar, Napoleon hoped to cut off British trade with Spanish America. But for the time being Spain retained unsteady control over her New World colonies, and this suited Whitehall's purposes well enough.

Forbes and Company may have anticipated the United States' making good its claim to West Florida. Indians above the thirty-first parallel owed this firm money. The United States urged the southern Indians, some of whom owed John Forbes large sums, to cede additional land. But many of these Indians did not want to adopt the white man's civilization, become small farmers, and sell their hunting lands. Forbes suggested that the United States advance him money owed by the Indians, and in turn the United States could require the southern Indians to reimburse the government with lands. Exchanging debts for lands was a traditional way of getting title to Indian territory. Prolonged negotiations ensued, and though at one point Forbes himself went to Washington, negotiations eventually broke down. It was significant not that there was no final agreement but that there might have been and that Forbes even visited Washington.[7]

British merchants, rivals of Forbes and Company with no unpaid Indian debts, wanted the Floridas to come under British rather than American dominion. They were outspoken in their criticism that this firm was becoming pro-American and furnishing munitions to Spain, Britain's wartime enemy. After the outbreak of the Anglo-Spanish war in 1804 Forbes and Company had to renew its license to trade with Spanish Florida. In his application to the Privy Council Forbes emphasized the advantages to the national economy of a Florida commerce established by the patriotism of Scottish merchants. To Forbes's rivals his patriotism was suspect, and it was worth noting that until now the firm had assumed that its British loyalty was self-evident.[8]

American occupation of Saint Louis in 1804 made upper Louisiana a new area where Britain and the United States quarreled. Previously Spain and Britain had disputed the Louisiana-Canadian boundary, and the United States inherited this controversy. The Missouri River Valley fur trade was at the heart of the disagreement. Canadian traders assumed they had a right to continue trading on the upper Missouri because it probably was in Canada, or, if not, that the Jay Treaty allowed Canadians to trade freely on American soil. But the American Indian superintendent for upper Louisiana demanded that fur traders take an oath of allegiance and that all foreigners leave the Missouri River.[9] This touched off a dispute lasting until 1818 when both parties agreed on the forty-ninth parallel as the boundary.

This new Louisiana controversy joined an old one—the Maine–New Brunswick boundary conflict. Commissioners from both sides had been meeting on and off since the Revolution to determine ownership of the Passamaquoddy Bay Islands and the exact location of the interior boundary. But this old quarrel, along with upper Louisiana's boundary and the final disposition of Spanish Florida, did not appear serious after 1803.[10]

It was fortunate for the preservation of the union that two disunion attempts occurred at this time. The brilliant, ambitious Aaron Burr was involved first in the project to establish a northern confederacy in 1804 and later to separate the West in 1805–6. In each instance he and his associates expected British cooperation. Burr in 1804 was supposed to help create an autonomous or independent northern state. High Federalists, led by Timothy Pickering of Massachusetts, William Plumer of New Hampshire, James Hillhouse and Uriah Tracy of Connecticut —all United States senators—were dejected by the Republican administration's policies and by Louisiana's acquisition. Secession seemed the only recourse, and if Burr, who had his own reasons for hating Jefferson, were elected governor of New York, he could bring that state over to the northern confederacy. Burr failed in his election bid, which helped bring about the downfall of any northern separatist movement.[11] After his duel with Hamilton in July 1804, Burr became a felon in the East. He sought refuge across the mountains and with

James Wilkinson worked to establish an independent western state at the expense of Spain and the United States.[12]

The British government from a variety of sources knew about New England dissatisfaction, the attempts to establish a northern confederacy, and Burr's projected role. Anthony Merry, the pompous British minister to the United States, visited New England and enjoyed High Federalist confidence.[13] Thomas Douglas, Lord Selkirk, who expected eventually to succeed Merry, also was in New England and conferred with Hamilton and disgruntled Federalists.[14] They, along with New Brunswick and Nova Scotia authorities, reported to the ministry the intensity of New England dissent. Plumer spent "gloomy hours in contemplating" separation.[15] Jedidiah Morse, conservative Congregational minister and "father of American Geography," thought the sooner New England broke away the better.[16] Pickering agreed reluctantly: "Only fifteen years ago we embraced [the Constitution] with so much ardor."[17]

Pitt and Henry Dundas (now Lord Melville) watched developments in New England and New York. They well knew that a successful northern confederacy undermined the Francophile Jefferson's authority and protected Canada. In principle they supported disunion but because there was no immediate threat to Canada, took no positive steps to encourage independence.

Burr's complicity in a western separation involved a longer time span —1802 to 1807—and allowed the ministry to consider this undertaking more closely. Charles Williamson, a ministerial advisor for almost two decades, had been in London since early 1803. Williamson and Burr had been friends for years, and the half-pay British officer was in London not only because he was Burr's spokesman but also because the Duke of York ordered him there.[18] Williamson consulted with cabinet ministers, the war office, and with Melville. This Scottish statesman, Pitt's confidant for the past two decades, based most of his views concerning North America on Williamson's information. Williamson suggested and Grenville, now nominally head of the "Ministry of All the Talents," agreed that Britain not aid Burr unless he operated independently of Jefferson's administration. This was no problem, because Burr detested the sage of Monticello.[19]

Williamson's reports in London and Merry's dispatches from Washington—Burr had taken the British minister into his confidence—kept Whitehall abreast of what Burr was up to in the West. But except for Melville and possibly Windham, few ministers immediately after 1803 wished to support Burr openly.[20] From Whitehall's point of view North America was relatively quiet after the Louisiana Purchase, and the ministry wanted to leave it that way. Canadians had just sent a double agent to interview the new French minister in Washington. Relieved Canadians discovered that France, at least for the moment, had no plan to rouse the French populace in Canada.[21] Burr, up until his capture on the lower Mississippi and the downfall of his project, always told his supporters that British warships and money were at his command. But this was not true. There were times after 1783 when Britain would have enthusiastically supported western independence. Unfortunately for Burr, 1804–6 was not one of them. Though Canadians wished him well, the ministry indeed was "slack in trying to gain a stronger interest in [the western] country."[22]

Burr wanted to include West Florida, Texas, and possibly other Spanish territory in his western state. The former vice-president expected Britain to aid him in conjunction with liberating all Spanish America. Britain, watching Spain fall under French control, feared Spanish American colonies and commerce might come into the French orbit. Restless British subjects were more anxious to free Spanish America than Whitehall. Sir Home Popham on his own initiative captured Buenos Aires in 1806.[23] Though Whitehall had refused direct assistance to Miranda, after he landed in Venezuela the impetuous Adm. Alexander Cochrane negotiated a treaty with this Creole implicating the British government.[24]

Pressures were building up on the ministry to take a more active role in overthrowing Spanish rule in America. Selkirk maintained it was better to have Miranda than Napoleon.[25] But a majority of the conservative ministers, preferring if necessary to rely on British soldiers to overturn Spanish rule, shied from inciting rebellion anywhere. Americans associated with the Burr conspiracy wanted to liberate Spanish America and solicited British assistance. But at the time of Burr's capture in February 1807 the ministry had not made up its mind and gave Burr no aid. Britain already had become more involved with Miranda than planned.[26]

An emergency suddenly forced Britain to reconsider her American policy. The U.S.S. *Chesapeake* in June 1807 sailed through the Virginia capes on a routine cruise. A British warship approached, and its bellicose commander demanded that the Americans hand over British deserters serving aboard. The Americans refused, and, after a lethal cannonade, officers of the Royal Navy seized the deserters. This insult to the flag aroused the nation, and Jefferson, with popular support, easily could have declared war. The president instead recommended levying a total embargo on exports from the United States. Like Napoleon and his Continental System, Jefferson determined to wage economic warfare. He felt this was the best way to force Britain to stop impressment and respect American maritime rights.

Despite Jefferson's caution there was the chance from the last half of 1807 to early 1809 that hotheads in each country would force a break. The *Chesapeake* incident made the ministry look afresh at America. When Burr and New England Federalists had plotted a northern confederacy around 1804, Whitehall was relatively uninterested—but not now. New England's disunion was the best way to insure Canada's safety. Admirals George Berkeley and Alexander Cochrane stationed in North American waters prodded the ministry to work for "the long expected separation of the northern states."[27] The opinionated Cochrane had served for years in America, traveled extensively in the north, had married the daughter of a New York merchant, and had firsthand knowledge of New England discontent. But as he informed the ministry, "I bear no goodwill toward the United States."[28]

Even if New Englanders seceded, Britain needed time to perfect her relationship with any new northern state. In the meantime Whitehall considered occupying northern Maine down to the Penobscot River and making it the new boundary. Upper Maine was a source for masts and timber for the navy. If by chance New England did not secede, then William Knox, New Brunswick's colonial agent, recommended acquiring East Florida from Spain and swapping it for northern Maine.[29] But he expected New England to break off and British occupation of the Penobscot to help bring this about.

There were approximately twenty-five thousand inhabitants between this river and the St. Croix, and some were loyalists who had previously indicated that they preferred living under British rule. New

Brunswick authorities urged Whitehall, after occupying the Penobscot, to grant the upper Maine inhabitants neutrality and commercial
concessions, at once demonstrating the advantages of British protection. British occupation of the Penobscot also forced the Americans
to give up any foolish notions about going after Quebec the way Benedict Arnold had in 1775.[30]

Officers of the Royal Navy on the North American station, the British minister in Washington, consuls in major ports, and Canadians all
thought separation of the northern states an excellent idea. This is
why, with Whitehall's blessing, the governors of Lower Canada, New
Brunswick, and Nova Scotia each dispatched confidential agents to
New England after the *Chesapeake* affair. These spies mingled with
leading New Englanders, reported the extent of Federalist dissatisfaction, and laid the groundwork for separation. Whitehall, needing
no prodding, early in 1808 ordered Canadians to make binding agree-
ments with New Englanders if the crisis worsened.[31] The British ministry subsequently denied that it had sent agents into New England to
foment separatism, but Robert Banks Jenkinson (in 1808 the second
earl of Liverpool) publicly told the parliamentary opposition one thing
and privately had instructed Canadian governors another.[32]

Without fanfare, Mr. Edwards in June 1808 stepped ashore at Halifax. This was none other than Aaron Burr on his way to London.
Though he still had many friends in the United States, he was politically discredited, in financial straits, and in September 1807 had been
lucky to secure acquittal in his treason trial. But Burr as well as anyone
understood the strength of particularism in New England and the
West. In the past Britain had refused to aid him, and it was ironic that
Burr's chances of British support were greater after his trial supposedly ending the Burr Conspiracy. Sir George Prevost, Nova Scotia's
lieutenant governor, a professional soldier, and Burr's kinsman by
marriage, eagerly greeted Burr at Halifax. Prevost, number ninety-six
on Burr's cypher and like most Canadians fascinated by disunionist
schemes, rushed Burr to England, wrote letters in his behalf, and made
arrangements for him to stay with English relations.[33]

Burr's friend, Charles Williamson, had been in London for some
time advising the ministry. With the advent of the *Chesapeake* affair
and the embargo, Williamson thought the time ripe to dismember the

United States, to divide it into thirds—the north, south, and west. Williamson hastened Burr to London and arranged for him to interview proper ministers.[34] Williamson knew that Britain was on the verge of working for American dismemberment and that Burr could be useful.

From the ministry's standpoint it was Jefferson's Republicans who caused all the trouble. A tripartite division of the United States had the advantage of dissipating the power of the "Negro Presidents and Negro Congresses."[35] Though New England had erred in 1775, according to the ministry's thinking, she was basically sound and anxious for a British connection. By controlling New Orleans and access to the Gulf, Britain expected to manipulate any independent western state. Jefferson, Madison, and their followers isolated in the southeastern Atlantic states could rant, be rendered impotent, and deserve every misfortune. Irascible Adm. George Berkeley, reflecting on the latent fidelity to the British nation of the Virginia slaves, thought it an excellent idea for the blacks to turn on their southern masters.[36]

British occupation of New Orleans and the Gulf Coast penalized the Republican south. If Britain employed southern Negroes against their white masters, as she did during the American Revolution and the War of 1812—and as Lincoln was to do during the Civil War—then British possession of the Gulf Coast had obvious advantages. New Orleans was the prize, though it was important primarily for reasons other than being a base to incite servile dissension. Jefferson, Whitehall, and Burr all realized New Orleans was vulnerable. Williamson closeted himself with Lord Melville; Melville's son, Robert Dundas; Robert Stewart, viscount Castlereagh; and George Canning, all except Melville ministers in the Duke of Portland's new administration. They discussed how easily three thousand British soldiers approaching New Orleans via Lake Pontchartrain could seize the city. General James Robertson, Williamson's friend, participated in the discussions and was considered for command. If British regulars needed help, Williamson said that he and Burr stood ready to enlist American recruits.[37]

Canadians in New Brunswick and Nova Scotia advocated not only New England's separation but also the West's dismemberment. One depended somewhat on the other. The New Brunswick governor sent an agent south on a confidential mission. His first stop was to be Massachusetts; his last, New Orleans.[38] The Nova Scotia governor, George Prevost, prepared an expedition at Halifax destined for the South. Eventually it sailed and captured the French West Indian island Martinique. But Whitehall just as easily could have ordered it to the Floridas and New Orleans. Prevost, who claimed West Florida lands, had a personal reason for preferring the Gulf Coast over Martinique.[39]

The controversy engendered by the *Chesapeake* affair and embargo coincided with another crisis. Napoleon summarily placed his brother, Joseph, on the Spanish throne in 1808, threatening French control of the Floridas and the rest of Spanish America. The British ministry assumed the ambitious Napoleon would not restrict himself to Spanish colonies. A large majority of the inhabitants in Louisiana were French and unhappy with their new American masters.[40] The celebrated French general, Jean-Victor Moreau, set out for Niagara in the fall of 1807 apparently planning to become "King of Acadie and both the Canadas."[41] When Williamson, Burr, and Canadian officials urged Whitehall to take the Floridas and New Orleans in 1808, there was added urgency.

Prime Minister William Cavendish, the duke of Portland, warned the aging and infirm George III that if Britain did not act swiftly, the New World was lost to France.[42] Lord Castlereagh, the aloof secretary of war and colonies, sent Williamson to the West Indies to encourage Spanish governors in the Floridas and Cuba not to recognize the usurper Joseph Bonaparte but to throw themselves on British protection. Williamson had money in his pocket to continue paying salaries of the Spanish troops.[43]

The war scare stemming from the *Chesapeake* affair and the prospect that overnight Napoleon might become master of Spanish America again raised the question of the Mississippi Valley's disposition. The Indians, conscious of this, renewed efforts to create a confederation, though because of growing hostility with the United States, they probably would have united anyway. Superintendent William Claus in 1805 watched a hostile confederation containing some five or six thousand warriors taking shape in the United States, while the Americans complained about a "designing . . . *Manitou* or *Prophet*" stirring up the western Indians.[44]

After the *Chesapeake* incident the confederation strengthened. According to Lt. Gov. Francis Gore of Upper Canada, it was only through Claus's influence that they had been restrained from taking up the hatchet against the Americans.[45] Americans did not appreciate Canadian Indian agents' "restraining" red men on United States soil. They got their hands on one such agent and clapped him into Michilimackinac's prison.[46] British traders at St. Louis, Prairie du Chien on the upper Mississippi, and on the Missouri River vented anti-American grievances.[47] Exaggerated accounts proclaimed that the Indians had already begun hostilities, had suspended navigation on the Ohio River, and awaited a large army sent from Britain.[48] It was the western Indians, not the Six Nations, who were so aggressive. The Iroquois confederacy, possessing lands both in Canada and in the United States, now realized that taking sides would probably cost them more territory.[49]

Both the American commanders at Detroit and their Canadian counterparts across the Detroit River at Amherstburg tried to maintain friendly relations with the Indians, because both expected the natives not to remain neutral. Claus, assembling the Indians at Amherstburg, distributed presents on a greater scale than at any time in recent years. James Craig, a professional soldier and contentious Canadian governor, supported Claus's efforts and assessed the sentiments of the Indians.[50] Craig was alarmed not only by the prospect of a probable war with the United States but also because France threatened to return to the lower Mississippi Valley: We "must win over the Indians."[51] The American general William Hull at Detroit watched hundreds of Indians regularly going to and from Amherstburg. Some of these Indians stopped by Detroit before returning to their villages. Though their anti-American bias was evident, Hull entertained them: "We had better feed them than fight them."[52]

As usual the Shawnees took the lead in organizing the western Indians. This tribe, directly in the path of the advancing Americans, better appreciated the need for a united front and was centrally located. Even before the *Chesapeake* incident Canadians noticed the

Shawnee Prophet. He was uniting the Indians and preaching a religious revival—shedding most of the white man's culture and reviving native virtues. Canadians heard that the Prophet had a brother of some consequence, Tecumseh, and suggested both visit Amherstburg.[53]

It was partly because of the Shawnee's pivotal position that Britain reinstated Matthew Elliott to the Indian Department. Accused of misappropriating Indian stores, he had been dismissed from the Indian Department in 1797. But he had a Shawnee family, personally knew the Prophet and Tecumseh, and had great influence among the Shawnees. This was why the government in 1808 reappointed Elliott Indian superintendent at Amherstburg. The illiterate Elliott along with the illiterate Girtys, all of whom had lived off and on for decades among the Shawnees and had apprised the Canadian Indian Department of what the Shawnees were up to.[54]

The Prophet proposed to include the southern Indians in his confederation and dispatched Shawnee messengers southward. They reported that the southern Indians were badly divided: one half was pro-American and disposed to accept Jefferson's program of civilization; the other half was bitterly opposed, natural allies of both the Prophet and Britain.[55]

During 1808 and into 1809 the Upper Canada governor and members of the Indian Department presumed war with the United States was imminent. This is why they were so interested in the Prophet and why they entertained with great pomp the numerous Indians encouraged to visit Amherstburg. They told the Indians that Britain was counting on their assistance, though "as a matter of course this [was] done with caution and delicacy."[56] Gore affirmed that Britain still held the 1768 Treaty of Fort Stanwix and the Ohio boundary sacred and that the Indians might soon have the opportunity to regain their lands.[57] The Prophet had heard all this before and knew about Britain's closing Fort Miamis' door. Promises were not enough.[58]

But Elliott believed—more so than his superiors—that one British regiment was all that was necessary. It and Tecumseh's warriors could bring the country between Detroit and the Ohio once again under Canadian control.[59] Success in the north must inspire the southern Indians. Williamson in London did not have Elliott's firsthand intelligence of western Indian affairs. But Williamson told the ministry that

Britain's North American colonies could yet amount to something.[60] He might have been right.

The dual emergency stemming from the *Chesapeake* affair and Joseph Bonaparte's threat to take over Spanish America subsided. This is not to say that Britons and Americans resolved their differences over impressment and maritime rights. After months of negotiation they decided not to go to war—at least for the time being. The Floridas, Texas, and all Spanish America were spared from French dominion, though not because any Bonapartes had a change of heart. Spanish Americans were saved from French rule because they, like residents of Old Spain, refused to accept it. Peninsular Spaniards spontaneously revolted against Joseph Bonaparte, proclaimed Ferdinand VII their legitimate king, and fought with success against French troops. Governors throughout Spanish America recognized Ferdinand rather than Joseph as their true king.

This sudden change caused the ministry in July 1808 to send Wellington's army not to the New World to subdue Spanish America but to the Iberian peninsula where it joined Spaniards and Portuguese fighting against the French. From this point Britain adopted a policy of maintaining the integrity of Spanish America in behalf of her new ally Ferdinand.[61] Wellington's troops never arrived in Pensacola, Mobile, and other Spanish American ports, and as a result Whitehall became less interested in the Gulf Coast and the American West. The government's main concerns were the bitter struggle against Napoleon in Europe and the attempt to maintain overseas commerce to keep Britain economically strong. Burr had arrived in England early in the summer of 1808 when Britain had been on the verge of sending Wellington to Spanish America. When he went to the Iberian peninsula instead, Burr was downcast: "I have no hope that the ministry will approve anything that might be proposed."[62]

But conditions were such in 1809 that Britain could not ignore the American frontier even if it wanted to. She had not resolved her maritime controversies with the United States, and Madison's policies were not much of an improvement over Jefferson's. An Anglo-American war, though not imminent, was still possible and the possibility kept alive the issue of Canadian security. It had been made clear to the ministry during the *Chesapeake* and embargo crisis that the best way to protect Canada was to divide the United States and that some Americans were willing to join in this endeavor. British authorities, retaining their contacts with New England Federalists, continued weighing chances of New England's secession.

The growing Indian confederation maintained the government's interest in the Mississippi Valley. It was not easy for Canadian Indian agents to manage Indians living on United States soil and at the same time to avoid war with the Americans. The ministry feared the Prophet's revival might get out of hand. With time running out for Indians east of the Mississippi River, they resolved regardless of British policy to retain their lands and culture. Elliott continued talks with the Shawnees, and his superiors, both in Canada and in London, read his dictated reports with more than customary interest.

It became obvious to Whitehall during the 1808 crisis that, though the United States had recently occupied New Orleans and St. Louis, her hold on Louisiana was weak. Over 80 percent of the white inhabitants were of foreign background, usually French, most of whom were disenchanted with American administration. Burr and Williamson had discussed with ministers at length New Orleans' weakness and how easy it would be for the navy to approach the city and help the Creoles throw off American rule.[63] New Orleans was no less vulnerable after 1809.

It was a United States governed by southern Republicans that had levied the embargo and caused Britain so much trouble. When ministers considered the plight of Negro slaves in the Old South, it in part reflected the increasing momentum of the British antislavery movement. But the ministry also recognized that tampering with the Old South's peculiar institution was a good way to take revenge on Republican slaveholders. The war scare of 1808 did not significantly alter conditions, though it again reminded Whitehall of American weaknesses and Washington's tenuous hold on various parts of the frontier.

10 • War

RELATIONS between the United States and Britain after Madison's inauguration in 1809 were unstable: there was neither peace nor war. Powerful forces pulled in each direction. A mutually beneficial commerce, a common language and heritage, and opposition to France by most Britons and some Americans were bonds drawing the countries together. But disputes threatened to bring about hostilities. Britain, whose existence depended on her navy, relied on impressment to furnish crewmen for her men-of-war and on her Orders in Council to regulate American commerce. The seizure of alleged British deserters aboard American merchant ships and losses resulting from the Orders in Council became more of a problem than ever. Many Americans were quick to believe that Britain was behind every Indian atrocity. George III's ministers in turn considered all Republicans in the United States pro-French and thought that Jefferson's embargo and Madison's less restrictive measures were merely extensions of Napoleon's Continental System. Britain's main concern was Europe rather than America as the administration supported Wellington's peninsular campaign and tried to weaken Napoleon's continental grip. But Canada's jeopardy in any break with the United States forced the ministry to watch America, and the Perceval administration realized that at any moment hostilities were possible.

Robert Banks Jenkinson, the second earl of Liverpool, eventually becoming chief minister in a rejuvenated Tory Party, had served in various ministries since the turn of the century. Appointed secretary for war and colonies under Spencer Perceval, he was charged with Canada's protection. Surveying North American affairs, Liverpool was both discouraged and optimistic. He accepted the prophecy of Sir James Craig, governor-in-chief at Quebec, that it was a question of time until hostilities broke out and, like Craig, felt it was possible to defend Canada: New England's separation was the means: "It will take place at no very distant period."[1] Neither Liverpool nor Craig in 1810 overly concerned himself with the exact boundaries of an independent New

England state or about its precise relationship with Canada. But Liverpool and Canadians expected a separate northern state not only to protect Canada but also to lead to favorable boundary adjustments.

Publicity attending the Henry exposé early in 1812 emphasized Britain's interest in a northern separation. John Henry, one of the agents Canadians had dispatched to New England during the 1807–9 crisis, achieved more notice than the others because he later disclosed all. On two occasions Henry had gone to New England to ascertain the depths of Federalist dissatisfaction and to lay the groundwork for separation. After completing his missions Henry wanted Craig to reward him liberally. But the governor gave Henry only £200. The furious Henry returned to the United States and offered to sell his correspondence with Craig that implicated both Britain and New England Federalists. Madison paid Henry $50,000 for the documents that incriminated Britain but mentioned no specific Federalist. Relieved Federalists in turn damned Madison for squandering secret service money on worthless letters.[2]

Parliament took up the Henry affair, and the opposition criticized the government for working to dismember the United States while professing peace. Defending the government, Liverpool argued that there had been a threat to Canada in 1808–9 and in an excess of zeal and without Whitehall's knowledge Craig had sent Henry among the New Englanders to promote dissension.[3] But Liverpool knew that Henry was one of several agents who had gone into New England to promote secession with the government's approval.[4] Publicity attending the Parliamentary debates and those in the American Congress highlighted conditions that were obvious: High Federalists were threatening to dissolve the union and Canadians were anxious to cooperate.

The Indian controversy further endangered the tenuous Anglo-American peace. A hostile confederation was evolving, and according to belligerent Americans, the British were responsible. As Americans made further inroads into the Old Northwest, the natives became alarmed about those lands supposedly guaranteed to them by the 1795 treaty with Anthony Wayne. They feared not only for the loss of their lands but also for their culture—their souls. The American policy of civilizing involved transforming the natives into self-sufficient, inde-

pendent small Christian farmers. After completing the transformation
the Indians, so Washington authorities reasoned, would readily sell
their excess hunting lands. There was a growing realization by Indians
that they must unite if they were to retain both their lands and their
heritage. For some time the Shawnee Prophet had been preaching a
religious revival, urging shedding most of the white man's ways and re-
vitalizing half-forgotten Indian traditions. His brother Tecumseh took
the lead in organizing the western Indians politically and sought British assistance. Presenting the British commander at Amherstburg with
an ancient belt the British had given the Indians after having "laid the
French on their back," he urged a liberal distribution of presents.[5]

Though the Perceval administration realized there might be war
with the United States, it hoped to avoid a conflict, certainly one initiated by the Indians. The governors of Upper and Lower Canada and
their London superiors went out of the way to restrain the Old Northwest Indians. Again and again the superintendents were ordered not
to encourage the natives overly, and Whitehall refused Tecumseh's
request for additional presents and munitions.[6] It is probably true,
however, that private traders and members of the Indian Department
exceeded Perceval's orders.[7]

The Prophet's band in 1811 resided on the upper Wabash at the
mouth of the Tippecanoe River. William Henry Harrison, autocratic
governor of the Indiana territory, had watched the developing confederation and increasing Indian truculence and assumed the British
were behind it all. He moved his army to the Tippecanoe. The Indians
attacked, and after a sharp encounter the natives withdrew, though
Harrison suffered heavier casualties. The American press in 1811—as
in the 1840 presidential campaign—hailed the battle as an American
triumph. British newspapers emphasized Harrison's losses and proclaimed the Indians victors. Tecumseh had not been with his brother at
the battle but had gone among the southern Indians to bring them into
the confederation.[8] These hostilities alarmed the British government,
which, having its hands full with Napoleon in Europe, did not want war
with the United States, and it again admonished the Indian superintendents to use all possible discretion.

Canada's safety depended both on friendly relations with the United
States and on Indian goodwill. Col. Isaac Brock, stationed in Upper

Canada and appointed its president and administrator in 1812, read speeches of the bellicose war hawks and pondered the anti-British indignation evoked by the Battle of Tippecanoe and the *President–Little Belt* incident, an Anglo-American naval encounter. Considering war a certainty, he assumed that Canada's security ought not to depend on an accommodation with the United States. Brock pleaded with the home government to increase presents to the Indians and allow Canadians more effectively to manage the red men in the Old Northwest, though without giving the United States "just cause" to complain. The veteran soldier harped upon the old argument that, if Britain did not supervise the Indians, the United States would.[9]

Britain and the United States also threatened to cross swords in the Old Southwest. This was true despite the fact that Spain and the United States claimed this territory and bickered about who owned what. Though the United States occupied Louisiana, Spain insisted that the Louisiana Purchase was fraudulent and that this province rightly belonged to Spain. The United States asserted that it had purchased not only Louisiana but also West Florida, that West Florida was part of Louisiana. It was no secret that the Americans craved not only West but also East Florida.[10]

Britain became entangled in the Gulf Coast imbroglio for several reasons: she became Spain's ally in January 1809, and it was in Britain's interest to maintain the integrity of Spanish territory both in Europe and in America. British merchants, loyalists, and interested citizens still urged Whitehall to take a more active interest in the Floridas, and there were renewed signs that Napoleon after all might take possession of the Gulf Coast. Aaron Burr arrived in Paris in 1810—he had left England after Spain demanded his expulsion—and solicited French support for an independent western state. Napoleon and some of his advisors were still interested in the Mississippi Valley, sparking new rumors in 1810 that in some fashion France was going to establish a client state on the Gulf Coast and in the Mississippi Valley.[11]

The fundamental dispute pitting Britain against the United States in the Floridas was that the United States wanted all of both Floridas and that Britain supported Spain diplomatically and perhaps militarily. The United States occupied Baton Rouge in 1810 after the local citizens revolted and menaced the remainder of West Florida. The peril was not diminished because the Americans had no valid claim. From his retirement Jefferson urged Madison promptly to take both Floridas. Delay, the former president reasoned, allowed the British to take root in St. Augustine and Pensacola; once entrenched in these ports they were likely to remain.[12]

On this point, as on most others, Madison saw eye to eye with his Albemarle County neighbor. According to the Spanish ambassador in Washington, it was through Madison's influence that Congress early in 1811 in secret session decided to appropriate both Floridas.[13] Madison's administration encouraged the nearly illiterate former Georgia governor, George Mathews, and John H. McIntosh to capture Fernandina on Amelia Island. Next their Patriot Army was to move against St. Augustine and the rest of Spanish Florida.[14]

Americans seized Baton Rouge in 1810 and Fernandina early in 1812; the Spanish government, fighting for its life against Napoleon, feared for the rest of the Floridas. Britain supported the exhausted Spanish regime in the Floridas during 1810–12, and this is what made the Florida controversy, along with impressment, the Orders in Council, and the Indians, an issue that threatened to bring on an Anglo-American war. The least dangerous—and least effective—way for Britain to bolster Spanish rule in the Floridas was through diplomacy. From the onset the British charge d'affaires in Washington, John P. Morier, protested American aggression against Spain, which was fighting a heroic battle against Napoleon. But neither Morier's remonstrances nor Britain's offer to mediate Spanish American differences over the Floridas had any effect.[15]

British naval and military support were the best means of preserving the Spanish Floridas. The British navy was responsible for Americans' not making even more inroads on the Floridas. Fernandina was an example. Commerce in this small port had boomed since the embargo, because it had become a center for contraband trade. The sixty to eighty British ships that called annually shipped cotton smuggled from the United States or timber and naval stores produced in East Florida.[16] The British navy stationed three warships at Fernandina in 1810, which was a good reason why the Americans did not take Fernandina in the same year they seized Baton Rouge. American gunboats outnumbered British vessels at Fernandina early in 1812 permitting

Mathews to capture this port. Immediately after Fernandina's fall British warships came to St. Augustine and deterred further American conquests. When the Americans eventually withdrew from Fernandina in May 1813 British warships returned and helped sustain Spanish dominion.[17]

There was a chance of not only British ships but also British soldiers arriving in the Floridas during the unsettled 1810–12 period. British newspapers asserted that American capture of Fernandina amounted to a declaration of war against both Spain and Britain. While Jefferson and Republicans in Congress wanted to send American soldiers into the Floridas to anticipate Britain, the British minister in Washington urged Whitehall to send over troops from the West Indies to forestall the Americans.[18] He expected Spain to welcome redcoats into the Floridas as readily as into the mother country.

There was growing pressure on the British ministry not only to station ships in the Floridas and to dispatch troops but also to make them outright British colonies. British merchants concerned with the Florida trade, Minorcans who had remained in Florida since they first came there under British rule in the 1760s, and even Spaniards who preferred British to American rule all importuned Whitehall to anticipate the United States.[19] Morier recommended that Spain's wisest course was to cede at least part of the Floridas to Britain. She had the power to restrain the Americans and protect Spain's remaining colonies.[20] Perceval's administration, considering reestablishing the British flag in the Floridas before 1812, made no final decision.

Mathews and his followers captured Fernandina in March 1812 but got no farther. Madison disavowed Mathews' conduct and the assistance lent by American gunboats. The president repudiated Mathews for a variety of reasons, but none was the fact that Madison opposed in principle seizing Florida by force. Federalist criticism and the danger that Mathews' invasions might bring on a war with Britain persuaded the president to back down. Mathews was furious, and for a while his Patriot Army still hoped to take St. Augustine. Ultraconservative Gouverneur Morris in New York was distraught: Madison's rashness was bad enough but Mathews' was even worse. Morris assumed the latter's conduct made a British war inevitable. From the New Yorker's standpoint it was fortunate that Mathews died and the Patriot Army disintegrated.[21]

With the Spanish peninsula engulfed in a civil war and large parts of Spanish America in actual or potential rebellion, it appeared that Spain must soon lose the Floridas. This is what worried the loyalist firm of Forbes and Company because it depended on Spanish beneficence. Overall the company had flourished under the Spaniards and expected to continue making a profit whenever the Americans or British took over. John Innerarity, a partner in Pensacola, told the Americans that he welcomed their dominion over Florida and wanted to assist in the transition.[22] The elderly John Forbes at the same time entreated the ministry to grab the Floridas before it was too late.[23]

The southern Indians observed the coming and going of British warships to Florida ports and indications that the now insane King George III was going to reestablish his authority on the Gulf Coast. The aged Creek chieftain, Hopoithle Micco, born before the British had come to Florida in 1763 and claiming to be spokesman for the principal southern tribes, begged the British king to return to Florida. Hopoithle Micco delivered his petition to William Munnings, acting Bahamian governor, who in turn forwarded it to London. With Whitehall's approval Munnings gave Hopoithle Micco and his followers presents and noncommittal words of encouragement.[24] At the same time Thomas Brown petitioned for the Bahamian governorship. Not enjoying his West Indian exile, Brown was as anxious to strengthen British ties with the southern Indians as Hopoithle Micco.[25]

Throughout the Indian country, from the Old Northwest to Florida, British presents, not always with the ministry's approval, reached Indian villages in increasing quantities. British merchants and Indian agents intimated that Britain was about to furnish more. Tecumseh knew that if he were to forge an effective confederation the Indians had to trade with someone other than the Americans. Britain seemed on the verge of playing that role. Tecumseh and his companions quickened their steps southward in 1811 to visit their Creek kinfolk and to dance the Shawnee war dance at the Sacred Hickory Ground and in Choctaw, Chickasaw, Cherokee, Creek, and Seminole council squares.[26]

Sir James Craig early in 1810, even after the *Chesapeake* controversy and embargo crisis subsided, had warned from Quebec that war was inevitable unless New England seceded. Craig's prophecy proved accurate. Though Federalists had denounced Madison before 1812 and had intimated the nation was about to dissolve, New England remained in the union. Canadians were not surprised when maritime and frontier disputes brought on an Anglo-American conflct in 1812. Neither side really wanted this war. Madison had succumbed to the strident demands of the war hawks who denounced the arbitrary policies of the Royal Navy and British tampering with the Indians. Though maritime grievances were more serious, the war hawks expected to punish Britain by taking over both Canadas and both Floridas.

Hoping if at all possible to avoid hostilities, Perceval suggested repealing the Orders in Council that Americans claimed violated their maritime rights. An assassin killed the resolute prime minister on May 11, 1812, and in the resulting confusion Britain's repeal did not reach Washington until after Congress had declared war. Britain and the United States were divided internally over the merits of hostilities, but militant spirits in both countries and British determination to defeat France regardless of the cost led to war.[27]

Britain, tied down in Europe, hard pressed to cope with Napoleon, was unable to send much aid to Canada during 1812 and 1813. The war hawks, expecting to take advantage of Britain's discomfiture, rallied to Henry Clay's cry of "on to Canada!" But the war in the Old Northwest went badly for the United States. Gen. William Hull, commanding American forces at Detroit, hoped to cross the Detroit River, seize Fort Malden at Amherstburg, and push Britain out of Upper Canada. Hull failed and, to the world's amazement, surrendered Detroit to the audacious Canadian general, Isaac Brock. There were several explanations. Hull had a long, overland supply route vulnerable to Indian disruption. The northwestern Indians, aroused by the Shawnees Tecumseh and the Prophet, had flocked to the British standard in surprising numbers. After assisting in the capture of Michilimackinac, they converged on Detroit and helped the wavering Hull decide to surrender. British naval superiority on Lake Erie had permitted Brock to reinforce Amherstburg and swiftly take the offensive. Hull, the scapegoat, was later court-martialed for treason.[28]

Later on in the war the Americans regained Detroit. Capt. Oliver H.
Perry defeated the British squadron on Lake Erie in September 1813,
and Britain then decided Detroit was untenable. In the ensuing retreat
Tecumseh was killed. At the other end of Lake Erie fighting during
1812 and 1813 on the Niagara frontier was bitter but indecisive. Iroquois warriors served in the armies of each side. Further east in the
Lake Champlain Valley opposing forces merely maneuvered while
the Maine–New Brunswick frontier was quiet.

Whitehall had been surprised by Brock's capture of Detroit largely
through the efforts of the Canadian militia and Indians. Detroit's ca-
pitulation, along with that of Michilimackinac and Fort Dearborn
(Chicago), meant that the upper part of the Old Northwest was more
firmly under British-Indian sway than at any time in recent years. One
outgrowth of Brock's initial victories was London's renewed interest in
an Indian buffer state in the Old Northwest. Britain probably could
not have taken Michilimackinac, Detroit, and Fort Dearborn without
the Indians. Brock promised at the beginning of hostilities that, if they
took up the hatchet once more for King George, their interests would
not be forgotten.

Canadians expected the tomahawk and musket to redraw the
boundary line and ten thousand warriors, backed up by Britain, to defend it. Canadian merchants recommended the Treaty of Greenville
line. During the war Canadians and Indians tried to keep the Americans below that line so that it could more easily become the fixed buffer
state boundary in the peace treaty.[29] Loyalist John Smyth Stuart offered to leave London at once and survey the new boundary wherever
it was located,[30] while contemporary pamphlets suggested making the
prince regent's brother king of an enlarged Canada.[31] Brock warned
the ministry that British honor and, more important, Canadian security depended on revising the boundary and not abandoning the Indians in peace negotiations. The general did not have a high opinion
of the "degenerate" Indian life style but understood the consequences
Canada faced if the natives got it into their heads that Britain was not
going to look after their interests in peace negotiations.[32]

News of British victories in the Old Northwest reverberated
throughout the southern Indian country and stimulated Tecumseh's
southern partisans and kinsmen. The western confederation strength-

ened. Creeks had fought and died at the Battle of Tippecanoe in 1811 and had sat in northern councils; Shawnees, including Tecumseh, regularly called on the southern Indians.[33] Tecumseh himself was half Creek..From Amherstburg in the north to Pensacola in the south and on both sides of the Mississippi British officials and merchants promised the Indians aid.

The Maine frontier had remained peaceful after the outbreak of hostilities basically because so many New Englanders opposed the war. It was hard to tell whether High Federalists or the British more virulently denounced "Mr. Madison's war." From the beginning New Englanders behaved exactly like the ministry thought they would. Americans living near the New Brunswick boundary "by the strongest assurances" declared to Canadians that they wanted no part of this unnatural conflict and that they were going to remain neutral.[34] Liverpool saw to it that this neutrality was reciprocal.[35] The Royal Navy blockaded the middle and southern states—but not New England.[36] Consul Andrew Allen remained in Boston for months after the declaration of war and munificently granted Massachusetts merchants licenses to trade not only with British territory but with Spanish and other foreign ports, all without interference by the British navy. Though the home government rebuked Allen for being so liberal in granting commercial favors, a considerable intercourse by one subterfuge or another flourished between New England and British colonies.[37] Authorities in New Brunswick and Nova Scotia happily sanctioned this mutually beneficial trade; Federalist members of the Massachusetts House of Representatives regularly corresponded with British naval commanders about circumventing Madison's commercial prohibitions.[38]

The ministry, the London press, naval officers on the North American station, and Canadian governors courted New England and assumed its opposition to the war must lead to separation. Gouverneur Morris expected New York to follow New England's lead toward neutrality or independence.[39] New Englanders met in great secrecy, blasting Madison and advocating neutrality, their conduct bordering on treason. They heartily approved the British navy's conduct when it encouraged contraband trade by dissident Americans.[40]

Adm. John Borlase Warren, appointed commander in chief on the

North American station early in 1813, had served in American waters
and always assumed New England's separation was inevitable. From
private sources and merely by reading current papers he presumed
the time was at hand. What the intrepid sailor wanted to know—and in
personal interviews he prodded Foreign Secretary Castlereagh and
First Lord of the Admiralty Robert Saunders Dundas, second viscount
Melville for guidance—was exactly how to deal with any independent
northern state and specifically how much protection he should afford
it.[41] Though the government in 1813 considered diverting Canadian
reinforcements to help redeem New England, the ministry did not
yet commit itself.[42]

New England was a large, diverse region. There were disenchanted
Federalists who wanted autonomy or independence. Others opposed
paying taxes for the war effort, letting the militia go outside the state,
and they perhaps condoned outright neutrality. A Republican faction
was as anxious to fight the redcoats in 1812 as in 1775. During 1812–13
New England neither actively supported the war effort nor left the
union. This was the main reason the second Earl of Liverpool was indecisive. He wanted New England to set its course before he fixed British policy. He retained contacts with discontented Federalists, adopted
measures to win their favor, and waited.

The Floridas and Louisiana, like the New England frontier, remained generally peaceful during 1812–13, though there were exceptions. The southern Indians grew increasingly angry with the
Americans. The more aggressive ones, the Red Sticks, strove for native
unity and looked to the British, both in the north and the south, for
assistance. Little Warrior and other Creek chiefs visited the northern
Indians after the outbreak of hostilities and returned home with talks
for war and promises of British aid.[43] Seminoles fought elements of the
Patriot Army and Georgia militia which ventured too far into East
Florida, and these Indians also solicited British munitions.[44]

The southern Indians wanted supplies sent by British ships calling
at Pensacola and St. Augustine rather than from Canada. With the in-
flux of Americans into the West it was more convenient for the Indians to communicate with the West Indies, particularly the Bahamas.
Both Sir John Johnson in Canada and Gov. Charles Cameron in
Nassau strengthened ties with the southern Indians and worked to

bring them into the struggle against the United States.[45] Through the Royal Navy, Indian agents, and private merchants, an increasing amount of munitions reached the southern Indians during 1812 and 1813 though the quantity fell short of Indian demands.

The Indians were not the primary reason for Whitehall's renewed interest in the Gulf Coast. Britain, because of loyalty to her Spanish ally and self-interest, saw she might have to fight to keep Americans out of Florida. Spain, though she had grounds enough, never declared war on the United States. She vacillated between aiding Britain and not provoking the United States to invade thinly garrisoned Florida. Castlereagh agreed that neutrality was a realistic policy for distraught Spain.[46] He also recognized that if, despite Spanish neutrality, the Americans invaded Florida, British forces were the only ones able to protect these colonies successfully. The British navy kept the sea lanes open to the Floridas and called on St. Augustine and Pensacola while the war hawks avowed that this was another reason why the Americans should have all the Floridas, "that sink of iniquity, the depot of Tories."[47]

In 1812 the ministry still equated the fate of the Mississippi Valley with New Orleans' status. At the commencement of hostilities admirals Warren and Alexander Cochrane told the ministry again and again what it already knew: New Orleans was vulnerable. Attacking it was the easiest way to get back at the United States, to initiate the process of dismemberment, and to force a humiliated Madison to seek terms.[48] Though Britain, struggling to defeat Napoleon in Europe, was not willing or able to begin a new campaign in America, the ministry agreed in principle with these naval commanders and at a more appropriate time adopted their plans. One can find in the 1812 Warren-Cochrane correspondence with the ministry the overall British strategy leading up to the Battle of New Orleans.

Cochrane and Warren realized that Britain did not have troops to spare in 1812 but argued that she did not need many. Outside assistance was available. Spain, still claiming Louisiana, might cooperate to keep alive her title and to weaken the United States.[49] Tecumseh and the northern Indians had been instrumental in Detroit's capture, and southern Indians were just as anxious to go against New Orleans.

The two naval commanders reminded the ministry that Negroes had no more affection for Madison and his fellow planters than did Britain. Approximately one third of the population from the Chesapeake Bay southward was black and in coastal areas—the region around New Orleans was one—the proportion was far greater. Louisiana slave insurrections in 1811 and 1812 highlighted the danger.[50] The British government was torn between inciting rebellion among the southern slaves, thereby bringing the war home to those responsible, and the specter of unleashing another Saint Domingue which might spread to the British West Indies. Another reason for caution was that tampering with the institution of slavery in Louisiana alienated the slaveholders. Most of them were French Creoles and others of foreign extraction who were potential British allies.[51]

Though the ministry had doubts about employing Negroes, admirals Warren and Cochrane had none. They continued to badger the government to take New Orleans and occupy it with red coats covering black skins. Warren thought the twelve-hundred-man Negro regiment stationed in the Bahamas just the force to garrison New Orleans after its capture. Its very presence must persuade slaves from a wide radius to desert and seek British protection and service in her armies. Warren looked beyond New Orleans and the Gulf Coast. British occupation of islands on the Atlantic seaboard, like Amelia Island and those in the Chesapeake Bay, provided havens for absconding slaves.[52] The military potential of the southern slaves was not lost on the British press, and with self-satisfaction it regularly reported how restless the blacks were, how there were revolts in Louisiana, South Carolina, and Virginia, and how eagerly the slaves sought British protection.[53]

Blacks, along with southern Indians and a few white British regulars, backed by the navy could bring the Gulf Coast under British sway and strike panic into the hearts of southern slaveholders. The beauty of this plan, according to Warren, was that Wellington's forces in the peninsula did not have to be weakened. Alexander Murray, Dunmore's son, assumed he was the logical one to bring over to the mainland black Bahamians and to send out the call for southern Negroes to rally to his standard. A controversial member of the Bahamian council, he constantly petitioned Whitehall to appoint him governor. Holding his deceased father's views about the Negroes' military potential, he had been charged with enlisting blacks into Bahamian military units and apprenticing them in appropriate trades on the islands. After Britain had abolished the slave trade in 1807, Murray was responsible for those Negroes brought into the Bahamas aboard ships illegally trafficking in slaves.[54]

Prime Minister Robert Banks Jenkinson, second earl of Liverpool, though not enthusiastic about the war, realized that the conflict offered an opportunity to whittle down a growing colossus. The United States' population had increased from about three million in 1783 to almost eight million in 1812. Fortunately, as Liverpool saw it, there were ways to render the United States impotent without sending large numbers of regulars from Europe. One was to encourage New England's separation and, if requested, to provide a small force to help maintain independence. Another was to wrest the Mississippi Valley from Washington's control. An Indian barrier state in the Old Northwest with the Greenville Treaty line as a possible boundary would be a start. More important was capturing New Orleans and divesting the United States of the Louisiana Purchase. Liverpool considered chances of establishing a client Indian (and Negro) state in the Floridas and Old Southwest as good as above the Ohio. This dream had faded in London after 1803. But at the end of 1812 the prime minister thought Britain might be placed "upon a footing in that quarter of the world on which we have never stood from the period of American independence" in spite of Madison's "vapouring."[55] Prime Minister Liverpool in 1812 was looking at the American frontier in essentially the same terms as his father (Hawkesbury) had in the years following the American Revolution. The veteran Lord Sheffield had no more use for the United States in 1812 than in 1783 when he had published his book predicting the upstart republic's inevitable failure. Sheffield was not sorry about the new war that enabled Britain to withdraw concessions made to the United States since the Revolution.[56]

Though Warren and Murray entreated the government to reestablish British dominion on the Gulf Coast, though British naval officers in 1813 entertained southern Indian chiefs aboard ship in Pensacola, and though these chiefs petitioned for British uniforms, swords, and commissions, there was little fighting in the south during 1812–13.

Even when the American army took over Mobile in 1813 there were almost no hostilities. The Spaniards grudgingly acquiesced and continued their precarious neutrality.[57]

There was one exception to the absence of southern hostilities—the Creek War which broke out in 1813. The Red Stick Creeks, who had close ties with Tecumseh and the Shawnee Prophet and who did not want Madison to civilize them, turned on the whites. Securing munitions from Forbes and Company, the Spaniards, and the British navy, in August 1813 they massacred some five hundred Americans at Fort Mims located close by the lower Alabama River. The Creek War was hotly contested, and during the latter part of 1813 the Indians had the upper hand. British naval officers who called at Pensacola and Governor Cameron in Nassau favored unleashing the Indians against the Americans. They regarded Indian hostilities as merely premature and wanted to restrain the natives until their efforts were coordinated with those of British regulars, Negroes, and the navy.[58] But the Indians had caught the Prophet's vision and did not wait.

By the end of 1813 there had been few significant changes anywhere on the frontier. An unofficial truce still existed on the Maine border. Detroit had swapped hands and was back under American control, though Britain still held Michilimackinac and Fort Dearborn. Neither side had made major inroads on the Niagara frontier. The Americans had gained Mobile in the south and another segment of Spanish West Florida. Tecumseh was dead and had failed to unite the Indians. But the Americans had not crushed the Indians: the United States had gotten the upper hand in the north but not in the south. Despite few major alterations during the first two years of the war, one of the most critical periods for the frontier and for the preservation of the union lay just ahead.

11 • Finis

THE YEAR 1814 witnessed great changes on both sides of the Atlantic. Wellington had led his victorious army across the Pyrenees into southern France, while Britain's allies invaded from the north and east. Conditions in 1814 contrasted with those of 1812. In the earlier year Napoleon dominated most of Europe and was on the verge of hurling six hundred thousand men into Russia to bring the Czar to heel. Britain at the same time had been unable to challenge Napoleon effectively on the continent, had suffered economic depression, and had acquired another enemy, the United States. But Napoleon lost his army in Russia, and his empire began to disintegrate. The defeated Napoleon abdicated in April 1814 and sought exile in Elba. Britain was elated with victory as Wellington, not Napoleon, reviewed troops in the Quai du Louvre. She expected to rectify her 1783 liberality toward the United States, and in so doing a considerable part of the frontier might again come under British dominion.

Diplomats made their way toward Vienna for the general peace conference while Wellington's army helped occupy France. Englishmen were relieved that the European carnage was over and that Europe for the first time in years was not at war. Britain had no continental enemies and was fighting only the United States. Despite concern about high taxes and the continuation on a war footing, the government resolved to "give Jonathan a good drubbing" for trying to take advantage of Britain in her hour of distress. The ministry had to dismiss thousands of soldiers if they were not employed, and there was little debate about sending some twenty thousand men over to America to hit "Mr. Madison a hard knock."[1] The government expected to set American matters right in one or two campaigns.

Whitehall's objective in 1814 was providing for Canadian security not only during current hostilities but permanently, and thus she tried to force the United States to concede an Indian buffer state in the Old Northwest. Britain up until the mid-1790s had actively supported this measure as a means to protect Canada and to promote the fur trade.

Indians regarded a buffer state as one step in fashioning a confederation and in stopping American expansion. Tecumseh and the Shawnee Prophet before the war had worked for a confederation propped up by Britain. But until William Hull's surrender of Detroit the British government was not very interested. At that point American influence disappeared from the Michigan peninsula, the future state of Wisconsin, and parts of upper Ohio, Indiana, and Illinois.

While Detroit was under British control during 1812–13 the ministry hoped to make the Americans concede what in fact existed—an Anglo-Indian protectorate in the Old Northwest. Canadian merchants took the initiative in suggesting proper limits. One recommendation was to demand Canada's 1774 boundary which had extended to the Ohio, but the newly acquired American population would outnumber English-speaking Canadians.[2] A more realistic boundary excluded the new state of Ohio and ran from Lower Sandusky on Lake Erie southward to the Ohio and down that river to its mouth.[3] The even less ambitious line established by Anthony Wayne's 1795 Treaty of Greenville appealed to Whitehall.[4] Canadians and Indians alike wanted no American forts anywhere in the Indian country. Advocates of the buffer state castigated the deceased Richard Oswald who had negotiated the Canadian boundary's location in 1783 for his "absolute ignorance —if not worse."[5]

The United States in 1783 had extended merely to the Mississippi River, but after the Louisiana Purchase her western limit was the Rocky Mountains. The Louisiana-Canadian boundary was as uncertain in 1812 as ever. Canadians and Indians hoped that Detroit's loss and other American defeats would force the United States to agree to a just boundary for Louisiana—the Missouri River.[6] Capt. Oliver H. Perry's victory on Lake Erie, American reoccupation of Detroit in 1813, and Tecumseh's death discouraged those who expected to constrict American limits both in upper Louisiana and in the Old Northwest. But in 1814 hopes revived. Britain and Indians still held Michilimackinac, Prairie du Chien on the upper Mississippi, and most of Michigan and Wisconsin. With Wellington's veterans preparing to embark from French ports and the United States on the verge of bankruptcy, fighting its most unpopular war, Britain and the Indians became optimistic about making territorial adjustments.

The prime minister, second earl of Liverpool, secretary for war and colonies, the earl of Bathurst, and other cabinet members in London, Field-Marshal Wellington, basking in his glory in Paris, and authorities in Quebec expected to adjust the entire Canadian boundary. They hoped to keep the Americans away from Lake Erie, admittedly a difficult tâsk because the Americans had naval superiority and occupied Detroit at one end and Buffalo at the other. Geographically upper Vermont and upper New York were tied to the St. Lawrence. British troops, with the possible cooperation of local inhabitants, especially Vermonters, could repair Oswald's 1783 blunder. During the war, trade flourished between Vermont and Canada. Vermont recalled its militia serving in New York, and when Gen. George Prevost finally invaded the United States in September 1814 it was no accident that he descended on New York, not Vermont. Ethan Allen and his brothers were dead or politically impotent, but there was still life and geographic logic in their dream of linking upper Vermont to Canada.[7]

Maine had grown dramatically since the Revolution, from 55,000 in 1783 to 242,000 in 1812.[8] But most of her population was west of the Penobscot River; in the one hundred miles between it and New Brunswick some 27,000 souls were scattered. This was the region Britain wanted to annex. She had set this area aside at the end of the Revolution as a loyalist asylum, and many refugees had arrived. Though it had become part of the United States, there were still loyalists and their descendants living there not opposed to union with New Brunswick. Disenchanted High Federalists were also there, in some cases old loyalists, who preferred to be oppressed by King George rather than by Mr. Madison and his Virginia dynasty and by Republicans who had increased at an alarming rate in Maine.[9] Britain hoped to push New Brunswick's boundary to the Penobscot and to settle permanently the fate of the Passamaquoddy Bay Islands.[10]

Indian agents and fur traders, Liverpool and fellow cabinet members, the London press, and Wellington's soldiers in France anxious to be off to America for the next campaign all displayed optimism in the spring of 1814. British confidence developed from her military successes on the continent, from Napoleon's exile, and from the United States' plight. Widespread American opposition to the war had emerged by 1814, varying from grumbling and refusal to volunteer for the army to High Federalists' hinting at disunion. Economic suffering was acute. The ministry assumed that internal stresses were increasing so rapidly that dismemberment was unavoidable.

Timothy Pickering and bitter High Federalists believed that Americans, i.e., Republicans—even those in Massachusetts—had betrayed the principles of '76 and were responsible for the present calamities. Only a thorough purging could make America sound, and part of the cure might include separation.[11] Gouverneur Morris, quick-witted spokesman for the New York Federalists, expected his party to make a comeback. He resented the pretensions of southern Republicans who tried to rule New Yorkers like plantation slaves, and he hoped to tie New York to New England.[12] Agitation for a New England convention to consider the current crisis and whether the northern states could remain in the union intensified.

Adm. Alexander Cochrane, new commander of the North American station, now blockaded New England in addition to the rest of the country. He retained his Federalist contacts, knew about plans for a convention, and assumed that "if they do not patch up a peace, then the much wished for [separation] will take place within a few months."[13] Overjoyed loyalists saw New England rejoining the Empire and advised the ministry how to govern her new American subjects: Britain must not repeat her previous mistakes and therefore must create an American nobility and allow New Englanders direct Parliamentary representation. These loyalists expected to bind prominent Federalists firmly to the mother country, lay the basis of well ordered British-American colonies, and prevent future revolution.[14] Though these particular recommendations had more merit in 1714 than in 1814, other proposals by loyalists and by British military and naval commanders in America greatly influenced the ministry.

The government relied on the redoubtable Cochrane as much as anyone. The admiral frequently called at Halifax, Britain's chief North American naval base. Nova Scotia was over two thousand miles from New Orleans, yet Cochrane concerned himself not only about New England but equally about conditions on the Gulf Coast that included: Louisiana's polyglot population and their feelings toward the American government, Spanish politics in the Floridas, the effects of the Creek War, and the number of southern blacks, slave or free, who were potential British allies.[15] Though New England and the Gulf Coast were remote from one another, their fates were intertwined. The *Times* (London) advised the government to inquire into the legality of the Louisiana Purchase, a not very subtle way of suggesting that Britain take over that territory.[16] Cochrane thought this a splendid idea; for almost two decades he had advocated just such a policy. Whereas in New England High Federalists were willing to work for separation and cooperate with Britain, in the south Indians, Negroes, loyalists, and an undetermined number of French and Spanish Creoles wanted to sever Louisiana from the union and place the Gulf Coast under British rule. Even contentious Winthrop Sargent, former governor of the Mississippi Territory and now a Natchez planter, believed in a quick "dissolution of the unnatural union."[17]

Cochrane, as he paced the deck under frozen rigging at Halifax, knew that not only might the northern states break off but Louisiana as well. The admiral did not care where disintegration started but was anxious to use British power to curtail Madison's domain. Cochrane was not alone in linking New England's fate with that of the Gulf Coast. Authorities in Nova Scotia and New Brunswick, ministers at Whitehall, and High Federalists all made the same kind of connection that Frenchmen had made a century beforehand.

New Orleans was the focal point on the Gulf Coast, and all considerations were subordinated to securing this port. Not only Britain but also Spain regarded the times appropriate to review the legality of the Louisiana Purchase, though Liverpool considered Spanish pretensions ridiculous.[18] But if Spain made over her title to Britain, that was another matter. Conquest of New Orleans and the Gulf Coast along with the Spanish title allowed Britain to claim as much of the Louisiana Purchase as she wanted. The ministry had not made up its mind about Louisiana and waited developments.

Regardless of Louisiana's future, the government agreed with Cochrane and did not question the wisdom of sending a strong force to the Gulf. British soldiers who first arrived in Florida late in 1813 were marines of the Royal Navy rather than regulars. The navy was on the scene, and its officers planned the strategy. Cochrane envisioned two simultaneous blows: the main one against New Orleans and a secondary one against southern Georgia. The British navy occupied islands at the mouth of the Apalachicola River and strategic spots on the adjacent mainland, while in the Atlantic the navy occupied Cumberland and similar islands on the Georgia coast. From these twin bases Cochranc expected British forces, which included large numbers of Indians and Negroes, to create a strong diversion in favor of the New Orleans expedition.[19]

The Royal Navy and peninsular veterans comprised the backbone of the Gulf Coast expedition, though supported by minorities living in the South: Indians, Negroes, French Creoles, British loyalists, and assorted other whites. Cochrane had primed those Indians in the Old Southwest to play as important a role as their brethren in the Old Northwest; now was the time to unleash the southern arm of the Indian confederation. The Upper Creek prophet, Francis (Hillis Hadjo), Tecumseh's friend who frequently had accompanied him, hated the Americans, became a Red Stick leader, and appreciated the necessity of native unity and British alliance.

It was unfortunate for both the Red Sticks and Britain that the natives had already initiated hostilities. Though the Red Sticks had been generally successful in 1813, Andrew Jackson solidly defeated them the following year at Horseshoe Bend and dictated a harsh peace supposedly ending the Creek War.[20] It did not. The surviving Red Sticks, including Francis, did not sign the peace treaty, fled to Florida, threw themselves on British protection, and continued fighting the Americans. Creek-Seminole-American hostilities persisted without interruption until 1818 if not 1842.[21] The hundreds of Red Sticks who sought refuge in Florida joined those natives who had successfully fought against George Mathews' Patriot Army in East Florida and had not tasted defeat.

Advance agents of the British expedition arrived in Spanish Florida late in 1813 and began to organize the southern Indians. Two prominent Florida chiefs—Thomas Perryman, king of the Seminoles, and the aged Kinache (Kinhega), chief of the Miccosukees, who perhaps was born when Oglethorpe ruled Georgia—were commissioned British generals.[22] The Red Sticks, Francis, and Peter McQueen, joined British forces at Pensacola in 1814. Cochrane sent at least six thousand stands of arms, one thousand swords, cannon, red coats, and so forth to arm and uniform Red Sticks who were fleeing into Florida and the several thousand Creek-Seminoles who were already there.[23] Marines built log forts to command the Apalachicola River: one on St. Vincent Island at the river's mouth, the principal one at Prospect Bluff fifteen miles upstream, and still another at the fork of the Apalachicola River. Col. Edward Nicholls and Lt. George Woodbine of the marines and Capt. Hugh Pigot of the Royal Navy supervised distributing the munitions, building the forts, and drilling the Indians. Cochrane pressed the government to guarantee all lands in Indian possession when both Floridas had been British colonies,[24] while others urged recognition of the Indian state of Muskogee.[25] These and similar arguments made Bathurst proclaim that the southern Indians had been continuously under British control since the early eighteenth century, and he avowed Britain was not now about to renounce that right.[26] British loyalists with pre-1783 land grants in the Floridas expected at last to make good their claims.[27]

The arrival of Nicholls with his stock of munitions alarmed Benjamin Hawkins, American agent to the Creek Indians. From his Creek agency on the upper Flint River he admonished the Indians: Britain sent William Augustus Bowles among you solely to make war, not "to spin and weave"; now she has the same policy. You err if you "sing the song of the Indians of the northern lakes and dance their dance."[28] But this song animated the thousands of Indians who assembled at Pensacola and on the Apalachicola River.

Since the American Revolution British subjects had recommended turning the southern slaves against their masters and relying on the freedmen to create a British Gulf Coast colony. The government in 1814 took these suggestions to heart. The ministry never went as far as to urge southern slaves to slit their masters' throats in the night. But blacks who sought protection of British forces in the Gulf of Mexico, coastal Georgia, and the Chesapeake Bay were promised freedom and land. British officers encouraged the able-bodied males to enlist in the army. Once the Negroes received arms and perfunctory training, Whitehall considered it perfectly legitimate for them to run their former masters through.[29] Negroes took advantage of Britain's overtures. Several thousand from the Chesapeake Bay and coastal Georgia sought refuge aboard British warships. Many were sent to Nova Scotia where the men usually enlisted in the army.[30]

Hundreds of Negroes living among the Florida Indians, though poorly equipped, already had fought effectively against Mathews' Patriot Army. These Florida Negroes were among the first who sought British assistance, and soon other Negroes, fleeing owners in both Georgia and the Floridas, joined them. Lieutenant Woodbine armed four hundred or more blacks and drilled them first in the plaza at Pensacola and subsequently at the Prospect Bluff fort. He expected these Negro soldiers to be part of the force that ascended the Apalachicola and Flint rivers and brought the war home to Georgia's heartland. Woodbine wanted thousands of Georgia fugitives to join his forces as they later flocked to Gen. William T. Sherman's army.[31] Loyalist John Morison had proposed to raise a Negro regiment at his own expense during the Revolution. Though the ministry turned down Morison's request in 1782, he repeated his offer in 1814 and hoped to have more success.[32] At the same time Alexander Murray, continuing to enlist blacks into the Bahamian military, was impatient to get over to the mainland.[33]

Britain anticipated assistance not only from southern blacks and Indians but from whites. Loyalists still lived in the Floridas, traded with these provinces, and managed the southern Indians and Negroes. Forbes and Company simultaneously cooperated with the British and the Americans. Since this company had one branch in American Mobile and another in Anglo-Spanish Pensacola, its conduct was not surprising.[34] The most numerous body of white potential allies was not the loyalists but the French and Spanish Creoles and assorted other non-Americans in Louisiana. Federalist John Windship, who knew them personally, advised his New England friends that many welcomed release from American dominion.[35]

Britain courted Louisiana whites—French and Spanish Creoles, those of British origin, even Jean Lafitte and his Baratarian "pirates"[36] —and hoped for their assistance or at least their neutrality. But the ministry was not sure their courtship should lead to marriage because it had not decided what to do with Louisiana. Britain was not ready to proclaim that her objective was to make Louisiana a British colony. Bathurst charged his subordinates to encourage the Creoles to turn against the Americans, to hint that Spain might return to New Orleans, and in the meantime to prepare the anti-American faction to welcome temporary British occupation.[37] But both Bathurst and Cochrane realized that "temporary" occupation had marked the beginnings of many a new colony.

The Louisiana French, both the *ancienne population* and recent immigrants, had mixed feelings about British overtures. These French did not like Americans and being engulfed by an alien culture. But they applauded the new 1812 state constitution that perpetuated their political control. Those who were slaveholders, some recently from Saint Domingue, wanted nothing to do with liberating Louisiana blacks.[38]

The Louisiana Purchase was sparsely settled, and Britain might decide to take it. Robert Dickson, veteran fur trader and Indian agent, enlisted Sioux and Winnebago Indians and voyageurs to retake Prairie du Chien (recently captured by the Americans) on the upper Mississippi River. For Dickson this was the first step in complete mastery of that river.[39] Lord Selkirk still resolved to settle Highlanders in Louisiana, either on the Red River in the north or, when Britain captured New Orleans, farther south. The indomitable Selkirk envisioned much of the Louisiana Purchase as an Indian preserve with mounted plains Indians sustaining Anglo-Indian dominion.[40]

Britain's course in 1814 depended largely on the achievements of the British army, whether it could "finish the good work which so happily begun in France."[41] The bulk of the troops went to Canada where Prevost assembled a large army to descend Lake Champlain and isolate New England. After many delays he invaded New York but got no further than Plattsburg. The Americans won naval control of Lake Champlain, and Prevost, remembering Burgoyne's fate, retired because of the threat to his supply lines. Hardest fighting, though indecisive, occurred on the Niagara frontier, of which the bloody battle of Lundy's Lane was typical. Britain, more successful in Maine, occupied Castine near the Penobscot River's mouth and established a military government for the one-hundred-mile stretch between Passamaquoddy Bay and the Penobscot River. What British diplomats had worked for in 1782 came to pass in 1814 as, with little fanfare, Maine inhabitants swore allegiance to the British crown.[42] Nantucket Islanders, threatened with starvation and short on fuel, also pledged neutrality, and their representatives withdrew from the Massachusetts general court.[43] In the West Britain repulsed an attack on Michilimackinac, recaptured Prairie du Chien, retained mastery of most of the Michigan-Wisconsin region, and improved her standing among the Indians. The British navy strengthened its blockade of the entire Atlantic seaboard, while roving forces sacked Washington and other exposed points.

The most crucial phase of the war came not in September when Prevost retreated after the Battle of Plattsburg but in the late fall and winter when the New England Federalists prepared to hold a convention in Hartford and Britain's expedition to the Gulf finally got underway. Either could have led to the union's dismemberment. Pickering reflected High Federalist thinking; he expected Britain to take New Orleans without difficulty, and "once Britain possesses New Orleans the union is severed."[44] Loss of the West did not distress Pickering. The Federalists might regain power in the East or the northern states might secede. Already Gouverneur Morris debated whether the Delaware, Susquehanna, or Potomac river was the best boundary, while British newspapers welcomed the return of New England as a prodigal son.[45]

Delegates from Massachusetts, Rhode Island, Connecticut, New Hampshire, and Vermont assembled at Hartford in mid-December and met in secret session. Varying degrees of opposition to the war and the Republican administration were manifest. Bitter John Lowell, not a delegate, wanted New England simultaneously to decare neutrality and negotiate a treaty with the southern states to protect New England as a minority section. If the southern states refused such a treaty or broke its provisions, then Lowell considered the union dissolved.[46] Gov. Caleb Strong of Massachusetts assumed separation unavoidable, though he wanted it to "take place without contention and with good will."[47] Comparative moderates, who controlled the convention throughout, opposed immediate secession and advocated amending the Constitution better to protect minority interests.[48]

A month before the Hartford Convention met, Thomas Adams, Federalist member of the Massachusetts general court, arrived at Halifax and opened negotiations with Gov. John C. Sherbrooke and Adm. Herbert Sawyer. Adams asserted he spoke for Governor Strong and other Massachusetts leaders and that not only Massachusetts but all New England was ready to declare neutrality and make a British alliance. If there were to be an alliance, Adams insisted Britain must cease hostilities, remove her blockade of New England, carry the war to the South, and, if necessary, help defend New England's independence.[49] Sherbrooke, with the home government's approval, said he would agree to all New England's demands the minute New England asserted her neutrality and sent a fully accredited minister to Halifax.[50]

After the Hartford Convention adjourned on January 5, the Massachusetts legislature praised the convention's accomplishments and dispatched three commissioners to present that state's case in Washington.[51] The Hartford delegates had not decided on the proper course should Madison's followers not agree to alter the Constitution. New Englanders in 1775 had not wanted to separate from the mother country but had expected George III's government to make concessions in favor of New England autonomy. George III had not given way, and independence resulted. Harrison Gray Otis, William Sullivan, and Thomas Perkins may have felt that history was about to be repeated as they made their way to Washington early in 1815.

Cochrane, calling at Halifax and aware of the Hartford deliberations and Adams' mission, agreed with Pickering that once New Orleans fell the union was severed. The outspoken British admiral expected his Louisiana expedition to strengthen the hands of querulous New England Federalists. This is why the admiral and his superiors in London so persistently advocated a Gulf Coast campaign.

When the British expedition arrived in the Gulf of Mexico early in December 1814, hostilities, already going on for some time in the south, generally had not favored the British cause. The Americans were opposed by three parties—Britain, Spain (technically neutral), and the Indians—and it proved difficult to coordinate the conduct of all three. British agents had tried to restrain the southern Indians until redcoats arrived in force, but the impatient Indians already had been defeated by Jackson at Horseshoe Bend.[52] Though survivors made their way to Florida and joined Nicholls, from the British standpoint the Indians should have waited.

The Spaniards simultaneously welcomed British forces to St. Augustine and Pensacola and fretted about whether their presence might lead to open warfare with the United States. But at first the British and Spaniards got along well enough. Colonel Nicholls and his advance party of marines arrived at Pensacola in August 1814 and in a formal ceremony the British flag was raised alongside the Spanish ensign at Fort San Miguel in Pensacola proper and at Fort Barrancas guarding the entrance to Pensacola Bay. The Spaniards even offered to turn over San Miguel and retire to Barrancas. Hundreds of Indians, primarily Red Sticks who had escaped Jackson's wrath, and a lesser number of Negroes arrived at Pensacola. Nicholls fed, clothed, and armed the Indians and located them on the city's outskirts, while Lt. George Woodbine drilled the Negroes and mulattoes in the heart of Pensacola.[53]

This port had become the focal point for enlisting the southern Indians and blacks, and it or nearby Mobile was to be the jumping-off point for the New Orleans attack. British warships and Nicholls' Indians tried to take Mobile but in an unsuccessful engagement failed to get by Fort Bowyer guarding the entrance to Mobile Bay. Pensacola was the only Gulf port available to Britain. Andrew Jackson, charged with New Orleans' defense, swiftly marched over three thousand men to Pensacola early in November and demanded its surrender. After brief fighting and changing his mind several times, the cowed Spanish governor obliged (Nicholls charged bribery), and without Spanish cooperation Nicholls' position became untenable. His Indians, Negroes, and marines abandoned the town, blowing up Fort Barrancas at the entrance to Pensacola Bay before departing.[54] After a brief occupation Jackson evacuated Pensacola. It suited the interests of Spain and the United States not to make the Pensacola incident cause for war, and the two countries retained their precarious neutrality. But both Pensacola and Mobile were denied to Britain. Her only base on the Gulf was on the Apalachicola River, and Nicholls retired from Pensacola to the Prospect Bluff fort.

When Wellington's brother-in-law, Gen. Edward Pakenham, arrived in the Gulf late in December to take command of the army, the overall strategy had already been devised, largely by Cochrane. He envisioned two attacks: the principal one directed at New Orleans and a secondary one to ravage Georgia's interior. Nicholls, from his base on the Apalachicola River, was to take his Indians, Negroes, and marines, ascend the Apalachicola and Flint rivers, prey on Hartford, Milledgeville, and other vulnerable frontier towns, and descend the Altamaha and join Adm. George Cockburn who had taken possession of Cumberland, St. Simons, and other Atlantic coastal islands. In this fashion Cochrane anticipated roasting the southerners between two fires.[55] Next he wanted to move against coastal South Carolina and also "punish those fellows."[56]

Britain expected her southern campaign to succeed. Even Wellington, despairing about chances in the north after the Americans won naval control of lakes Erie and Champlain, was optimistic about British fortunes in the south. He predicted New Orleans' capture and advised keeping the city.[57] Liverpool late in October thought the Americans were about to face a humiliation from Cochrane greater than any yet experienced.[58] The cabinet wanted British forces to occupy New Orleans and adjacent territory but still had not yet made up its mind whether to retain permanent possession. But once again the British press reviewed the merits of Louisiana, and tracts appeared acclaiming the Gulf Coast and lamenting the fact that Britain in 1783 unwisely surrendered the Floridas.[59]

Cochrane and Pakenham perfected their plans just as British and American diplomats on December 24 concluded a peace treaty at Ghent. Negotiators had been in the Flemish city since midsummer but for a long time had made little progress. At first Britain planned to dictate peace terms and constrict American limits not only along the Canadian frontier but also on the Gulf Coast and in the Louisiana Purchase. Britain insisted that provisions be made for her Indian allies, and Secretary for War Bathurst made it clear that the government regarded both northern and southern natives as allies.[60] The ministry insinuated that the United States did not have valid title to Louisiana. Britons with pre-1783 Florida land grants wanted the Americans to recognize these claims in the peace treaty.[61]

A combination of circumstances forced Britain to retreat from her imperious position taken in the summer and early fall of 1814. Prevost retired from Plattsburg, and Britain could not win naval control of lakes Champlain and Erie. British landowners groaned under high taxes. European allies who had beaten Napoleon, began quarreling among themselves, threatening a resumption of hostilities; rumors abounded that the exiled Napoleon thought the times ripe for his return to France. As a result Britain in the fall made concessions, though none touched on the vital issue of maritime rights that supposedly had started the war. She abandoned demands for an independent Indian barrier state in the Old Northwest and for keeping occupied territory south of the Canadian boundary. The treaty, signed on Christmas eve, stipulated that hostilities would not cease immediately but only after the exchange of ratifications, which would take several months.[62]

Liverpool, not sure the Americans would ratify a treaty ignoring maritime grievances, half expected Madison to play "some trick on us in ratification."[63] The *Times* (London) cautioned celebrating a peace that might never take place.[64] Thomas Brown, assuming the treaty would never go into effect, pleaded with Liverpool to send him to the southern states to lead the Indians.[65]

The government rushed Anthony Baker to America with the treaty for Madison's signature. In the meantime Britain continued her aggressive southern campaign and prepared to sign a treaty with New England separatists the minute Baker reported that the Americans delayed ratification.[66] The cabinet knew that if there were any spectacular success in the south or if New England seceded, Britain could refuse to comply with the Treaty of Ghent in the same manner she had gotten around the 1783 treaty. Or she could argue that Louisiana and the Floridas belonged to Spain and were not encompassed by the peace treaty.

Even after British negotiators reached a settlement at Ghent, the cabinet expected New Orleans to fall; Pickering regarded it as "a moral certainty."[67] Castlereagh, having expected to alter the boundaries of the Floridas and Louisiana at American expense in the summer of 1814, apparently had not given up that idea.[68] By occupying major Gulf Coast ports Britain could continue to make her weight felt in the Mississippi Valley and pick up the threads of western disunion and slave insurrection at any future time. As the recent war had demonstrated, a British presence on the Gulf Coast protected Canada. If by any remote chance Britain regained the thinly populated Louisiana Purchase, then Canada would be connected to the Gulf as of old.

The success of Jackson's forty-five hundred men, primarily militia, against over six thousand veteran redcoats on January 8 was astounding. It was at this point—and soon afterwards when Madison's administration ratified the Treaty of Ghent—that Britain's ambition of controlling the Gulf Coast and Mississippi Valley and linking them to Canada died. One of the main reasons Jackson won was that few of the Louisiana whites supported Britain. Both the French Creoles and Lafitte and his Baratarians fought for the Americans, not the British. British tampering with slavery in Louisiana, encouraging the Creoles to side with the Americans, was a decisive factor in Jackson's victory. It was ironic that Cochrane's attempts to free Negro slaves, alarming the French planters, helped perpetuate the "peculiar institution" in Louisiana for several additional decades. At the crucial moment Nicholls' Indians and Negroes proved ineffective. They were scattered —some had gone against Mobile—and he was unable to concentrate them to invade Georgia when Pakenham attacked New Orleans. As a result Nicholls took less than one hundred Creek-Seminoles and a few Choctaws to New Orleans where they played a minor role in the fighting.[69]

Even after the New Orleans failure British commanders continued hostilities on the Gulf Coast uncertain whether or not Madison would ratify the treaty and confused about the Spanish Floridas' fate. Britain in February 1815 successfully attacked Fort Bowyer while Nicholls readied his two thousand Indians and Negroes to invade Georgia. Although Jackson's victory insured that the Americans kept Louisiana, the Floridas' status was in question. Spain was unlikely to retain these provinces for long; if Britain did not take them the Americans would. Having seized Baton Rouge and Mobile they had already made a good start.

Nicholls and Cochrane in America and Brown in London urged keeping bases on the Apalachicola River and retaining the Floridas. But the ministry regarded the Floridas of little consequence unless attached to New Orleans and the Mississippi Valley. Madison's signed treaty reached London on March 13, and hostilities quickly ceased. Napoleon had returned to France, and "little did they [the Americans] think what kind genius was at work for them in Europe!"[70] Britain, thankful for the American peace, tried to erase memories of conflict in the New World and the thought of the New Orleans debacle.

Between 1783 and 1815 the concept of bringing the Mississippi Valley and the Gulf Coast under British sway and of expanding Canada's boundary into New England and the Old Northwest had preoc-

cupied assorted British subjects, and upon occasion, such as in the recent war, they had persuaded the ministry to support this design.
Geography, the Indians, loyalists, land speculators, and separatists
within the United States over the years all had worked in behalf of this
scheme. But 1815 marked the end of an era in both Europe and America. Napoleon met defeat at Waterloo, and for the first time in a quarter
century Britain was not embroiled with France and enjoyed a sustained
peace. The government, coming more under the influence of Adam
Smith's free trade doctrines, saw less need for American colonies.
Commerce with the United States flourished, and after the successful
Latin American revolutions of the 1820s Britain dominated all New
World trade without the expense of administering and defending colonies. Geography that had separated the West from the East and had
forced westerners and Vermonters to look to Canada and the St. Lawrence was less significant after 1815. The Erie Canal, completed in
1825, tied the Great Lakes and the upper Mississippi Valley to the
Hudson and made them less dependent on the St. Lawrence. Similar
canals and turnpikes bound the West to the East and weaned upper
Vermont from the St. Lawrence.

The Treaty of Ghent killed hopes for an Indian confederation.
Thousands of Indians had taken to heart the teachings of Tecumseh
and the Shawnee Prophet and had fought the Americans with a
vengeance in both the north and south. There had been remarkable
Indian cooperation. Shawnee talks had helped ignite the Creek War in
1813, while that same year Red Sticks arrived at Amherstburg. They
joined the British and Indians in the north, were at Tecumseh's side
at his death, and, along with southern Indians who arrived later,
fought on the Niagara frontier until the war's end.[71] Six months
before Jackson's New Orleans victory, Dickson's militia and Indians
had retaken Prairie du Chien on the upper Mississippi. Once reinforced, Dickson hoped to move against St. Louis. He assumed that British success in the north coupled with New Orleans' capture placed
much of the Mississippi Valley under the Anglo-Indian dominion.
Americans at St. Louis tended to agree.[72] But Dickson heard of the New
Orleans disaster and shortly afterward his garrison at Prairie du Chien
and the one at Michilimackinac received orders to retire. Neglect of the
Indians in the Treaty of Ghent, Tecumseh's death, and the setbacks at

Horseshoe Bend and New Orleans destroyed hopes of Indian unity.

At the war's onset Britain had promised the Indians that if they fought alongside the redcoats she would look after their interests in the peace settlement. The Canadian governor summoned Tecumseh's sister to Quebec in 1814 after the great warrior's death and, while her followers performed the calumet dance, promised that King George would force the Americans to deal fairly with the red men.[73] Across the ocean Prime Minister Liverpool exclaimed: "God forbid we abandon the Indians!"[74] But the Treaty of Ghent did not safeguard the Indians and their lands within United States boundaries, and Tecumseh's sister was not the only bitter Indian. Americans soon surged into the Michigan and Illinois territories, forcing out the Indians; on the upper Missouri the United States exerted pressure resulting in the eventual expulsion of the Canadian fur traders. In the south the Red Sticks abandoned their lands in southern Alabama which, with British assistance, they had expected to regain. The Red Sticks, relocated in the Floridas, joined their Seminole kinsmen and continued fighting the Americans. Britain pensioned the widows of fallen warriors and principal chiefs and urged the Americans to treat Indian tribes living within the United States as sovereign "nations" and respect their rights. In defending the treaty, Liverpool asserted that the Americans had avoided the issue of maritime rights, while Britain had fulfilled her engagements to the Indians.[75] The natives were dumbfounded.

The loyalists posed no threat to the frontier after 1815. Though time had taken its toll, there was a surprising number of Revolutionary veterans active during the War of 1812, and they were delighted at the renewed attention paid them by the government. Seventy-year-old Sir John Johnson, superintendent general at Montreal, encouraged the Indians anew. He volunteered once more to lead war parties into New York and hoped to even scores with the rebels who had pillaged his Mohawk Valley property early in the Revolution and had caused the death of his young child.[76] Soldiers who had marched with Prevost alongside Lake Champlain in 1814 had traveled that same route with Burgoyne in 1777.[77] Seventy-three-year-old Matthew Elliott left his Amherstburg home in 1812 and, with less spring in his step, again led the Indians against the long knives.[78] Alexander Murray, whom Patrick Henry had run out of Virginia, was in the Bahamas and anxious to turn the blacks against recalcitrant southern planters. Thomas Brown, scarred where rebels had burned his feet and scalped him, wanted to resume his Indian superintendency during the War of 1812. Loyalists in London tried to influence Liverpool's handling of the war. Daniel Coxe, formerly a member of the council of colonial New Jersey, and Sir John Sinclair, a Pennsylvanian whose father died in Braddock's defeat, were but two examples.[79] John Eardley Wilmot, who since 1783 had worked to obtain compensation for the loyalists, thought 1814 an appropriate time to publish his *Historical View of the Commission for Inquiring into the . . . Claims of the American Loyalists* and hoped to get it in print in time to influence the proceedings at Ghent.[80] John Smyth Stuart was beside himself in 1814 when after thirty-one years' delay and many false starts Britain was finally sending an expedition to the Gulf Coast. He revived plans for creation of an independent, pro-British, southern Indian state, gave Pakenham his charts and previous correspondence, was delighted that Pakenham's soldiers whiled away the time reading his *Tour of the United States*, volunteered to go to Ghent and advise the government's representatives about points concerning the frontier, and in his excitement stepped off a sidewalk and was run over and killed by a carriage.[81] Loyalists who refused to accept the verdict of 1783 if they were still alive acknowledged the one of 1815.

New England separatism had run its course, though even in February 1815 Governor Strong still regarded secession inevitable.[82] Canadians had set great store by this, and their hopes were never higher than during the winter of 1814–15. But the Massachusetts delegation as it approached Washington was greeted by news of Jackson's victory and the Treaty of Ghent. Later members of the Hartford Convention explained away their conduct as a great mistake or argued that equating the Hartford Convention with disunionism was unfair. But in truth it was not. Late in December both Liverpool and Chancellor of the Exchequer Nicholas Vansittart, aware of Strong's overtures and much more, had the best reasons for thinking there would be a separation should the war continue.[83]

With some effort one can continue evaluating Britain's policies toward the frontier after 1815, but the issues, personnel, and territory involved usually differed. Britain during the 1840s negotiated with the independent Lone Star Texas Republic and had designs on Oregon and California. In the East the disputed Maine–New Brunswick boundary was yet to be established. It was not immediately clear in 1815 to all Indians that Britain had abandoned them. Tecumseh's friend, the Red Stick Creek chief Francis, had relocated in Florida and in 1815 went to London, beseeching the prince regent to take the southern Indians, both in the Floridas and the United States, under his wing. Nicholls supported Francis and hoped to be appointed Indian superintendent. But Francis got only a token monetary present. He returned to Florida where in 1818 Jackson captured and hanged him.[84]

Even in the twentieth century some of the old Indian aspirations remained faintly alive. The Six Nations, located both in western New York and in Canada, still insisted they were independent and in 1930 sent delegates to London, as did Joseph Brant in the eighteenth century, but to no avail.[85] And when in the 1950s the Six Nations dispatched representatives to the Florida Miccosukee Indians encouraging them to assert their independence, one might argue—with a great stretch of imagination—that Brant's, Tecumseh's, and Francis's hopes for confederation were not dead.[86]

Britain still flirted with supporting American disunion after 1815, but along new lines. During the War of 1812 the ministry had been aware that if it did not dismember the United States, in time Britain would find it almost impossible to defend Canada. Ministers could read articles to this effect in the press or heed the warnings of English travelers: "It belongs to the present generation of Englishmen to take care that the discovery of America does not produce . . . the ruin of this country."[87] Britain made her supreme effort in 1814–15 and failed. Until the early 1860s she stopped trying to detach New England, the West, and other areas from the union. During the American Civil War, however, the cabinet weighed once again the merits of dismembering the United States, though by a curious twist this time the government negotiated with the southern slavocracy rather than New Englanders or westerners.

But 1815 marked the end of an era that began in 1783. No longer was there any question about the disposition of the Mississippi Valley; Britain did not aspire to assume France's role in North America; the western Indian confederation lay in shambles, and soon removal or annihilation became the choices for most natives; Federalist sectionalists already were beginning to transform themselves into outspoken nationalists. Britain had tried to shape the American frontier to suit her own needs and had failed.

Abbreviations

Add. MSS.	Additional Manuscripts, British Museum
Adm.	Admiralty, Public Record Office
A.G.I.	Archivo General de Indias
A.H.N.	Archivo Histórico Nacional
A.O.	Audit Office, Public Record Office
ASP,IA	*American State Papers, Indian Affairs*
B.M.	British Museum
B.T.	Board of Trade, Public Record Office
C.O.	Colonial Office, Public Record Office
F.O.	Foreign Office, Public Record Office
Gifts	Gifts and Deposits Group, Public Record Office
Hist. MSS. Com.	Great Britain, Historical Manuscripts Commission
L.C.	Library of Congress
MPHC	Michigan Pioneer and Historical Society, *Historical Collections*
N.L.S.	National Library of Scotland
N.Y.P.L.	New York Public Library
P.A.C.	Public Archives of Canada
RA	Royal Archives
Supt. Gen. and Insp. Gen.	Superintendent General and Inspector General
T.	Treasury, Public Record Office
W.O.	War Office, Public Record Office

Notes

CHAPTER 1

1. Nathaniel W. Wraxall, *Historical Memoirs of My Own Time*, 2:103.

2. Anglo-American treaty, Paris, 3 September 1783, David Hunter Miller, ed., *Treaties and Other International Acts of the United States of America*, 2:151–57; Anglo-Spanish treaty, Versailles, 3 September 1783, Frances G. Davenport and Charles O. Paullin, eds., *European Treaties Bearing on the History of the United States and Its Dependencies*, 4:159.

3. Evarts B. Greene and Virginia D. Harrington, *American Population before the Federal Census of 1790*, pp. 7, 119, 192–93; Stella H. Sutherland, *Population Distribution in Colonial America*, p. 161.

4. U. S. Bureau of the Census, *Historical Statistics of the United States, Colonial Times to 1957*, p. 7; Greene and Harrington, *American Population*, pp. 193–94; U. S. Census Office, "Population of States and Territories by Counties, at Each Census: 1790 to 1900," *Twelfth Census of the United States, Taken in the Year 1900*, 1:20, 36, 37, 39, 45; Clarence E. Carter, ed., *The Territorial Papers of the United States*, 2:470. Sutherland says 1790 population was only 3,700,000 in *Population Distribution*, p. 271.

5. This figure is a crude estimate, because data on Indian population, if available, is notoriously unreliable. Helpful estimates are in Greene and Harrington, *American Population*, pp. 199–200; 205–6.

6. Carl Van Doren, *Secret History of the American Revolution*, pp. 138–39, 239–40, 404; Charles A. Jellison, *Ethan Allen: Frontier Rebel*, pp. 242–74; Levi Allen to Lord Sydney, London, 3 May 1789, F.O. 4/7.

7. Thomas McKean to John Adams, Philadelphia, January 1814, in John Adams, *The Works of John Adams, Second President of the United States; with a Life of the Author*, ed. Charles F. Adams, 10:87.

8. Paul H. Smith, "The American Loyalists: Notes on Their Organization and Numerical Strength," p. 269.

9. Minute of cabinet, 17 October 1782, in John W. Fortescue, ed., *The Correspondence of King George the Third from 1760 to December 1783*, 6:114.

10. Louise P. Kellogg, *The British Régime in Wisconsin and the Northwest*, pp. 177, 179; Randolph C. Downes, *Council Fires on the Upper Ohio: A Narrative of Indian Affairs in the Upper Ohio Valley until 1795*, pp. 269–76.

11. Richard B. Morris, *The Peacemakers: The Great Powers and American Independence*, pp. 262–63, 277.

12. George III to Shelburne, Windsor, 3 November 1782, Letters of George III to Shelburne, Bancroft Collection, N.Y.P.L.

13. Alfred L. Burt, *The United States, Great Britain and British North America from the Revolution to the Establishment of Peace after the War of 1812*, pp. 26–29; Robert Raskleigh, Robert Hunter, James Strachan, *et al.* to Shelburne, New York Coffee House, 6 February 1783, Shelburne Papers, LXXII, William L. Clements Library, Univ. of Mich., Ann Arbor; Hunter to Haldimand, London, 27 March 1783, Add. MSS. 21,735; representation of Quebec merchants, 31 January 1783, Gifts 30-8/346.

14. Townshend to Haldimand, 28 February 1783, Add. MSS. 21,705; Morris, *The Peacemakers*, pp. 350–52.

15. Earl of Carlisle's speech in House of Lords, 17 February 1783, William Cobbett, ed., *The Parliamentary History of England, from the Earliest Period to the Year 1803*, 23:377.

16. John Connolly to Shelburne, Portland Chapel, London, September 1782, Shelburne Papers, LXXII; Connolly to Shelburne, 1 February 1783, Correspondence of Peace Commissioners, VI, Bancroft Collection; John F. D. Smyth (Stuart) to commissioners, London, 21 November 1787, A.O. 13/62.

17. Minutes of cabinet, 17 October 1782, minutes of secret negotiations, July 25, 1782–January 20, 1783, Townshend Collection, Henry E. Huntington Library and Art Gallery, San Marino, Calif.; Shelburne to Strachey, 20 October 1782, Henry Strachey Letters, Bancroft Collection.

18. Thomas P. Abernethy, *Western Lands and the American Revolution*, p. 285; Irving Brant, *James Madison*, 2:194.

19. Carleton to Paterson, New York City, 24 September 1782, America, 1782, IV, Bancroft Collection; Strachey to Townshend, Calais, 8 November 1782, Correspondence of peace commissioners, Bancroft Collection; Wilbur H. Siebert, "The Exodus of the Loyalists from Penobscot and the Loyalist Settlements at Passamaquoddy," 3:485 ff.

20. James B. Wilbur, *Ira Allen, Founder of Vermont, 1751–1814*, 1:162 ff.; Jellison, *Ethan Allen*, pp. 242 ff.

21. Intelligence by Johnson, Niagara, N.Y., 9 May 1782, Add. MSS. 21,762; intelligence, [8?] January 1783, Sir Guy Carleton Papers, 6721, Public Record Office, London.

22. Ethan Allen to Haldimand, 16 June 1782, Carleton Papers, 4524; Ethan Allen [?] to Haldimand, Quebec, 11 July 1782, Carleton Papers.

23. Sherwood to Mathews, Loyal Block House, Vt., 27 April 1783, Add. MSS. 21,838.

24. Haldimand to Townshend, Quebec, 14 February 1783, Add. MSS. 21,716.

25. Ethan Allen [?] to Haldimand, Quebec, 11 July 1782, Carleton Papers, 4524; Sherwood to Mathews, 27 April 1783, Add. MSS. 21,838.

26. Arnold to Germain, 3 February 1783, Shelburne Papers, LXVII; intelligence, 2 August 1783, Carleton Papers, 8612.

27. North to Haldimand, London, 8 August 1783, Add. MSS. 21,705.

28. For West Florida see Cecil Johnson, *British West Florida, 1763–1783*,

p. 149; and J. Barton Starr, "Tories, Dons, and Rebels: The American Revolution in British West Florida"; for East Florida see Charles L. Mowat, *East Florida as a British Province, 1763–1784*, pp. 64, 146–47.

29. John Graham to Carleton, Tybee, Ga., 20 July 1782, Carleton Papers, 5108; James Bruce to Shelburne[?], 22 August 1782, Shelburne Papers, LXVI.

30. James Penman to Leslie, Charleston, S.C., 5 June 1782, Carleton Papers, 4739; Tonyn to Carleton, St. Augustine, 11 October 1782, Carleton Papers, 5850.

31. Tonyn to Sydney, St. Augustine, 14 June 1784, in John W. Caughey, ed., *East Florida, 1783–1785: A File of Documents Assembled and Many of Them Translated by Joseph Byrne Lockey*, p. 289; John Cruden to John Maxwell, St. Marys River, Fla., 28 October 1784, C.O. 23/25.

32. Memorial of sundry inhabitants of East Florida to Leslie, 1782[?], Carleton Papers, 10,275.

33. Dunmore to Clinton, Charleston, S.C., 2 February 1782, C.O. 5/175; Ross to Dunmore, Charleston, S.C., 3 March 1782, C.O. 5/175; Dunmore to Townshend, London, 24 August 1782, Sydney Papers, William L. Clements Library, Ann Arbor, Michigan; J. Leitch Wright, Jr., "Lord Dunmore's Loyalist Asylum in the Floridas," pp. 371–72.

34. Oswald to Townshend, Paris, 2 October 1782, Shelburne Papers, LXX; Oswald to Henry Strachey, Paris, 4 December 1782, Shelburne Papers, LXX; minute of cabinet, 25 October 1782, Townshend Collection; Vaughan to Shelburne, Paris, 18 January 1783, Benjamin Vaughan Papers, William L. Clements Library, Univ. of Mich., Ann Arbor.

35. Penman to Leslie, Charleston, S.C., 5 June 1782, Carleton Papers, 4739; Thomas Brown to Carleton, St. Augustine, 28 April 1783, Carleton Papers, 7571; George Townshend to commissioners, Argyle St., London, 28 April 1787, T. 77/17; address of British subjects resident in East Florida to Tonyn, St. Augustine, 15 February 1785, Caughey, *East Florida Documents*, p. 522; Wilbur H. Siebert, ed., *Loyalists in East Florida, 1774 to 1785*, 2:307–8.

36. Memorial of Mary Oswald, 11 November 1786, A.O. 12/3.

37. Memorial of the earl of Dunmore, London, 25 February 1784, A.O. 12/54.

38. Silas Deane to Edward Bancroft, Ghent, 10 February 1783, in Silas Deane, *The Deane Papers, 1774–1790*, ed. Charles Isham, 5:129–30.

39. Deane to James Wilson, London, 1 April 1783, Deane, *The Deane Papers*, p. 152; Deane to Isaac Moses, London, 29 April 1783, in Deane, *The Deane Papers*, p. 159; memorial of the earl of Dunmore, 25 February 1784, A.O. 12/54.

40. Wilbur H. Siebert, "The Loyalists of Pennsylvania," pp. 14–15; Wilbur H. Siebert, "Kentucky's Struggle with Its Loyalist Proprietors," p. 114.

41. Memorial of John Connolly, 2 February 1784, A.O. 12/54; Siebert, "Kentucky's Struggle with Its Loyalist Proprietors," p. 113.

42. Memorial of Sir John Johnson, 1786[?], A.O. 12/20; memorial of Daniel

Claus, 24 January 1786, A.O. 12/21; James T. Flexner, *Mohawk Baronet: Sir William Johnson of New York*, pp. 344–50.

43. Major Arent De Peyster to Haldimand, Detroit, 15 June 1782, Add. MSS. 21,783; McKee to De Peyster, Shawanese Town, 24 May 1783, Add. MSS. 21,763.

44. John McDonald to McKee, 25 October 1782, Claus Papers, III, P.A.C.; McArthur to Carleton, St. Augustine, 9 January 1783, Carleton Papers, 10,049.

45. A convenient summary of the Indian conflict in the West is in John R. Alden, *A History of the American Revolution*, pp. 423–42.

46. Downes, *Council Fires*, pp. 208, 272–76; John Bakeless, *Daniel Boone*, pp. 156 ff.

47. Resolution of the Continental Congress, 1 May 1783, Worthington C. Ford et al., eds., *Journals of the Continental Congress, 1774–1789*, 24:319–20.

48. Downes, *Council Fires*, pp. 441–45; Louis De Vorsey, *The Indian Boundary in the Southern Colonies, 1763–1775*, pp. 164–72.

49. John Ehrman, *The Younger Pitt: The Years of Acclaim*, pp. 133–34.

50. Earl of Carlisle's speech in House of Lords, 18 February 1783, in *Quebec Gazette*, 1 May 1783.

51. Townshend to Thomas Brown, Whitehall, 14 February 1783, Carleton Papers, 6908; North to Haldimand, Whitehall, 10 April 1783, Add. MSS. 21,705; Carleton to McArthur, New York, 26 March 1783, Carleton Papers, 7220.

52. Brown to Carleton, St. Augustine, 1 June 1783, Carleton Papers, 10,116.

53. John Johnson's speech to Six Nations, Niagara, N.Y., 13 July 1783, Claus Papers, III; Allan Maclean and John Butler's meeting with chiefs and principal warriors of Six Nations, Shawnees, Delawares, and Cherokees, Niagara, N.Y., 2 October 1783, C.O. 42/15.

CHAPTER 2

1. Thomas J. Wertenbaker, *Father Knickerbocker Rebels: New York City during the Revolution*, p. 268.

2. Anglo-American Treaty, Paris, 3 September 1783, Miller, *Treaties*, 2:151.

3. Marquis of Carmarthen to David Hartley, St. James, 25 March 1784, David Hartley Papers, IV, William L. Clements Library, Univ. of Mich., Ann Arbor.

4. Fox to Hartley, 4 August 1783, Hartley's negotiations, I, Bancroft Collection; memo for the definitive treaty, Hartley Papers, II.

5. William Twiss to Haldimand, London, 3 December 1783, Add. MSS. 21,735; John Steven Watson, *The Reign of George III, 1760–1815*, pp. 261–72.

6. Anna L. Lingelbach, "The Inception of the British Board of Trade,"

pp. 701–11; Helen T. Manning, *British Colonial Government after the American Revolution, 1782–1820*, pp. 75–96.

7. John A. Cannon, *The Fox-North Coalition: Crisis of the Constitution, 1782–4*, pp. 230–35; Archibald S. Foord, "The Waning of 'The Influence of the Crown,'" p. 506.

8. The work most satisfactorily describing British politics in the years immediately after the Revolution is John Ehrman, *The Younger Pitt: The Years of Acclaim*. Lewis Namier's *The Structure of Politics at the Accession of George III*, and *England in the Age of the American Revolution* are most helpful. See also Lewis Namier and John Brooke, *The House of Commons, 1754–1790*, 1:1–204; Keith G. Feiling, *The Second Tory Party, 1714–1832*, pp. 143–83; Ian R. Christie, *The End of North's Ministry, 1780–1782*, pp. 267–372; Donald G. Barnes, *George III and William Pitt, 1783–1806*; Arthur Aspinall, "The Cabinet Council, 1783–1835," pp. 145–252.

9. Andrew C. McLaughlin, "The Western Posts and British Debts," pp. 416–18, 427–30; Burt, *United States, Great Britain and British North America*, pp. 85–95, argues that Britain's fear of an Indian war prevented her from turning over the forts; Gerald S. Graham, ed., "The Indian Menace and the Retention of the Western Posts," p. 46.

10. Haldimand to Washington, Sorel, Lower Can., 11 August 1783, Add. MSS. 21,835.

11. Anglo-American treaty, Paris, 3 September 1783, Miller, *Treaties*, 2:155.

12. Townshend to Haldimand, Whitehall, 28 February 1783, Add. MSS. 21,705.

13. Horace Walpole, *Journal of the Reign of King George the Third, from the Year 1771 to 1783*, August 1783, 2:634.

14. William Twiss to Haldimand, London, 3 December 1783, Add. MSS. 21,735.

15. Haldimand to Washington, Sorel, Lower Can., 11 August 1783, Add. MSS. 21,835.

16. Haldimand to North, Quebec, 6 August 1783, Add. MSS. 21,716.

17. Haldimand to Major Ross, Quebec, 26 April 1783, Add. MSS. 21,785; Haldimand to John Johnson, Quebec, 22 May 1783, Add. MSS. 21,775.

18. Haldimand to William Pollock, Quebec, 19 November 1783, Add. MSS. 21,727.

19. Haldimand to Daniel Robertson, Quebec, 6 May 1784, Add. MSS. 21,723.

20. Ibid.; Haldimand to Arent S. De Peyster, Quebec, 29 March 1784, Add. MSS. 21,723.

21. Sydney to Haldimand, Whitehall, 8 April 1784, Add. MSS. 21,705.

22. Arthur B. Darling, *Our Rising Empire, 1763–1803*, p. 113; Samuel F. Bemis, *Jay's Treaty: A Study in Commerce and Diplomacy*, pp. 10–11.

23. William Twiss to Haldimand, London, 3 December 1783, Add. MSS. 21,735.

24. Robert Hunter to Haldimand, London, 27 March 1783, Add. MSS. 21,735; Wayne E. Stevens, *The Northwest Fur Trade, 1763–1800*, pp. 72–87.

25. Burt, *United States, Great Britain, and British North America*, pp. 84–85.

26. Haldimand to Robertson, Quebec, 6 May 1784, Add. MSS. 21,723; Bemis, *Jay's Treaty*, p. 256.

27. First report of bill, 25 September 1781[?], Indian Papers, Philip Schuyler Papers, XIV, N.Y.P.L.

28. John Deseronto to Daniel Claus, Lachine, Lower Can., 8 January 1784, Claus Papers, XXIV.

29. Joseph Brant to Robert Mathews, Montreal, 7 April 1784, Add. MSS. 21,772.

30. "Measures suggested as the most probable to retain the Six Nation Indians in the Kings Interest," 1785[?], Add. MSS. 21,779.

31. Sydney to Haldimand, Whitehall, 8 April 1784, Add. MSS. 21,705.

32. Ibid.

33. Franklin to Oswald, Passy, Paris, 26 November 1782, Hartley Papers, III.

34. Resolution of town of Boston, 9 April 1783, in *Gentleman's Magazine*, 53 (1783), 528; resolution of officers and men of 5th regiment, Delaware militia, in *Gentleman's Magazine*, 53 (1783), 704; American intelligence, *Gentleman's Magazine*, 59 (1784), 223; William H. Nelson, *The American Tory*, p. 166; William Schaw and Lord Cathcart to earl of Carlisle, Walton's, London?, 12 June 1783, in Benjamin F. Stevens, *B. F. Stevens's Facsimiles of Manuscripts in European Archives relating to America, 1773–1783*, 1:130.

35. Thomas Pitt's speech in Parliament, 17 February 1783, *Gentleman's Magazine*, 53 (1783), 293.

36. Evan Nepean to Haldimand, Wednesday night, 1785, Add. MSS. 21,736; Haldimand to George Yonge, Curzon St., London, 10 May 1785, Add. MSS. 21,727.

37. *Daily Universal Register* (London), 1 April 1785.

38. Siebert, *Loyalists in East Florida*, 1:161, 209.

39. Brown to North, St. Augustine, 15 September 1783, C.O. 5/182; Tonyn to Carleton, St. Augustine, 11 September 1783, Carleton Papers, 9094.

40. Conde de Floridablanca to Bernardo del Campo, el Pardo, 23 March 1784, Simancas, estado, leg. 2617, no. 40, A.G.I.; Floridablanca to Conde de Aranda, Madrid, 2 January 1783, in Caughey, *East Florida Documents*, p. 42.

41. George III to Lord Grantham, St. James, 19 December 1782, in Fortescue, *Correspondence of George III*, 6:192.

42. John Cruden to John Maxwell, St. Marys River, 28 October 1784, C.O. 23/25.

43. Tonyn to Sydney, St. Augustine, 14 June 1784, in Caughey, *East Florida*

Documents, pp. 289–92; John Cruden to Charles III, St. Marys River, 28 October 1784, East Florida Papers, 195M15; Cruden to Earl of Dartmouth, St. Marys River, 28 October 1784, in Hist. MSS Com., *The Manuscripts of the Earl of Dartmouth. Fourteenth Report*, 2:483; *Daily Universal Register* (London), 13 July 1785.

44. Kenneth Coleman, *The American Revolution in Georgia, 1763–1789*, p. 266; Caughey, *East Florida Documents*, pp. 11–12; J. Leitch Wright, Jr., *William Augustus Bowles: Director General of the Creek Nation*, pp. 140–41.

45. John Dalling to Lord George Germain, Jamaica, 25 October 1780, C.O. 137/79; Dalling to Germain, Jamaica, 25 April 1781, C.O. 137/80; John Rydjord, *Foreign Interest in the Independence of New Spain: An Introduction to the War for Independence*, pp. 90–92.

46. Andrew Turnbull to Haldimand, Charleston, 2 November 1783, Add. MSS. 21,735; Francisco de Miranda to Henry Knox, London, 19 February 1785, Henry Knox Papers, XVII, Massachusetts Historical Society, Boston; William S. Robertson, *The Life of Miranda*, 1:34–58.

47. Dunmore to Townshend, London 1, 24 August 1782, Sydney Papers.

48. Brown to North, St. Augustine, 15 September 1783, C.O. 5/82.

49. Stevens, *Northwest Fur Trade*, pp. 93–97.

50. Arthur P. Whitaker, ed. and trans., *Documents Relating to the Commercial Policy of Spain in the Floridas, with Incidental Reference to Louisiana*, pp. xxvii–xxxix; Marie T. Greenslade, "William Panton," pp. 109–14.

51. Zéspedes to José de Gálvez, Havana, 22 March 1784, estado, leg. 3901, A.H.N. (photostat L.C.); memorial by Panton, Leslie, and Co. to Spanish Crown, St. Augustine, 31 July 1784, in Duvon C. Corbitt, ed., "Papers Relating to the Georgia-Florida Frontier, 1784-1800," 21:80.

52. Bernardo de Gálvez to José de Gálvez, Madrid, 20 December 1783, in Whitaker, *Documents*, p. 39.

53. Wright, *Bowles*, pp. 26–34.

54. Arthur P. Whitaker, "Alexander McGillivray, 1783–1789," pp. 184–95; "return of extra officers, interpreters, and war conductors," July 1783[?], Carleton Papers, 10,140; John W. Caughey, "The Natchez Rebellion of 1781 and Its Aftermath," p. 82.

55. There is no satisfactory account of the Canadian Indian Department in the post-Revolutionary period. Of value are Reginald Horsman, "The British Indian Department and the Resistance to General Anthony Wayne, 1793–1795," p. 270; Consul W. Butterfield, *History of the Girtys*, pp. 212–32; and Ernest A. Cruikshank, *The Story of Butler's Rangers and the Settlement of Niagara*, pp. 111–14.

56. Tonyn to Sydney, St. Augustine, 6 December 1784, in Caughey, *East Florida Documents*, p. 325.

57. Robert Treat's testimony, 27 July 1786, Benjamin Lincoln Papers, VII, Massachusetts Historical Society, Boston; Shawnee chiefs to McKee, Shawa-

nese Town, 20 March 1785, Lyman Draper Manuscripts, Frontier Wars, U23, State Historical Society of Wisconsin, Madison.

58. Leslie F. S. Upton, *The Loyal Whig: William Smith of New York and Quebec*, pp. 144–45.

59. Edward Bancroft to William Frazer, Philadelphia, 8 November 1783, Correspondence of Sir John Temple, 1783–86, Bancroft Col.

60. George III to North, Windsor, 12 July 1783, George III and Lord North, Bancroft Col.; George III to Fox, Windsor, 7 August 1783, in Charles James Fox, *Memorials and Correspondence of Charles James Fox*, 2:128–29.

61. Chittenden to Haldimand, Arlington, 12 July 1784, Add. MSS. 21,835; Ira Allen to Haldimand, Montreal, 10 September 1784, Add. MSS. 21,835.

62. John Baker Holroyd, first earl of Sheffield, *Observations on the Commerce of the American States with Europe and the West Indies, including the Several Articles of Import and Export, and on the Tendency of a Bill Now Depending in Parliament, with Additional Notes on the Commerce of the United States* (Philadelphia, 1783), pp. 1 ff.; Sheffield to William Knox, Sheffield Place, 3 July 1783, William Knox Papers.

63. *Quebec Gazette*, 1 September 1785.

64. Sydney to Haldimand, Whitehall, 8 April 1784, Add. MSS. 21,705.

65. Haldimand to Ira Allen, Quebec, 17 September 1784, Add. MSS. 21,835; Robert Mathews to Ira Allen, Quebec, 27 September 1784, Add. MSS. 21,724.

66. Sydney to Haldimand, Whitehall, 8 April 1784, Add. MSS. 21,705; Sydney to Haldimand, Whitehall, 2 August 1784, Add. MSS. 21,705.

67. James Clarke to Brook Watson, Halifax, 25 May 1785, C.O. 217/57.

68. Thomas Carleton to Sydney, St. Johns, 4 November 1785, C.O. 188/3; Michael Wallace to Anthony Stewart, Halifax, December 1785, C.O. 217/59.

69. Jellison, *Ethan Allen*, pp. 317–19; William Montgomery to the Pennsylvania Council, Northumberland, 20 May 1786, in Julian P. Boyd and Robert J. Taylor, eds., *The Susquehannah Company Papers*, 8:336; occurrences from 5 August to 5 October 1787, New York, 5 October 1787, America and England, no. 301, Bancroft Col.

70. Monroe to Thomas Jefferson, New York, 25 August 1785, in Edmund C. Burnett, ed., *Letters of Members of the Continental Congress*, 8:203.

71. Whitaker, *Spanish-American Frontier*, pp. 108–19.

72. Gentleman at the Falls of the Ohio to his Friends in New England, 4 December 1786, in Samuel C. Williams, *History of the Lost State of Franklin*, pp. 123–24.

73. Wilkinson to Estevan Miró and Martín Navarro, in Miró and Navarro to Antonio Valdes, New Orleans, 25 September 1787, Pontalba Collection, Filson Club, Louisville, Ky.

74. George Sharpe to Governor Hay, Detroit, 2 June 1785, Add. MSS. 24,322.

75. Tobias Lear to Lincoln, Mount Vernon, 26 February 1787, Lincoln Papers, VIII.

76. Robert Ernst, *Rufus King, American Federalist*, pp. 74–75; Monroe to Patrick Henry, New York, 12 August 1786, in Burnett, *Letters of Continental Congress*, 8:424–25.

CHAPTER 3

1. Bemis, *Jay's Treaty*, pp. 10–11.

2. Ibid., p. 207.

3. Charles M. Johnston, ed., *The Valley of the Six Nations: A Collection of Documents on the Indian Lands of the Grand River*, pp. xxxii–xli.

4. William L. Stone, *Life of Joseph Brant-Thayendanegea, including the Border Wars of the American Revolution*, 2:239–40, 248, 264–69; Anthony F. C. Wallace, *The Death and Rebirth of the Seneca*, pp. 154–65.

5. John Johnson to Evan Nepean, Montreal, 7 November 1785, C.O. 42/17.

6. John Adams to John Jay, Grosvenor Square, 15 December 1785, in William R. Manning, ed., *Diplomatic Correspondence of the United States: Canadian Relations, 1784–1860*, 1:339–40.

7. *Daily Universal Register* (London), 6 January 1786.

8. Brant to Sydney, London, 4 January 1786, C.O. 42/49.

9. Downes, *Council Fires*, pp. 141–45, 283–84; Johnson to Haldimand, Montreal, 11 August 1783, Add. MSS. 21,775.

10. Of value in understanding the Indians' legal claim to land is Wilcomb E. Washburn, "The Moral and Legal Justifications for Dispossessing the Indians," pp. 24–32; and Reginald Horsman, *Expansion and American Indian Policy, 1783–1812*, pp. 5–15, 53–65, 170–73.

11. Johnson's speech to Six Nations, Niagara, 13 July 1783, Claus Papers, III; Gen. Allan Maclean and Col. John Butler's meeting with chiefs of Six Nations, Shawnees, Delawares, and Cherokees, Niagara, 2 October 1783, C.O. 42/15.

12. General Maclean and Colonel Butler's meeting with chiefs of Six Nations, Shawnees, Delawares, and Cherokees, Niagara, 2 October 1783, C.O. 42/15; in council, Lower Sandusky, 6 September 1783, minutes of Detroit councils, 1781–90, R.G. 10, A, 4, P.A.C.

13. Brant to Sydney, London, 4 January 1786, C.O. 42/49.

14. Sydney to Hope, Whitehall, 6 April 1786, C.O. 42/49.

15. Ibid.; "Nepean Papers, Secret Service Payments," 31 March 1786, Sydney Papers.

16. Haldimand Diary, 20 January 1786, Add. MSS. 21,890.

17. *Daily Universal Register* (London), 1 April 1786.

18. Ibid., 23 June 1786.

19. Ibid., 31 January 1786.

20. Ibid., 6 April 1786.

21. Samuel Kirkland journal, 7 July 1788, Lyman Draper Manuscripts, Brant Papers, F11, State Historial Society of Wisconsin, Madison.

22. "Lake Champlain, from Lt. Gov. Skene, this given by Silas Deane to me and put into Lord Dorchester's hands before he set off," 1786 [?], Add. MSS. 38,222; Deane to Sheffield, Chapel St., 25 November 1788, in Silas Deane, *The Deane Papers: Correspondence between Silas Deane, His Brothers and Their Business and Political Associates, 1771–1795*, pp. 233–34; William Smith diary, P.A.C.

23. Levi Allen to Sydney, London, 3 May 1789, F.O. 4/7; Dorchester to Hawkesbury, Quebec, 13 June 1787, C.O. 42/12; Chilton Williamson, *Vermont in Quandary: 1763–1825*, pp. 151–64.

24. Jellison, *Ethan Allen*, pp. 300–303.

25. Sydney to Dorchester, Whitehall, 5 September 1788, C.O. 42/61.

26. Simcoe to Nepean, Wolford Lodge, Devonshire, 3 December 1789, Ernest A. Cruikshank, ed., *The Correspondence of Lieut. Governor John Graves Simcoe, with Allied Documents Relating to His Administration of the Government of Upper Canada*, 1:8.

27. Observations, political and commercial relating to Canada, 1788, C.O. 42/112.

28. Robert S. Cotterill, *History of Pioneer Kentucky*, pp. 209–22.

29. "Memorandum of the present political sentiments of the United States," by Henry Hope [?], Quebec, 8 September 1785, C.O. 42/17.

30. "Extract of the new system of English politics respecting North America," in Jefferson to Jay, Paris, 11 August 1786, in Manning, *Diplomatic Correspondence*, 1:353.

31. Timothy Bloodworth to North Carolina Assembly, 16 December 1786, in Burnett, *Letters of the Continental Congress*, 8:522.

32. Madison to Jefferson, New York, 19 March 1787, ibid., 561.

33. Dorchester to Sydney, Quebec, 11 April 1789, C.O. 42/64; Grenville to Dorchester, Whitehall, 20 October 1789, C.O. 42/65.

34. E. Wilson Lyon, ed., "Moustier's Memoir on Louisiana," p. 251.

35. Dorchester to Connolly, Quebec, 15 January 1788, C.O. 42/60.

36. Nicholas B. Wainwright, *George Croghan, Wilderness Diplomat*, pp. 287–91, 301; Reuben G. Thwaites and Louise P. Kellogg, eds., *Documentary History of Dunmore's War, 1774; Comp. from the Draper Manuscripts in the Library of the Wisconsin Historical Society*, p. 42.

37. Connolly to Dorchester, Detroit, 4 May (say June) 1788, C.O. 42/59; Arthur St. Clair to John Wyllys, Ft. Harmar, 28 November 1788, in William H. Smith, ed., *The St. Clair Papers: The Life and Public Services of Arthur St. Clair, Soldier of the Revolutionary War, President of the Continental Congress, and Governor of the North-Western Territory*, 2:98–99; James R. Jacobs, *Tarnished Warrior: Major-General James Wilkinson*, p. 90; Thomas Marshall to Washington, Fayette

County, Ky., 12 February 1789, in Thomas M. Green, *The Spanish Conspiracy. A Review of Early Spanish Movements in the South-West. Containing Proofs of the Intrigues of James Wilkinson and John Brown; of the Complicity Therewith of Judges Sebastian, Wallace, and Innes*, pp. 251–52.

38. Wilkinson to Miró, New Orleans, 17 September 1789, Pontalba Collection.

39. Jared Sparks, ed., *Correspondence of the American Revolution: Being Letters of Eminent Men to George Washington*, 4:248–51; George Morgan to Diego de Gardoqui, Pittsburgh, 19 December 1788, estado, leg. 3888 bis., doc. 2041; Abernethy, *Western Lands*, p. 358.

40. *Daily Universal Register* (London), 6 February 1786.

41. Adam Mabane to Haldimand, Quebec, 15 February 1787, Add. MSS. 21,736.

42. Bond to Duke of Leeds, Philadelphia, 10 November 1789, F.O. 4/7.

43. Observations on the colony of Kentucky, in Dorchester to Sydney, 27 August 1789, C.O. 42/65.

44. Ibid.; Grenville to Dorchester, Whitehall, 29 October 1789, C.O. 42/65.

45. *Daily Universal Register* (London), 8 November 1786.

46. *Bahama Gazette* (Nassau), 25 February 1786; noticias Anglo-Americanas, December 1786, Simancas, estado, leg. 8143, A.G.I.

47. *Daily Universal Register* (London), 23 October 1786.

48. Minutes of the Committee of Trade, 1 May 1787, Add. MSS. 38,390.

49. James Cruden to Hawkesbury, Sackville Street, London, 18 May 1787, Add. MSS. 38,222; John Cruden to [?], New Providence, 22 December 1785 [?], Add. MSS. 38,218.

50. Archibald McArthur to Sydney, Nassau, 13 April 1787, C.O. 23/27.

51. House of Commons debates, 27 June 1786, *The Scots Magazine*, 48 (1786), 533; John Nutt to Henry Dundas, 27 March 1787, Broad Street, Melville Papers, William L. Clements Library, Univ. of Mich., Ann Arbor.

52. Gentleman long resident in America to Mr. Woodford, upon the interests of Spain, London, 18 October 1788, Add. MSS. 38,223; William Knox to Grenville, 22 March 1788, William Knox Papers, VII.

53. [?] to John Temple, New York, 12 May 1788, Gifts 30-8/343.

54. Zéspedes to José de Gálvez, St. Augustine, 30 March 1787, estado, leg. 3901, apartado 1, núm. 16, A.H.N.; *Daily Universal Register* (London), 30 August 1787.

55. Sheffield to Hawkesbury[?], Sheffield Place, Sussex, 14 July 1786, Add. MSS. 38,219; Wright, "Dunmore's Loyalist Asylum," p. 377.

56. "Kings, chiefs, and head warriors of Creek and Cherokee Nation," Coweta, second windy moon, 1789, C.O. 42/87.

57. Stephen Sayre to Henry Knox, London, 29 June 1789, Henry Knox Papers, XXIV; Haldimand diary, 27 December 1789, Add. MSS. 21,891.

58. Levi Allen to William Pitt, London, 25 December 1789, Gifts 30-8/107.

59. Grenville to Dorchester, Whitehall, 20 October 1789, C.O. 42/65.

60. *Times* (London), 28 March 1788; ibid., 7 May 1788.

61. Henry Knox to Arthur St. Clair, War Office, 8 December 1788, in Smith, *St. Clair Papers*, 2:101.

62. David Owen to Dundas, 28 March 1788, Melville Papers, Clements Library; John Cochrane to Pitt, London, 10 September 1788, Gifts 30-8/124.

63. *Times* (London), 31 March 1788.

CHAPTER 4

1. William R. Manning, *The Nootka Sound Controversy*. In *Annual Report of the American Historical Association for the Year 1904*, pp. 312–43.

2. Julian P. Boyd, *Number 7, Alexander Hamilton's Secret Attempts to Control American Foreign Policy, with Supporting Documents*, pp. 4–13.

3. Ibid., pp. 11–13, 34–54; Beckwith's memorandum, in Dorchester to Grenville, Quebec, 25 September 1790, C.O. 42/69; Beckwith to Grenville, Philadelphia, 3 March 1791, Grenville Papers (Boconnoc MSS.), B.M.

4. Board of Trade to Grenville, Whitehall, 19 April 1790, B.T. 3/2; Grenville to Dorchester, Whitehall, 6 May 1790, C.O. 42/67; "Letters from a Gentleman at New York," *Times* (London), 9 October 1790.

5. Arthur St. Clair to commanding officer of Detroit, Marietta, 19 September 1790, *ASP,IA*, I, 96; Beckwith to Grenville, New York, 3 November 1790, C.O. 42/21.

6. Josiah Harmar to Henry Knox, Ft. Washington, 4 November 1790, *ASP,IA*, 1:104.

7. Dumas Malone, *Jefferson and His Time*, 2:310.

8. J. Leitch Wright, Jr., "Creek-American Treaty of 1790: Alexander McGillivray and the Diplomacy of the Old Southwest," p. 386.

9. Beckwith's report, in Dorchester to Grenville, Quebec, 25 September 1790, C.O. 42/69.

10. Beckwith to Grenville, New York, 3 November 1790, C.O. 42/21; Dorchester to Beckwith, Quebec, 27 June 1790, C.O. 42/68.

11. Memoranda and letters concerning Miranda's 1790 conferences with Pitt are in Francisco de Miranda, *Archivo del General Miranda*, 15:106–26; Robertson, *Miranda*, 1:97–112.

12. Miranda to Knox, London, 15 March 1790, Henry Knox Papers, XXV.

13. Stephen Sayre to Knox, London, 10 May 1790, ibid., XXVI.

14. Jonathan Williams to Knox, London, 4 January 1790, ibid., XXV.

15. Douglas S. Freeman, *George Washington, A Biography*, 6:269–71.

16. Duke of Gloucester to Prince of Wales, Geneva, 20 September 1786, RA, p. 17(b), 54, 378; Gloucester to George III, 17 September 1792, ibid., 54, 403.

17. William B. Willcox, *Portrait of a General: Sir Henry Clinton in the War of Independence*, pp. 463–91.

18. Clinton to Simcoe, January 1790, Sir Henry Clinton Papers, William L. Clements Library, Univ. of Mich., Ann Arbor.

19. Clinton memorandum (notes for speech in Parliament?), January 1790, Clinton Papers.

20. Ibid.

21. Simcoe to Clinton, 23 April 1790, Clinton Papers.

22. Simcoe to Evan Nepean, 1 April 1790, Add. MSS. 38,225; Simcoe to Clinton, 23 April 1790, Clinton Papers; Simcoe's observation on the force necessary for the protection of the interior part of Canada, 1 November 1790, Gifts 30–8/178.

23. Clinton to Simcoe, January 1790, Clinton Papers.

24. Alexander Ross to George Chalmers, New Providence, 8 November 1790, Add. MSS. 22,900.

25. Arthur Campbell to Pitt, Upper Harley Street, 28 October 1790, Gifts 30–8/120.

26. Wright, "Dunmore's Loyalist Asylum," pp. 370–78.

27. Wright, *Bowles*, pp. 11–35.

28. Winthrop Sargent to St. Clair, Ft. Steuben, 17 August 1790, Carter, *Territorial Papers*, 2:301; Wellbank to McKee, Cherokee Nation, 12 April 1791, Claus Papers, IV.

29. Dorchester to Grenville, Montreal, 26 July 1790, C.O. 42/68.

30. Grenville to Dorchester, 5 October 1790, C.O. 42/68.

31. Bond's report of occurrences from 6 August to 4 September 1790, F.O. 4/8.

32. Ibid., 5 July to 3 August 1790.

33. *Times* (London), 22 December 1789.

34. Clinton memorandum (notes for speech in Parliament?), January 1790, Clinton Papers; Grenville to Dorchester, Whitehall, 6 May 1790, in Canada, Public Archives, *Report, 1890*, p. 132.

35. John Holroyd, Lord Sheffield, *Observations on Commerce of the American States*, p. 38.

36. Board of Trade to Grenville, Whitehall, 19 April 1790, B.T. 3/2.

37. Bond's pertinent reports are scattered throughout F.O. 4/8.

38. Grenville to Dorchester, Whitehall, 29 October 1789, C.O. 42/65.

39. Simcoe's observations on the force necessary for the protection of the interior part of Canada, 1 November 1790, Gifts 30–8/178.

40. Board of Trade to Grenville, Whitehall, 19 April 1790, B.T. 3/2.

41. Ibid.

42. Ibid.

43. Clinton memorandum, 5 September 1790, Clinton Papers.

44. Levi Allen to Simcoe, Onion River, received 16 February 1792, C.O. 42/316.

45. Samuel Peters to Grenville, Grosvenor Place, London, 15 November 1791, Grenville Papers.

46. Grenville to Dorchester, Whitehall, 20 October 1789, C.O. 42/65.

47. Grenville to Dorchester, Whitehall, 6 May 1790, C.O. 43/10.

48. Board of Trade to Grenville, Whitehall, 19 April 1790, B.T. 3/2.

49. Clinton memorandum (notes for speech in Parliament?), January 1790, Clinton Papers.

50. Simcoe to Clinton, 23 April 1790, Clinton Papers; Van Doren, *Secret History*, pp. 395–400.

51. Jefferson to James Monroe, New York, 11 July 1790, Julian P. Boyd, ed., *The Papers of Thomas Jefferson*, 17:25.

52. Case of Benjamin Baynton, 30 July 1789, A.O. 12/102; Benjamin Baynton, *Authentic Memoirs of William Augustus Bowles, Esquire, Ambassador from the United Nations of Creeks and Cherokees, to the Court of London*.

53. Wright, *Bowles*, p. 50.

54. Edmund Fanning to Nepean, Island of St. John, 20 November 1790, C.O. 226/13.

55. Clinton memorandum (notes for a speech in Parliament?), January 1790, Clinton Papers.

56. Sargent to St. Clair, Ft. Steuben, 17 August 1790, Carter, *Territorial Papers*, 2:301; Wellbank to McKee, Cherokee Nation, 12 April 1791, Claus Papers, IV.

57. Thomas Brown to Pitt, Nassau, 2 November 1790, C.O. 23/30. For undisclosed reasons Brown did not accept the Spanish offer.

58. Beckwith's report, in Dorchester to Grenville, Quebec, 25 September 1790, C.O. 42/69.

59. Simcoe to Clinton, 18 October 1790, Clinton Papers.

60. Wright, *Bowles*, pp. 22, 28, 66.

61. Manning, *Nootka Sound Controversy*, pp. 453–61.

62. James O'Fallon to Miró, Crabb-Orchard [Kentucky], 18 February 1791, Lawrence Kinnaird, ed. and trans., *Spain in the Mississippi Valley, 1765–94, Translations of Materials from the Spanish Archives in the Bancroft Library*, 2:403; Arthur P. Whitaker, *The Spanish-American Frontier: 1783–1795; The Westward Movement and the Spanish Retreat in the Mississippi Valley*, p. 143; Simcoe to Dundas, London, 12 August 1791, Cruikshank, *Simcoe Papers*, 1:50.

63. Simcoe to Clinton, 23 April 1790, Clinton Papers.

64. Simcoe to Dundas, Weymouth, Eng., 19 September 1791, Gifts 30–8/178.

CHAPTER 5

1. John C. Miller, *The Federalist Era, 1789–1801*, p. 183.

2. Grenville to Hawkesbury[?], St. James Square, 14 January 1791, Add. MSS. 38,226.

3. Glimpses of loyalist sentiment in Natchez are in Dorris C. James, *Antebellum Natchez*, pp. 55–56, and in Jack D. L. Holmes, *Gayoso: The Life of a Spanish Governor in the Mississippi Valley, 1789–1799*, pp. 16–20, 114–17.

4. Grenville to Hawkesbury[?], St. James Square, 14 January 1791, Add. MSS. 38,226.

5. Bond's report on occurrences from 7 December 1786 to 5 January 1787, F.O. 4/5.

6. Forsyth, Richardson, and Co., and Todd, McGill, and Co. to John Johnson, Montreal, 10 August 1791, C.O. 42/83.

7. Horsman, *Expansion and American Indian Policy*, pp. 88–89.

8. Grenville to Hammond, Whitehall, 2 September 1791, F.O. 115/1.

9. Alexander Macomb to Henry Knox, New York, 16 February 1792, Henry Knox Papers, XXX; the best published account of the battle from the American point of view is James R. Jacobs, *The Beginning of the U.S. Army, 1783–1812*, pp. 85–123.

10. Extract of a letter from Vincennes, 15 June 1792, in *Bahama Gazette* (Nassau), 28 September 1792.

11. Henry Clinton, incomplete draft, 1791–92, Clinton Papers; Clinton to Prince William Henry, Duke of Gloucester, Orwell Park, 8 August 1792, Clinton-Gloucester Correspondence, William L. Clements Library, Univ. of Mich., Ann Arbor; Simcoe to McKee, Navy Hall, 30 August 1792, C.O. 42/317.

12. Grenville to Hammond, Whitehall, 17 March 1792, F.O. 115/1; ibid., 25 April 1792.

13. Clinton to Gloucester, Orwell Park, 8 August 1792, Clinton-Gloucester Corr..

14. Clinton, draft, 1792, Clinton Papers.

15. Clinton to Gloucester, Orwell Park, 8 August 1792, Clinton-Gloucester Corr.

16. Ibid.; Clinton to Gloucester, draft, 1792, Clinton Papers.

17. Clinton to Gloucester, Orwell Park, 8 August 1792, Clinton-Gloucester Corr.

18. Clinton to Joseph Brant, 1792, Clinton Papers.

19. Simcoe to Dundas, London, 12 August 1791, C.O. 42/316.

20. Simcoe to Dundas, 26 August 1791, C.O. 42/316.

21. Simcoe to Clinton, Quebec, 14 January 1792, Clinton Papers; Connolly to McKee, Montreal, 21 July 1793, Supt. Gen. and Insp. Gen., VIII, R.G. 10, P.A.C.

22. Wayne to Knox, Legion Ville, 16 February 1793, in Richard C. Knopf, ed., *Anthony Wayne, a Name in Arms: Soldier, Diplomat, Defender of Expansion Westward of a Nation; the Wayne-Knox-Pickering-McHenry Correspondence*, p. 190.

23. Smith to Simcoe, Montreal, 7 June 1792, John Graves Simcoe Papers, William L. Clements Library, Univ. of Mich., Ann Arbor.

24. Duke of Kent to George III, Quebec, 30 September 1792, RA 45,872–45,873; Kent to Major Cliffe, Halifax, 26 May 1795, RA 45,567–45,568.

25. Simcoe to McKee, 23 June 1793, Claus Papers, V.

26. Grenville to Hammond, Whitehall, 3 January 1792, F.O. 115/1.

27. Ibid.

28. Reginald Horsman, "The British Indian Department and the Abortive Treaty of Lower Sandusky, 1793," pp. 193–97.

29. Proceedings of a council between the Shawnees and Delawares and Captain Brant, at the Rapids, 28 October 1792, Supt. Gen. and Insp. Gen., VIII, R.G. 10, P.A.C.

30. Timothy Pickering to Rebecca Pickering, Niagara, 27 May 1793, Timothy Pickering Papers, II, Massachusetts Historical Society, Boston; ibid., 9 July 1793.

31. Simcoe to McKee[?], Navy Hall, 28 June 1793, Claus Papers, V.

32. Speech of the general council to the commissioners of the United States, 13 August 1793, Supt. Gen. and Insp. Gen., VIII, R.G. 10, P.A.C.; Timothy Pickering to Rebecca Pickering, on Lake Erie, 21 August 1793, Pickering Papers, II.

33. Wayne to Knox, Hobsons Choice, 2 July 1793, in Knopf, *Wayne Correspondence*, p. 253.

34. Simcoe to Clinton, York, 25 September 1793, Clinton Papers.

35. Clinton to Gloucester, Orwell Park, 8 August 1792, Clinton-Gloucester Corr.; Gloucester to George III, 17 September 1792, RA, p. 17(b), 54,403.

36. Representations of Bowles . . . to George III, Osborne's Hotel, 3 January 1791, F.O. 4/9.

37. Grenville to Hawkesbury[?], St. James Square, London, 14 January 1791, Add. MSS. 38,226.

38. Ibid.; Grenville to Dorchester, Whitehall, 7 March 1791, C.O. 42/73.

39. Bowles to Grenville, Adelphi, London, 25 January 1791, F.O. 4/9.

40. Wright, *Bowles*, pp. 55–86.

41. Beckwith to Dorchester[?], Philadelphia, 2 December 1791, in Frederick J. Turner, ed., "English Policy toward America in 1790–1791," pp. 734–35; Stevenson to Clinton, New York, 31 January 1792, Clinton Papers.

42. Hammond to Jefferson, Philadelphia, 14 December 1791, F.O. 115/1; Hammond to Simcoe, Philadelphia, 19 October 1792, Cruikshank, *Simcoe Papers*, 1:233.

43. Simcoe to Clinton, Quebec, 14 January 1792, Clinton Papers.

44. John McDonald to Panton, Cherokees, 6 October 1792, in Duvon C. Corbitt, ed., "Papers Relating to the Georgia-Florida Frontier," 23:197–98; Moses Price to Panton, New Seneca, 24 July 1793, ibid., p. 387; Price to McKee, 27 August 1793, Claus Papers, V.

45. Dunmore's Commission to Philatoulche Upiahatche, Bahamas, 5

February 1793, East Florida Papers, 114J9, L. C.; Dunmore to Dundas, Nassau, 28 August 1792, C.O. 23/31.

46. McKee to Dragging Canoe, Foot of the Miamis Rapids, 22 July 1791, Claus Papers, IV.

47. Simcoe to Clinton, Quebec, 14 January 1792, Clinton Papers

48. Proceedings of a general council of the several Indian nations, Glaize, 30 September 1792, Supt. Gen. and Insp. Gen., VIII, R.G. 10, P.A.C.

49. Wellbank to Dunmore, Usechas, 18 June 1792, C.O. 23/31; Wellbank to McKee, Cowetah Old Town, 6 February 1793, Upper Canada, Indian Affairs, I, M.G. 19, F16, P.A.C.

50. Simcoe to McKee, Navy Hall, 23 July 1793, Claus Papers, V; Wellbank to McKee, Glaize, 18 September 1793, Claus Papers, VI.

51. Simcoe to Alured Clarke, Navy Hall, 29 July 1793, Cruikshank, *Simcoe Correspondence*, 1:392–93.

52. Simcoe to McKee, Navy Hall, 23 July 1793, Claus Papers, V; speech of the general council to the commissioners of the United States, 13 August 1793, Supt. Gen. and Insp. Gen., VIII, R.G. 10, P.A.C.; Simcoe to Clinton, York, Upper Can., 25 September 1793, Clinton Papers.

53. Charles Storer to Pickering, New York, 4 October 1793, Pickering Papers, LIX; Jacob Lindley, Joseph Moore, and Oliver Paxson, "Expedition to Detroit, 1793: The Quakers, the United States Commissioners, and the Proposed Treaty of Peace with the Northwestern Indian Tribes," p. 614.

54. Simcoe to Clinton, York, 25 September 1793, Clinton Papers.

55. Simcoe to Clarke, Navy Hall, 29 July 1793, Cruikshank, *Simcoe Correspondence*, 1:393; Thomas Duggan to McKee, Detroit, 25 August 1793, Claus Papers, V; Wellbank to Richard England, Glaize, 23 September 1793, Claus Papers, VI.

56. Barthélemi Tardiveau to minister of France, Kaskaskia, 22 May 1791, in Wellbank to Dunmore, Usechas, 18 June 1792, C.O. 23/31; a convenient summary of French designs on the Floridas and Louisiana is Frederick J. Turner, ed., *Correspondence of the French Ministers to the United States, 1791–1797, Annual Report of the American Historical Association for the Year 1903*, pp. 10–12.

57. Stevenson's suggestions to Dundas, 31 July 1793, C.O. 42/317.

58. Price to Panton, New Seneca, 24 July 1793, Corbitt, "Papers Relating to the Georgia-Florida Frontier," 23:387.

59. Simcoe to Baron de Carondelet, Rapids of Miami River, 11 April 1794, C.O. 42/100.

60. Simcoe to McKee[?], Navy Hall, 28 June 1793, Claus Papers, V; Wayne to Knox, Legion Ville, 16 February 1793, Knopf, *Wayne Correspondence*, p. 190.

61. Beckwith to Dorchester, Philadelphia, 14 January 1793, Cruikshank, *Simcoe Correspondence*, 1:299.

62. Robert Dickson to Robert Hamilton, Michilimackinac, 14 July 1793, C.O. 42/318.

63. Simcoe to Dundas, Weymouth, Eng., 19 September 1791, Gifts 30–8/178.

64. Simcoe to Dundas, London, 12 August 1791, C.O. 42/316.

65. Stevenson to Simcoe, New York, 7 February 1792, Cruikshank, *Simcoe Correspondence*, 1:110.

66. Simcoe to Dundas, London, 2 June 1791, RA 6815–6822; Samuel Peters to Grenville, Pimlico, Eng., 19 November 1791, C.O. 42/88.

67. Clinton, draft, 1792, Clinton Papers.

68. Stevenson to Dundas, Orchard St., 1 August 1793, Cruikshank, *Simcoe Correspondence,* 1:413; Stevenson to Clinton, 26 December 1793, Clinton Papers.

CHAPTER 6

1. Simcoe to Roger Hale Sheaffe, Navy Hall, 10 August 1794, Simcoe Papers, folder 4, P.A.C.

2. Thomas Carleton to Dundas, Fredericton, N.B., 4 July 1794, C.O. 188/5.

3. United States controversies with Britain and France are discussed in Bemis, *Jay's Treaty*, pp. 142–60, Charles R. Ritcheson, *Aftermath of Revolution: British Policy toward the United States, 1783–1795*, pp. 273–313, and Alexander De Conde, *Entangling Alliances: Politics and Diplomacy under George Washington*, pp. 204–310.

4. Les français libres a leurs frères les canadiens, ca. 1794, C.O. 42/101.

5. Pickering's remarks on Lord Dorchester's speech of 10 February 1794, Pickering Papers, LIX.

6. Dorchester to Indians of the Seven Villages of Lower Canada as deputies from all the nations who were at the general council held at the Miamis in 1793, Quebec, 10 February 1794, C.O. 42/98.

7. Dundas to Dorchester, Whitehall, 5 July 1794, C.O. 42/98; Portland to Dorchester, Whitehall, 15 July 1794, C.O. 42/98.

8. Simcoe to Pitt, Plymouth, Eng., 30 November 1799, Grenville Papers.

9. Simcoe to Clinton, York, Upper Can., 25 September 1793, Clinton Papers.

10. Stevenson to Clinton, 26 December 1793, Clinton Papers.

11. Simcoe to McKee[?], 6 August 1794, Claus Papers, VI.

12. Pickering's remarks on Lord Dorchester's speech of 10 February 1794, Pickering Papers, LIX.

13. Dorchester to Simcoe, Quebec, 17 February 1794, C.O. 42/98.

14. Merchants of Detroit to Richard G. England, Detroit, 23 May 1794, Cruikshank, *Simcoe Correspondence*, 2:244–45.

15. Henry Motz to John Johnson, Quebec, 1 August 1791, C.O. 42/83.

16. McKee to Joseph Chew, Miamis Rapids, 8 May 1794, ibid., 234.

17. Simcoe to Dorchester, 14 March 1794, C.O. 42/319.

18. Simcoe to Dorchester, Navy Hall, 10 July 1794, Cruikshank, *Simcoe Correspondence*, 2:316; Simcoe to Dundas, Navy Hall, 5 August 1794, W.O. 1/14.

19. Simcoe to Dundas, Navy Hall, 21 June 1794, C.O. 42/318; Samuel Kirkland to Pickering, Paris near Oneida, 8 December 1794, Pickering Papers, LXII.

20. Memorandum by William Jarvis in Simcoe to Dundas, Navy Hall, 5 August 1794, C.O. 42/318; Simcoe to Portland, Navy Hall, 17 May 1795, Canada, Public Archives, *Report*, *1891*, p. 71.

21. Wayne to Henry Knox, Greenville, 11 June 1794, Henry Knox Papers, XXXV.

22. Presley Neville to Thomas Mifflin, Pittsburgh, 10 June 1794, *ASP,IA*, I, 510.

23. Thomas Carleton to Dundas, Fredericton, N. B., June 14, 1794, C.O. 188/5.

24. John McDonald to McKee, Cherokees, 10 April 1794, Upper Canada, Ind. Affairs, I, M.G. 19, F 16, P.A.C.

25. William Hartshorne's diary of a journey from New York to Detroit with other Quakers to treat with the Indians, 4 May–17 Sept. 1793, N.Y.P.L.

26. Wellbank to McKee, Cherokee Nation, 12 April 1794, Claus Papers, VI.

27. Simcoe to Carondelet, Rapids of Miami River, 11 April 1794, C.O. 42/100.

28. Bowles to Grenville, 5 June 1798, Cuba, leg. 2371, A.G.I.

29. Deposition of William Jones, Scriven County, 15 August 1794, *ASP,IA*, I, 497.

30. Abraham P. Nasatir, *Spanish War Vessels on the Mississippi, 1792–1796*, p. 57.

31. Carondelet to Simcoe, New Orleans, 2 January 1794, C.O. 42/100.

32. Simcoe to Carondelet, Rapids of Miami River, 11 April 1794, C.O. 42/100.

33. Simcoe to Zenon Trudeau, 11 April 1794, Rapids of Miami River, Kinnaird, *Spain in the Mississippi Valley*, 3:265; Simcoe to Dorchester, Navy Hall, 29 April 1794, Cruikshank, *Simcoe Correspondence*, 2:222.

34. Simcoe to Dundas, Navy Hall, 21 June 1794, C.O. 42/318; Dorchester to Carondelet, Montreal, 24 August 1794, C.O. 42/104.

35. Whitaker, *Spanish-American Frontier*, pp. 163–70; Holmes, *Gayoso*, pp. 151–60.

36. Diary of an officer in the Indian camp opposed to Wayne, Glaize, 14 June 1794, Claus Papers, VI.

37. Bemis, *Jay's Treaty*, pp. 219–31; Jerald A. Combs, *The Jay Treaty: Political Battleground of the Founding Fathers*, pp. 137–48; Ephraim D. Adams, *The Influence of Grenville on Pitt's Foreign Policy, 1787–1798*, pp. 25–29.

38. Dundas to Dorchester, Whitehall, 5 July 1794, C.O. 42/98; Dundas to Simcoe, Whitehall, 4 July 1794, C.O. 42/318.

39. Marquis of Buckingham to Grenville, Weymouth, Eng., 10 August 1794, in Hist. MSS. Com., *Report on the Manuscripts of J. B. Fortescue, Esq., Preserved at Dropmore*, 2:614.

40. England to Simcoe, Detroit, 9 July 1794, in Cruikshank, *Simcoe Correspondence*, 2:314; Simcoe to England, 26 August 1794, ibid., 3:5; Jacobs, *Beginning of the U.S. Army*, pp. 168–70.

41. Wayne to Knox, Grand Glaize, 28 August 1794, Knopf, *Wayne Correspondence*, pp. 351–55; McKee to Joseph Chew, near Ft. Miamis, 27 August 1794, Cruikshank, *Simcoe Correspondence*, 3:7–8; Jacobs, *Beginning of the U.S. Army*, pp. 171–77.

42. Jacobs, *Tarnished Warrior*, p. 143.

43. Treaty of Greenville, 3 August 1795, Charles J. Kappler, ed., *Indian Affairs. Laws and Treaties*, 2:39–45.

44. Simcoe's reply to Indian nations assembled at the Wyandot village, 13 October 1794, C.O. 42/318; Simcoe to McKee, 25 October 1794, Claus Papers, VI.

45. Portland to Simcoe, Whitehall, 4 October 1794, C.O. 42/318; Dundas to Simcoe, Whitehall, 10 November 1794, ibid.

46. Simcoe to Clinton, Ft. Erie, 18 September 1794, Clinton Papers.

47. Simcoe to Portland, Kingston, 20 December 1794, C.O. 42/319; Peter Russell to Clinton, Niagara, 10 November 1794, Clinton Papers.

48. Edmund Randolph to Jay, Philadelphia, 18 August 1794, *ASP,FR*, I, 483; Samuel F. Bemis, *Pinckney's Treaty: America's Advantage from Europe's Distress, 1783–1800*, p. 245; Leland D. Baldwin, *Whiskey Rebels: The Story of a Frontier Uprising*, pp. 141, 299; *Times* (London), 22 October 1794.

49. Wayne to Henry Knox, Greenville, 29 January 1795, Knopf, *Wayne Correspondence*, p. 383.

50. Hawkesbury's comments on project of proposals to be made to M. Jay, 1794, Add. MSS. 38,354; memorial of the merchants of London trading to the province of Canada to Portland, 20 November 1794, Portland Manuscripts, 9908, University of Nottingham Library, Nottingham, England. Both Graham, "Indian Menace and the Retention of the Western Posts," p. 46, and Burt, *The United States, Britain, and British North America*, pp. 88–94, 132, overemphasize the importance the ministry placed on a possible Indian war in the Old Northwest.

51. Council at Canandaigua, 25 October 1794, Pickering Papers, LX.

52. Dorchester to Dundas, Quebec, 4 September 1794, W.O. 1/14.

53. Simcoe to Pitt, Plymouth, 30 November 1799, Grenville Papers.

54. Dorchester to Portland, Quebec, 25 April 1795, C.O. 42/101; Dundas to Dorchester, Whitehall, 5 July 1794, C.O. 42/98.

55. Conference at Tellico Block House between Blount and John Watts, Hanging Maw, and other chiefs of the Cherokee nation, 7–8 November 1794, *ASP,IA*, I, 538.

56. Pickering to Wayne, War Office, 30 June 1795, Knopf, *Wayne Correspondence*, p. 387; Wayne to Pickering, Greenville, 8 March 1795, ibid., pp. 387–88.

57. Blount to Knox, Knoxville, 3 November 1794, *ASP, IA*, I, 532.

58. John McDonald to McKee, Lower Cherokees, 26 December 1794, Upper Canada, Ind. Affairs, M.S. 19, F16, 1, P.A.C.

59. Bowles to Grenville, 5 June 1798, Cuba, leg. 2371, A.G.I.

60. Wright, "Dunmore's Loyalist Asylum," pp. 378–79.

61. Horsman, *Elliott*, pp. 95–99; 117–41.

62. Connolly to Dorchester, Quebec, 17 November 1794, C.O. 42/102.

63. Simcoe to Dorchester, Kingston, 9 March 1795, C.O. 42/319.

64. J. V. Campbell, "Account of a Plot for Obtaining the Lower Peninsula of Michigan from the United States in 1795," pp. 407–11; John Askin to John Askin, Jr., Detroit, 5 July 1795, in Milo M. Quaife, ed., *The John Askin Papers*, 1:550; [?] to Alexander Henry, Greenville, 8 August 1795, ibid., pp. 559–60.

65. Morris to Patrick Colquhoun, Philadelphia, 22 December 1794, Robert Morris Papers, IX, Library of Congress, Washington, D.C.

66. Morris's land speculations are discussed in Shaw Livermore, *Early American Land Companies: Their Influence on Corporate Development*, pp. 162–74; and Aaron M. Sakolski, *The Great American Land Bubble: The Amazing Story of Land-Grabbing, Speculations, and Booms from Colonial Days to the Present Time*, pp. 57–63, 142–49, 158–65.

CHAPTER 7

1. E. Wilson Lyon, *Louisiana in French Diplomacy, 1759–1804*, pp. 79–86.

2. Georges H. Victor Collot, *A Journey in North America, Containing a Survey of the Countries Watered by the Mississippi, Ohio, Missouri, and Other Affluing Rivers*, 2:55ff.

3. James A. James, *The Life of George Rogers Clark*, p. 437.

4. LeClerc de Milfort, *Memoir, or A Quick Glance at My Various Travels and My Sojourn in the Creek Nation*, pp. 99–103.

5. Portland to Simcoe, Whitehall, 24 October 1795, C.O. 42/319; Portland to Dorchester, Whitehall, 4 December 1795, C.O. 42/104.

6. Robert Liston to Grenville, Philadelphia, 6 September 1796, F.O. 115/5; Crown to Bute, Downing Street, 3 June 1796, F.O. 72/41.

7. Simcoe to Portland, Navy Hall, 17 May 1795, Canada, Public Archives, *Report, 1891*, p. 71.

8. Stevenson to Dundas in Stevenson to Portland, Portman Square, London, 1 April 1796, C.O. 42/320.

9. Ira Allen to Portland, London, 19 March 1796, C.O. 42/107.

10. George Morgan to McKee, Prospect, N.J., 16 April 1796, Claus Papers, VII. Other than insisting that Morgan was a strong nationalist, Max Savelle, *George Morgan, Colony Builder*, pp. 227–29, has little to say about Morgan after the downfall in the early 1790s of his colony at New Madrid.

11. St. Clair to James Ross, Pittsburgh, 6 September 1796, Smith, *St. Clair Papers*, 2:411.

12. William Tatham to John King, 15 November 1796, C.O. 42/107; G. Melvin Herndon, *William Tatham and the Culture of Tobacco*, pp. 370–76.

13. Romayne to Pulteney, Guilford St., 23 December 1795, Melville Papers, Clements Library.

14. [?] to [?] (copy made by George Chalmers), Nassau, 1 January 1796, C.O. 23/34.

15. Oliver Wolcott to Oliver Wolcott, Jr., 21 November 1796, William Plumer, Jr., *Life of William Plumer*, p. 283.

16. William Knox to New Brunswick Committee, Soho Square, London, 2 September 1795, William Knox Papers, VIII.

17. Hawkesbury to Bond, London, 14 January 1796, Add. MSS. 38,310.

18. Timothy Dwight to a friend, 1793, in Plumer, *Life of Plumer*, p. 283.

19. Duc de La Rochefoucauld Liancourt, *Travels through the United States of North America, the Country of the Iroquois, and Upper Canada, in the Years 1795, 1796, and 1797*, 2:478.

20. Robert Prescott to Robert Liston, Quebec, 1 December 1796, C.O. 42/108.

21. Burt, *United States, Britain, and British North America*, p. 177; Portland to Peter Hunter, 10 February 1801, Despatches from the Colonial Office to the Governor General, LIII, P.A.C.

22. Isaac Ogden to Prince Edward Augustus, Duke of Kent, New York, 3 April 1797, C.O. 217–71; Pickering to Rufus King, Dept. of State, 15 February 1797, in Manning, *Diplomatic Correspondence, Canada*, 1:101; Liston to Grenville, Philadelphia, 2 April 1798, F.O. 115/6.

23. Ira Allen to Portland, London, 19 March 1796, C.O. 42/107; Simcoe to Portland, 11 December 1796, C.O. 42/320.

24. John White to Herman W. Ryland, 19 December 1796, C.O. 42/108; Burt, *United States, Britain, and British North America*, pp. 170–73.

25. Miller, *Federalist Era*, pp. 126–28, 198–202.

26. Hamilton to King, New York, 22 August 1798, in Charles R. King, ed., *The Life and Correspondence of Rufus King, Comprising His Letters Private and Official, His Public Documents, and His Speeches*, 2:659; Gilbert L. Lycan, *Alexander Hamilton and American Foreign Policy: A Design for Greatness*, pp. 373–90.

27 T Pickering to Rebecca Pickering, Washington, 16 December 1814, Pickering Papers, III; John Temple to marquis of Carmarthen, 7 December 1786, F.O. 4/4.

28. Portland to Simcoe, Whitehall, 24 October 1795, C.O. 42/319.

29. William H. Masterson, *William Blount*, pp. 296–98.

30. Romayne to Blount, New York, 15 March 1797, U. S. Congress, *The Debates and Proceedings in the Congress of the United States . . . Fifth Congress*, pp. 2344–45.

31. Deposition of Romayne, 15–20 July 1797, ibid., p. 2361; Romayne to William Pulteney, New York, 12 June 1798, Melville Papers, Clements Library.

32. Romayne to Blount, 15 March 1797, *Debates and Proceedings . . . Fifth Congress*, pp. 2344–45.

33. Russell to Simcoe, Niagara, 22 September 1796, Ernest A. Cruikshank and Andrew F. Hunter, eds., *The Correspondence of the Honourable Peter Russell, with Allied Documents Relating to His Administration of the Government of Upper Canada during the Official Term of Lieut.-Governor J. G. Simcoe, While on Leave of Absence*, 1:40; Oche Haujo to Benjamin Hawkins[?], Tuckabatchee, 27 May 1798, Supt. Gen. and Insp. Gen., R.G. 10, A, 5b, P.A.C.

34. Deposition of John Franklin, 2 September 1797, *Debates and Proceedings . . . Fifth Congress*, pp. 2380–81.

35. Liston to Grenville, Philadelphia, 15 February 1797, F.O. 115/5.

36. Liston to Grenville, Philadelphia, 17 February 1797, W.O. 1/746; Liston to Grenville, Philadelphia, 16 March 1797, F.O. 115/5; Liston to Hammond, Philadelphia, 8 April 1797, Sir Robert Liston Papers, 5593, N.L.S.

37. Robert Prescott to Portland, Quebec, 18 February 1797, C.O. 42/108.

38. Chisholm to Isaac Shelby, Knoxville, 24 January 1795, Kings Mountain Papers, Draper MSS., 11 DD.

39. Rogers C. Harlan, "A Military History of East Florida during the Governorship of Enrique White: 1796–1811," pp. 135–36.

40. Memorandum, 1797, Cochrane Papers.

41. Ebenezer Jacob to Dundas, 28 December 1797, Melville Papers, N.L.S.; ibid., 7 January 1798.

42. Arthur P. Whitaker, "The Muscle Shoals Speculation, 1783–1789," pp. 365–86; Masterson, *Blount*, pp. 71–74, 268; Arthur Campbell to Pickering, 7 August 1797, Pickering Papers, XXI.

43. Malmesbury's notes on conference with French, 8 July 1797, in James Harris, 1st earl of Malmesbury, *Diaries and Correspondence of James Harris, First Earl of Malmesbury*, 3:370; Malmesbury to Pitt, Lille, 16 July 1797, ibid., pp. 384–85.

44. Blount to Carey, 21 April 1797, *Debates and Proceedings . . . Fifth Congress*, pp. 2349–50.

45. Masterson, *Blount*, pp. 315–23, 339.

46. Liston to Hammond, Philadelphia, 7 September 1797, Liston Papers.

47. Chisholm to Melville, Newgate, London, 9 October 1797, Melville Papers, N.L.S., XXIV; report of examination of Chisholm by Rufus King, · London, 9 December 1797, in Frederick J. Turner, ed., "Documents on the Blount Conspiracy, 1795–1797," p. 604.

48. Ibid.; Chisholm to Rufus King, London, 29 November 1797, ibid., pp. 595–600.

49. Deposition of Romayne, 15–20 July 1797, *Debates and Proceedings . . . Fifth Congress*, p. 2362.

50. Grenville to Liston, Downing St., 8 April 1797, F.O. 115/5.

51. Pickering to Samuel Sitgreaves, Abraham Baldwin, Robert G. Harper et al., Philadelphia, 26 July 1797, Pickering Papers, VI.

52. King to Grenville, London, 25 August 1797, Grenville Papers.

53. Liston to Hammond[?], Philadelphia, 8 April 1797, Liston Papers; Liston to Grenville, Philadelphia, 15 February 1797, F.O. 115/5; Prescott to Portland, Quebec, 18 February 1797, C.O. 42/108; Liston to [?], 10 May 1797, Liston Papers.

54. Liston to Grenville, Philadelphia, 10 May 1797, F.O. 115/5.

55. Miller, *Federalist Era*, pp. 205–8.

56. Examination of David McLane, Montreal, 22 May 1797, C.O. 42/109; William Kingsford, *The History of Canada*, 7:439–55; *Quebec Gazette*, 13 July 1797; ibid., 27 July 1797.

57. Pickering to Andrew Ellicott, Dept. of State, 28 July 1797, Pickering Papers, XXXVII; Pickering to Arthur Campbell, Philadelphia, 18 August 1797, Pickering Papers, VII.

58. Edward Winslow, Jr., to [?], Boston, 17 August 1797, Winslow Papers, VII.

59. Morton Eden to G. Morris, Vienna, 24 December 1796, Gouverneur Morris Papers, Columbia University Library, New York City; Howard Swiggett, *The Extraordinary Mr. Morris*, p. 313.

60. Morris to Washington, London, 3 July 1795, Grenville Papers.

61. Hamilton to Rufus King, 22 August 1798, in King, *Correspondence of King*, 2:659.

62. Andrew Ellicott to Pickering, Natchez, 14 November 1797, Pickering Papers, XXI.

63. *Morning Post and Gazetteer* (London), 26 October 1798.

64. Pickering to Rufus King, Philadelphia, 2 April 1798, Pickering Papers, VIII.

65. Portland to John Wentworth, Whitehall, 3 September 1798, C.O. 217/69.

66. Pickering to John Adams, Trenton, 11 September 1798, Pickering Papers, XXXVII.

67. Grenville to Liston, Downing St., 8 June 1798, F.O. 115/6.

68. Pickering to Richard Alsop, Trenton, 10 September 1798, Pickering Papers, IX.

69. William Sabatier to Dundas. Westminster, London, 9 May 1799, Melville Papers, XXXII, N.L.S.; Bowles to Grenville, 5 June 1798, Cuba, leg. 2371, A.G.I.

70. Wright, *Bowles*, pp. 95–103.

71. Portland to Russell, Whitehall, 7 June 1798, Despatches from Colonial Office to Governor General, LIII, P.A.C.; Prescott to John Johnson, Quebec, 18 February 1799, Claus Papers, XV.

CHAPTER 8

1. Burt, in *The United States, Great Britain, and British North America*, and Bradford Perkins in his trilogy consisting of *The First Rapprochement: England and the United States, 1795–1805, Prologue to War: England and the United States, 1805–1812*, and *Castlereagh and Adams: England and the United States, 1812–1823*, emphasize Anglo-American collaboration even after 1800.

2. James M. Banner, Jr., *To the Hartford Convention: The Federalists and the Origins of Party Politics in Massachusetts, 1789–1815*, pp. 35–52; Samuel E. Morison, *Harrison Gray Otis, 1765–1848: The Urbane Federalist*, pp. x, 354–70.

3. Wentworth to John King, Halifax, 21 December 1799, C.O. 217/73.

4. Winslow[?] to [?], Fredericton, N.B., 21 June 1800, Winslow Papers, VIII, P.A.C.

5. William Cobbett to William Gifford, 4 November 1799, Gifts 30–8/124; observations respecting the Canada road, 1801, Winslow Papers, VIII.

6. Franco-Spanish Treaty, San Ildefonso, 1 October 1800, Davenport and Paullin, *European Treaties*, 4:181–82.

7. Henry Dundas' memorandum for the consideration of His Majesty's ministers, Wimbledon, Eng., 31 March 1800, Gifts 30–8/243; Ralph Abercromby to Dundas, Edinburgh, 20 November 1799, Melville Papers, Clements Library.

8. Windham to [?], 5 October 1799, Add. MSS. 37,878.

9. Dundas' memorandum, 31 March 1800, Gifts 30–8/243; Dundas to Miranda, 30 June 1800, Melville Papers, Clements Library.

10. Simcoe to Pitt, Plymouth, 30 November 1799, Gifts 30–8/222.

11. Stevenson to Windham, 27 Adams St., 8 May 1802, Add. MSS. 37,880.

12. Simcoe to John King, Plymouth, 25 January 1800, Simcoe Papers, folder 9, P.A.C.

13. Hunter to Portland, Quebec, 28 December 1799, C.O. 42/325; Addington to John Sullivan, Treasury, 26 May 1802, C.O. 42/330.

14. Dundas' memorandum, 31 March 1800, Gifts, 30–8/243.

15. Carlos De Vilemont to Nathaniel Folsom, Arkansas Post, 21 June 1800, Winthrop Sargent Papers, V, Massachusetts Historical Society, Boston.

16. Bowles's proclamation, Apalachicola, 26 November 1799, Add. MSS. 37,878.

17. John King to James Jackson, St. Marys, Ga., 12 July 1800, East and West Fla., 1764–1850, Georgia Department of Archives and History, Atlanta.

18. James, *Antebellum Natchez*, pp. 72–77, 101–4.

19. Bowles to[?], Kingston, 14 July 1799, Cuba, leg. 212B, A.G.I.

20. Ernst, *King*, p. 269.

21. Hawkesbury to R. King, Downing St., 7 May 1802, Manning, *Diplomatic Correspondence, Canada*, 1:532.

22. Bowles to Reeves, Portsmouth, 1 March 1799, Add. MSS. 37,878.

23. John F. D. Smyth Stuart to Dundas, 25 February, 27 March 1798, Hist. MSS Com., *Report on the Manuscripts of Earl Bathurst, Preserved at Cirencester Park*, p. 23.

24. Arthur Wellesley, memorandum, 18 November 1806, in Arthur Wellesley, First Duke of Wellington, *Supplementary Despatches and Memoranda of Field Marshal Arthur, Duke of Wellington, K.G.*, 6:35–38; ibid., 20 November 1806, p. 42.

25. Thomas McKee to William Claus, Sandwich, 15 August 1800, Claus Papers, VIII; George Ironside to William Claus, Amherstburg, 12 June 1801, Supt. Gen. and Insp. Gen., R.G. 10, A, 5b, P:A.C.

26. Ironside to Prideaux Selby, Amherstburg, 15 June 1801, Claus Papers, VIII; William Claus to Selby, Ft. George, 14 September 1801, ibid.; Brant to Johnson, Grand River, November 1801, Stone, *Brant*, 2:408.

27. Bowles to John Adams, Wekiva, 31 October 1799, Add. MSS. 37,878; Bowles to Reeves, Apalachicola, 26 November 1799, ibid.

28. Liston to Grenville, Philadelphia, 13 December 1799, F.O. 115/7.

29. Act for Preservation of Peace with the Indian Tribes, 17 January 1800, in U. S. Congress, *The Public Statutes at Large of the United States of America, from the Organization of the Government in 1789 to March 3, 1845*, 2:6–7.

30. Pitt to Dundas, Park Place, London, 2 October 1801, Pitt Papers, III, William L. Clements Library, Ann Arbor, Mich.

31. Grenville's speech in House of Lords, 3 November 1801, in Cobbett, *Parliamentary History*, 36:163–71.

32. John Bowles, *Reflections at the Conclusion of the War: Being a Sequel to "Reflections on the Political and Moral State of Society, at the Close of the Eighteenth Century."*

33. Cobbett to William Gifford, 4 November 1799, Gifts 30–8/124.

34. Cobbett to Windham, 27 March 1803, Add. MSS. 37/853.

35. Cobbett to Hawkesbury, 27 March 1802, ibid.

36. Cobbett to Windham, 23 November 1802, ibid.

37. Cobbett to Windham, 22 August 1802, ibid.

38. Windham to[?], Pall Mall, 3 November 1802, Add. MSS. 37,881.

39. Edward Cooke to Lord Castlereagh, London, 6 April 1802, in Charles Vane, marquis of Londonderry, ed., *Memoir and Correspondence of Viscount Castlereagh, Second Marques of Londonderry*, 5:40.

40. Malmesbury, *Harris Diaries and Correspondence*, 8 April 1802, 4:64–66.

41. Proceedings in Parliament, 3 May 1802, *Gentleman's Magazine*, 72 (1802), 764.

42. Cooke to Castlereagh, 6 April 1802, Londonderry, *Correspondence of Castlereagh*, 5:38, Hawkesbury to Rufus King, Downing St., 7 May 1802, Manning, *Diplomatic Correspondence, Canada*, 1:532.

43. Sheffield to George Chalmers[?], Sheffield Place, 21 December 1802, Add. MSS. 22,901.

44. Charles Whitworth to Hawkesbury, Paris, 16 December 1802, in Charles Whitworth, *England and Napoleon in 1803: Being the Despatches of Lord Whitworth and Others*, pp. 28–29; John H. Frere to Hawkesbury, Madrid, 27 January 1803, F.O. 72/48.

45. Lord St. Vincent, Thomas Troubridge, and John Markham to Adm. Edward Thornbrough, 31 March 1803, Adm. 1/4353.

46. Peter Russell to William Henry Clinton, York, 16 May 1803, Clinton Papers.

47. Jefferson to Robert R. Livingston, Washington, D.C., 18 April 1802, in Paul L. Ford, ed., *The Works of Thomas Jefferson*, 9:365.

48. Rufus King to Madison, London, 2 April 1803, Manning, *Diplomatic Correspondence, Canada*, 1:552; Madison to Livingston and James Monroe, Dept. of State, 28 May 1803, Pickering Papers, LIV.

49. Extract from *Philadelphia Daily Advertiser* in *Quebec Gazette*, 20 January 1803.

50. Pickering's speech in the House of Representatives, 26 and 28 February 1814, Pickering Papers, XLIX.

51. *Times* (London), 28 August 1802.

52. Malmesbury to Thomas Pelham, Park Place, 20 March 1803, Add. MSS. 33,111.

53. W. [?] A. to Charles Williamson, New York, 4 March 1803, Grenville Papers; [?] to Williamson, 18 May 1803, ibid. Evidence concerning Burr's western schemes at any period is sketchy or nonexistent, and the 1802–3 period is no exception. W.[?] A., who may have written both of these letters, was a New Yorker and a mutual friend of Charles Williamson and Burr. Williamson was Henry Dundas's confidant and advisor on American affairs. Several years later Williamson without question was Burr's most important contact with the British government, and, though the evidence is sketchy, there seems little doubt that Williamson acted as Burr's intermediary with the ministry during the winter of 1802–3.

54. William Plumer to[?], Epping, New Hampshire, 20 December 1828, in Henry Adams, ed., *Documents Relating to New-England Federalism, 1800–1815*, pp. 145–46; Pickering to Richard Peters, Washington, D.C., 24 December 1803, ibid., p. 338; Lynn W. Turner, *William Plumer of New Hampshire, 1759–1850*, pp. 134–42; Banner, *To the Hartford Convention*, p. 116.

55. Lord Selkirk's diary, II, 7 October–14 November 1803, Earl of Selkirk Papers, LXXIV, P.A.C.; Selkirk to Grenville, St. Mary's Isle, 15 October 1806, in John P. Pritchett, "Selkirk's Views on British Policy toward the Spanish-American Colonies, 1806," p. 393.

56. Wright, *Bowles*, pp. 162–68.

57. Rufus King to Livingston, London, 7 May 1803, Pickering Papers, LIV; Hawkesbury to Rufus King, 19 May 1803, ibid.

58. *Times* (London), 15 September 1803.

59. J. Leitch Wright, Jr., *Anglo-Spanish Rivalry in North America*, pp. 177–78.

60. Louis N. Baudry des Lozières, *Second voyage à la Louisiane, faisant suite au premier de l'auteur de 1794–98. Contenant la vie militaire du général Grondel . . . qui commanda long-temps à la Louisiane*, and George Orr, *The Possession of Louisiana by the French, Considered, as it Affects the Interests of Those Nations More Immediately Concerned, viz. Great Britain, America, Spain and Portugal*, exemplify contemporary literature treating Louisiana's fate.

61. Alexander Stephens, ed., *The Life of General W. A. Bowles, A Native of America—Born of English Parents in Frederick County, Maryland, in the Year 1764*.

CHAPTER 9

1. Isaac J. Cox, *The West Florida Controversy, 1798–1813: A Study in American Diplomacy*, pp. 81–87.

2. John Norton to Melville, Fulham, 20 October 1804, Melville Papers, 3848, N.L.S.

3. John H. Frere to Hawkesbury, Madrid, 14 May 1804, F.O. 72/152; *Gentleman's Magazine*, 74 (Supplement, 1804), 1232.

4. Cameron to Edward Cooke, New Providence, 4 September 1808, C.O. 23/55.

5. William C. C. Claiborne to James Madison, New Orleans, 10 May 1805, in Dunbar Rowland, ed., *Official Letter Books of W. C. C. Claiborne, 1801–1816*, 3:52.

6. William Jacob's "Plans for Occupying Spanish America," 26 October 1804, Gifts 30–8/345.

7. John Forbes to Henry Dearborn, Pensacola, 5 September 1806, *ASP,IA*, I, 750–751; ibid., Feb. 7, 1807, 751.

8. Privy Council to John King, Council Office, Whitehall, 8 August 1805, P.C. 2/168.

9. Thomas Dunn to Anthony Merry, 15 November 1805, C.O. 42/192.

10. Burt, *United States, Britain, and British North America*, pp. 185–98.

11. Selkirk's diary, 21 February–4 June 1804, Selkirk Papers, IV; Ernst, *King*, pp. 280–81; Henry Adams, *History of the United States of America*, 2:160–66.

12. Thomas P. Abernethy, *The Burr Conspiracy*, pp. 24–32.

13. Merry to Hawkesbury, Washington, 1 March 1804, F.O. 115/12; Adams, *History of the U.S.*, 2:391.

14. Selkirk's diary, 21 February–4 June 1804, Selkirk Papers, IV; Charles J. Fox to [?], Arlington St., 1803–6, North Papers, Bodleian Library, Oxford, England.

15. Plumer to Bradbury Cilley, 5 January 1804, in Plumer, *Life of Plumer*, p. 285.

16. Jedidiah Morse to Plumer, 3 February 1804, ibid., p. 289.

17. Pickering to Theodore Lyman, Washington, 14 March 1804, Pickering Papers, XIV.

18. Williamson to [?], Lancaster Square, London, 9 October 1804, Gifts 30–8/190; Abernethy, *Burr Conspiracy*, pp. 15–16, W. [?] A. to Williamson, New York, 4 March 1803, Grenville Papers.

19. Grenville to Selkirk, London, 15 November 1806, in Pritchett, "Selkirk's Views," p. 396; Melville to Castlereagh, Dunera, 8 June 1808, in Londonderry, *Correspondence of Castlereagh*, 7:446–47.

20. "State of that part of the United States of N. America laying beyond the Alleghenny Mountains," 1 January 1806, Add. MSS. 37,885.

21. Robert S. Milnes to Earl of Camden, Quebec, 24 May 1805, C.O. 42/127.

22. [?] to [?], 1 February 1804[?], C.O. 42/126; *Quebec Gazette*, 27 November 1806.

23. William W. Kaufmann, *British Policy and the Independence of Latin America, 1804–1828*, pp. 23–24.

24. Howick to Cochrane, Admiralty, 3 June 1806, Cochrane Papers, 2571; William Ocn to Cochrane, Admiralty, 19 July 1806, ibid.

25. Selkirk's observations on South America (delivered to Windham and Grenville), 1806, Selkirk Papers, LII.

26. Howick to Cochrane, Admiralty, 19 July 1806, Cochrane Papers, 2571.

27. Cochrane to Thomas Grenville, *Northumberland*, at sea, 20 April 1807, Cochrane Papers, 2297; George Berkeley to Bathurst[?], Halifax, N.S., 13 August 1807, Hist. MSS Com., *Bathurst MSS.*, pp. 63–64.

28. Cochrane to Grenville, 20 April 1807, Cochrane Papers, 2297.

29. William Knox to New Brunswick Committee, Ealing, 7 September 1808, William Knox Papers, VIII.

30. W. Cottnam Yonge to Maj. Gen. Skerrett, Halifax, 12 October 1807, C.O. 217/81; Knox to Cooke, Ealing, Eng., 27 January 1808, William Knox Papers, VIII.

31. [?] to Lords Commissioners of the Admiralty, Downing St., 13 February 1808, C.O. 217/84.

32. Liverpool's speech in House of Lords, 5 May 1812, in Thomas C. Hansard, ed., *The Parliamentary Debates*, 23:14–17.

33. Prevost to Castlereagh, Halifax, N.S., 17 June 1808, C.O. 217/83; Prevost to Edward Cooke, 18 June 1808, ibid.; *Aaron Burr's Celebrated Cipher Letter and Key*, broadside, Aaron Burr Papers, Personal Miscellaneous, Box 2, N.Y.P.L.

34. Williamson to Burr, off Cadiz, 19 June 1808, in Aaron Burr, *The Private Journal of Aaron Burr, during his Residence of Four Years in Europe, with Selections from His Correspondence*, 1:24; Williamson to Melville, Devon, Eng., 16 January 1808, MSS. 8886, N.L.S.; Williamson to Melville, 5 February 1808, ibid.

35. Ernst, *King*, p. 281.

36. Berkeley to Bathurst, September 1807, Canada, Public Archives, *Report, 1910*, pp. 85–86.

37. Williamson to Melville, Devon, 16 January 1808, MSS. 8886, N.L.S.; Williamson to Dundas, Craven St., London, 4 May 1808, Melville Papers, Clements Library; Melville to Castlereagh, Dunira, 8 June 1808, Londonderry, *Correspondence of Castlereagh*, 7:446–47.

38. Girod to Wentworth, Halifax, N.S., 28 May 1808, C.O. 217/82.

39. Prevost to Cooke, Halifax, N.S., 27 April 1808, C.O. 217/82; Howe's report in Prevost to Cooke, Halifax, N.S., 19 May 1809, C.O. 217/85; memorial to Canning, London, 15 December 1807, *ASP, Public Lands*, II, 595.

40. Charles E. A. Gayarré, *History of Louisiana*, 4:204–5, 212.

41. Wentworth to Castlereagh, Halifax, N.S., 19 September 1807, C.O. 217/81; *The Royal Gazette and Bahama Advertiser* (Nassau), 17 October 1807.

42. Portland to George III, 21 April 1808, Portland MSS. 4117; Castlereagh to Portland, 24 April 1808, ibid., 8584.

43. Castlereagh to Williamson, Downing St., 4 June 1808, Londonderry, *Correspondence of Castlereagh*, 6:369; Castlereagh to Duke of Manchester, Downing St., 4 June 1804, ibid., p. 368.

44. Claus to Lt. Col. Green, Ft. George, 24 July 1805, Supt. Gen. and Insp. Gen., R.G. 10, X, P.A.C.; J. Dunham to Dr. Wheelock, Ft. Michilimackinac, 24 July 1807, *Quebec Gazette*, 8 October 1807.

45. Gore to Castlereagh, York, Upper Can., 7 October 1807, C.O. 42/347.

46. Joseph Cheniguy to Robert Peel, London, 10 May 1812, C.O. 42/148.

47. Meriwether Lewis to Henry Dearborn, St. Louis, 20 August 1808, in Carter, *Territorial Papers*, 14:213.

48. William Wells to Dearborn, Ft. Wayne, 5 December 1807, ibid., 7:498–99; *Gentleman's Magazine*, 77 (1807), 968.

49. Diary or narrative, by a British subject, of a journey from New York City ... to Niagara Falls, 6 August–6 September 1808, N.Y.P.L.

50. Craig to Gore, Quebec, 28 December 1807, *MPHC*, 25 (1898), 230; Claus to Gore, Amherstburg, 27 February 1808, Claus Papers, IX.

51. Craig to Gore, 11 May 1808, Canada, Public Archives, *Report*, 1893, pp. 9–10.

52. William Hull to Dearborn, Detroit, 24 November 1807, *ASP,IA*, I, 746.

53. Gore to Craig, York, Upper Can., 5 January 1808, C.O. 42/136; Claus to Gore, Amherstburg, 27 February 1808, Claus Papers, IX.

54. Craig to Castlereagh, Quebec, 15 July 1808, C.O. 42/136; Horsman, *Elliott*, pp. 163–69.

55. Gore to Craig, York, Upper Can., 27 July 1808, Supt. Gen. and Insp. Gen., R.G. 10, XI, P.A.C.; Elliott to Claus, Amherstburg, 28 June 1809, ibid.; Wellbank to Alexander McKee, Cherokee Nation, 12 April 1794, Claus Papers, VI.

56. John Johnson to Claus, York, Upper Can., 29 January 1808, ibid., X.

57. Gore's speech to the western confederacy, Amherstburg, 11 July 1808, ibid., XI.

58. Gore to Craig, York, Upper Can., 27 July 1808, ibid.

59. Gore to Craig, York, Upper Can., 20 February 1809, *MPHC*, 15 (1888), 15; Claus to Gore, Amherstburg, 20 April 1808, Canada, Public Archives, *Report, 1893*, p. 8.

60. Williamson to Gen. James Robertson, London, 7 December 1807, MSS. 8886, N.L.S.

61. Wright, *Anglo-Spanish Rivalry*, pp. 166–70.

62. Burr to Jeremy Bentham, London, 14 October 1808, in Burr, *Burr Journal*, 1:70.

63. Gayarré, *Louisiana*, 4:204–12.

CHAPTER 10

1. Liverpool to Craig, London, 4 April 1810, Add. MSS. 38,323.

2. Samuel E. Morison, "The Henry-Crillon Affair of 1812," pp. 267–80.

3. Liverpool's speech, House of Lords, 5 May 1812, in Hansard, *Parliamentary Debates*, 23:14–17; *Times* (London), 29 April, 1 May, and 6 May 1812.

4. Craig to Castlereagh, Quebec, 10 April 1808, C.O. 42/136.

5. Tecumseh's speech, Amherstburg, 15 November 1810, Supt. Gen. and Insp. Gen., R.G. 10, A, 5b, P.A.C. The most recent biography of Tecumseh is Glenn Tucker, *Tecumseh, Vision of Glory*.

6. Craig to Liverpool, Quebec, 29 March 1811, C.O. 42/143; Gore to Claus, York, Upper Can., 26 February 1811, C.O. 42/351.

7. Horsman, *Elliott*, pp. 173–74.

8. *Gentleman's Magazine*, 82 (1812), 79; Tucker, *Tecumseh*, pp. 218–29.

9. Brock to Prevost, York, Upper Can., 25 February 1812, in William C. H. Wood, ed., *Select British Documents of the Canadian War of 1812*, 1:170; Brock to Liverpool, York, Upper Can., 25 May 1812, Hist. MSS Com., *Bathurst MSS.*, p. 175.

10. Cox, *West Florida Controversy*, pp. 83–101.

11. *Gentleman's Magazine*, 80 (1810), 170; Charles Roberts to Capt. Byng, Amelia Island, 27 July 1810, Adm. 1/500.

12. Jefferson to John W. Eppes, Monticello, 5 January 1811, Richard K.

Murdoch, "A British Report on West Florida and Louisiana, November, 1812," p. 36.

13. Luis de Onís to Eusebio Bardaxi y Azara, Philadelphia, 31 January 1811, estado, leg. 5637, A.H.N.; Cox, *West Florida Controversy*, p. 523.

14. Rembert W. Patrick, *Florida Fiasco: Rampant Rebels on the Georgia-Florida Border, 1810–1815*, pp. 55–69.

15. John P. Morier to Robert Smith, Washington, 15 December 1810, in Great Britain, Foreign Office, *British and Foreign State Papers*, 5:739–40.

16. Fagan Lenox and Co. to John W. Croker, Liverpool, 21 February 1811, Adm. 1/4356; Richard Wellesley to Henry Wellesley, Foreign Office, 22 January 1810, F.O. 72/93.

17. Warren to Croker, Halifax, N.S., 31 August 1810, Adm. 1/500; Juan José de Estrada to Thomas Thomson, St. Augustine, 15 April 1812, Adm. 1/502; Onís to Warren, Philadelphia, 25 November 1813, Cochrane Papers, 2337.

18. Augustus Foster to Wellesley, Washington, 5 August 1811, F.O. 115/22; *Bahama Gazette* (Nassau), 9 April 1812.

19. Joseph Hibberson to Wellesley, Liverpool, 5 January 1811, F.O. 72/125; James Wallace to Morier, Savannah, 28 January 1811, F.O. 115/22.

20. Morier to Crown, Washington, 3 December 1810, F.O. 115/21.

21. Anne C. Morris, ed., *The Diary and Letters of Gouverneur Morris, Minister of the United States to France, Member of the Constitutional Convention, etc.*, 16 April 1812, 2:538; Patrick, *Florida Fiasco*, pp. 120–27.

22. John Innerarity to Mr. Sanderson, Pensacola, 23 November 1810, West Florida Papers, V, L.C.

23. John Forbes to Hibberson, St. Augustine, 18 September 1810, F.O. 72/125.

24. Hopoiethle Micco to George III, Apalachicola River, 1 September 1811, C.O. 23/58; William V. Munnings to Hopoiethle Micco, Nassau, 9 December 1811, C.O. 23/58; Crown to Munnings, Downing St., 29 February 1812, C.O. 23/58.

25. Thomas Brown to Liverpool, Strand, London, 6 December 1810, C.O. 23/57.

26. Testimony of Tus-te-nuck-o-chee, 22 August 1883, Tecumseh Papers, Draper MSS., 4YY; Tucker, *Tecumseh*, pp. 195–214.

27. Perkins, *Prologue to War*, pp. 300–417.

28. J. Mackay Hitsman, *The Incredible War of 1812: A Military History*, pp. 62–76.

29. Prevost to Bathurst, Montreal, 5 October 1812, C.O. 42/147; memorial of Canadian merchants to Prevost, Montreal, 14 October 1812, C.O. 42/159; Prevost to Robert Dickson, Quebec, 14 January 1813, *MPHC*, 15 (1888), 221.

30. Smyth Stuart memorial, 16 March 1813, Add. MSS. 38,363.

31. Francis Armstrong to Duke of Sussex, 14 July 1812, in Francis Arm-

strong, *Letters to His Royal Highness the Duke of Sussex, relative to His Majesty, and Other Important Matters*, pp. 13–14.

32. Brock to Prevost, Ft. George, 7 September 1812, *MPHC*, 15 (1888), 140; Brock to Prevost, York, 28 September 1812, Wood, *Canadian War Documents*, 1:596.

33. Elliott to Brock, Amherstburg, 12 January 1812, ibid., p. 282; Hawkins to Tustunnuggee Thlucco, Oche Haujo, and Upper Creek Chiefs, Creek Agency, 29 March 1813, *ASP,IA*, I, 839.

34. George S. Smyth to Liverpool, St. John, N.B., 4 July 1812, C.O. 188/18.

35. Liverpool to Smyth, Downing St., 30 September 1812, C.O. 188/18.

36. Liverpool to John Gladstone, Fife House, 28 July 1813, Add. MSS. 38,253.

37. Andrew Allen to Herbert Sawyer, Boston, 18 July 1812, Adm. 1/502; Mr. Chetwynd to Croker, Whitehall, 8 December 1812, Adm. 1/4358.

38. Seward Porter to Warren and John Sherbrooke, in Warren to Bathurst, Halifax, N.S., 26 November 1813, C.O. 217/92.

39. G. Morris to Harrison G. Otis, 29 April 1813, Morison, *Otis*, pp. 84–85.

40. Allen to Sherbrooke, Boston, 23 July 1812, C.O. 217/89.

41. Warren to Melville, Upper Grosvenor St., London, 8 August 1812, John B. Warren Papers, National Maritime Museum, Greenwich, England.

42. David D. Roche to Bathurst, Cork, Ire., 14 January 1813, C.O. 42/152.

43. Hawkins to Tustunnuggee Thlucco, Oche Haujo, and Upper Creek Chiefs, Creek Agency, 29 March 1813, *ASP,IA*, I, 839.

44. Patrick, *Florida Fiasco*, pp. 179–236.

45. Johnson to Claus, Montreal, 16 March 1813, *MPHC*, 15 (1888), 260; Edward Handfield to Cameron, Nassau, 28 October 1813, C.O. 23/60.

46. Castlereagh to Wellesley, Foreign Office, 9 September 1812, F.O. 72/128.

47. Henry S. Halbert and Timothy H. Ball, *The Creek War of 1813 and 1814*, p. 243; letter from Ft. Stoddert, 22 August 1812, *National Intelligencer*, 19 September 1812, in Murdoch, "British Report," p. 41.

48. Warren to Melville, Halifax, 11 November 1812, Warren Papers; unsigned draft, 1812[?], Cochrane Papers.

49. Onís to Antonio Cano Manuel, Philadelphia, 31 December 1813, estado, leg. 5557, expediente 1, A.H.N.

50. Anthony Baker to Castlereagh, Washington, 31 October 1812, C.O. 42/149; Herbert Aptheker, *American Negro Slave Revolts*, pp. 249–51, 254.

51. John Windship to William Plumer, Jr., State of Louisiana, 1 November 1813, in Everett S. Brown, ed., "Letters from Louisiana, 1813–1814," p. 571.

52. Warren to Duke of Buckingham, Chesapeake Bay, 2 May 1813, Huntington Library; Warren to Melville, Halifax, N.S., 18 November 1812, Warren Papers.

53. *Gentleman's Magazine*, 83 (1813), 278; ibid., p. 491.

54. Alexander Murray to Liverpool, London, 11 December 1809, C.O. 23/56; Murray to Liverpool, Nassau, 24 January 1812, C.O. 23/59.

55. Liverpool to Wellington, Fife House, 7 October 1812, Wellington, *Supplementary Despatches*, 7:445.

56. Sheffield to Charles Abbot, Sheffield Place, 6 November 1812, Charles Abbot, ed., *The Diary and Correspondence of Charles Abbot, Lord Colchester*, 2:409.

57. John K. Mahon, *The War of 1812*, p. 202.

58. Alexander Durant to Cameron, Creek Nation, 11 September 1813, C.O. 23/60; Cameron to Bathurst, Nassau, 30 November 1813, C.O. 23/60.

CHAPTER 11

1. Bathurst to Wellington, Downing St., 28 January 1814, in Wellington, *Supplementary Despatches*, 8:547; Thomas Grenville to Marquis of Buckingham, 12 April 1814, in Richard P. Grenville, duke of Buckingham and Chandos, *Memoirs of the Court of England, during the Regency, 1811–1820. From Original Family Documents*, 2:61; John Sinclair to Liverpool, Edinburgh, 1 May 1814, Add. MSS. 38,257.

2. Memorial of North American merchants . . . to Bathurst, London, 7 May 1814, Add. MSS. 38,257; *Quebec Gazette*, 9 June 1814.

3. James Irvine and John Richardson to Prevost, 14, 24 October 1812, C.O. 42/159.

4. Castlereagh to Commissioners at Ghent, Foreign Office, 14 August 1814, Henry Goulburn Papers, I, William L. Clements Library, Univ. of Mich., Ann Arbor.

5. Daniel Coxe to Liverpool, Surry, 27 June 1814, Add. MSS. 38,258.

6. Memorial of the committee of merchants interested in the trade and fisheries of British North America to Bathurst, London, 7 May 1814, C.O. 42/159.

7. Liverpool to British commissioners, 31 August 1814, in Charles D. Yonge, *The Life and Administration of Robert Banks, Second Earl of Liverpool, K. G., Late First Lord of the Treasury*, 2:64–66; Prevost to Bathurst, Montreal, 5 August 1814, C.O. 42/157.

8. Ronald F. Banks, *Maine Becomes a State: The Movement to Separate Maine from Massachusetts, 1785–1820*, p. 5.

9. Sherbrooke to Bathurst, Castine, 10 September 1814, C.O. 217/93; Siebert, "Exodus of Loyalists from Penobscot," pp. 485–520.

10. Bathurst to Goulburn, 12 September 1814, Goulburn Papers, II; Sherbrooke to Bathurst, Halifax, 18 August 1814, C.O. 217/93.

11. T. Pickering to John Pickering, Washington, 8 January 1815, Pickering Papers, IV.

12. Morris to Rufus King, 31 January 1814, Morris, *Gouverneur Morris Diaries*, 2:556–59.

13. Cochrane to Viscount Melville, Bermuda, 10 March 1814, Cochrane Papers, 2345.

14. John Morison to Liverpool, 27 Axendon St., 20 April 1814, Add. MSS. 38,257; Thomas Morgan to Liverpool, Winkton, 4 December 1814, Add. MSS. 38,260.

15. Pigot to Cochrane, New Providence, 13 April 1814, Cochrane Papers, 2328; Pigot to Cochrane, New Providence, 8 June 1814, Adm. 1/506.

16. *Times* (London), 15 April 1814.

17. Gilbert Aspinwall to Sargent, New York, 21 July 1814, Sargent Papers, VII.

18. Liverpool to Castlereagh, Fife House, 8 February 1814, in Charles K. Webster, *The Foreign Policy of Castlereagh, 1812–1815, Britain and the Reconstruction of Europe*, p. 520.

19. Cochrane to Croker, Halifax, N.S., 3 October 1814, Adm. 1/4360.

20. Halbert and Ball, *Creek War*, pp. 275–84.

21. J. Leitch Wright, Jr., "A Note on the First Seminole War as Seen by the Indians, Negroes, and Their British Advisers," pp. 566–75.

22. Woodbine to Pigot, Prospect Bluff, 25 May 1814, Cochrane Papers, 2328.

23. Cochrane to Melville, Bermuda, 3 September 1814, Cochrane Papers, 2345.

24. Cochrane to Croker, Bermuda, 22 June 1814, Cochrane Papers, 2348.

25. Smyth Stuart to Liverpool, 18 March 1814, Add. MSS. 38,257.

26. Bathurst to Goulburn, Downing St., 4 October 1814, Goulburn Papers, II.

27. Castlereagh to Lord Gambier, Henry Goulburn, and William Adams, Foreign Office, 28 July 1814, Goulburn Papers, I.

28. Hawkins to Big Warrior, Little Prince, and other Creek Chiefs, Creek Agency, 16 June 1814, *ASP,IA*, I, 845.

29. Goulburn to Croker, Downing St., 19 January 1814, Cochrane Papers, 2342; Bathurst to Ross, War Dept., 10 August 1814, ibid., 2326.

30. C.O. 217/96 (1815) deals with Negroes Cochrane sent to Nova Scotia.

31. Nicholls to Cochrane, Apalachicola Bay, 12 August 1814, Cochrane Papers, 2328; Cochrane to Nicholls, *Tonnant* off Apalachicola, 3 December 1814, Cochrane Papers, 3346.

32. Morison to Henry Torrens, Oxendon St., 8 February 1814, C.O. 42/159; Morison to Fox, Charleston, S.C., 27 May 1782, C.O. 5/82.

33. Alexander Murray to Cameron, 9 December 1815, C.O. 23/63; Alexander Murray to Cameron, 3 January 1816, ibid.

34. Extracts of letters from Pensacola in Cameron to Bathurst, Nassau, 17 April 1814, C.O. 23/61; John Innerarity to James Innerarity, Pensacola, 10 November 1814, in John Innerarity, "Letters of John Innerarity: The Seizure of Pensacola by Andrew Jackson, November 7, 1814," pp. 127–30.

35. John Windship to William Plumer, Jr., Rapide, La., 18 February 1814, in Brown, "Letters from Louisiana," p. 572; Windship to Plumer, Natchitoches, Louisiana, 20 March 1814, ibid., p. 574.

36. Nicholls to Mos. Laffite or Commandant at Barataria, Pensacola, 31 August 1814, in Great Britain, Foreign Office, *British and Foreign State Papers*, 6:351.

37. Bathurst to Robert Ross, War Dept., 6 September 1814, W.O. 6/2; Bathurst to Pakenham, Downing St., 24 October 1814, W.O. 6/2.

38. Joseph G. Tregle, Jr., "Political Reinforcement of Ethnic Dominance in Louisiana, 1812–1845," pp. 78–83.

39. Robert Dickson to Noah Freer, Prairie du Chien, 17 January 1815, *MPHC*, 16 (1889), 44–45; Kellogg, *British Régime in Wisconsin*, pp. 316–17.

40. American Treaty, Western Indians, 1814, Selkirk Papers, LII.

41. "Recolonization of the American States, 1814," in William Cobbett, *Letters on the Late War between the United States and Great Britain: Together with other Miscellaneous Writings, on the Same Subject*, p. 155.

42. Edward Griffith to Cochrane, off Castine, 9 September 1814, Adm. 1/507; Griffith to Croker, 13 September 1814, ibid.

43. Cochrane to Henry Hotham, Patuxent River, 30 August 1814, Cochrane Papers, 2349; Hotham to gentlemen of the committee who stipulated for neutrality of Island of Nantucket, off New London, 22 September 1814, W.O. 1/142.

44. Pickering to Hillhouse, Washington, 16 December 1814, Pickering Papers, XV.

45. G. Morris to Lewis B. Sturges, Morrisania, 1 November 1814, in Jared Sparks, *The Life of Gouverneur Morris, with Selections from His Correspondence and Miscellaneous Papers*, 3:319; Pickering to Jay, Washington, 22 October 1814, John Jay Papers, Columbia University Library, New York City; *Bahama Gazette* (Nassau), 25 August 1814.

46. John Lowell to Pickering, Boston, 3 December 1814, Pickering Papers, XXX.

47. Caleb Strong to Pickering, Boston, 7 February 1815, Pickering Papers, XXX.

48. Banner, *To the Hartford Convention*, pp. 328–44.

49. Proposals of Massachusetts agent, in Sherbrooke to Bathurst, Halifax, N.S., 20 November 1814, C.O. 217/93. Morison, *Otis*, p. 540, identified Adams as the agent, and J. S. Martell, ed., "A Side Light on Federalist Strategy during the War of 1812," pp. 560–63, published the proposals.

50. Bathurst to Sherbrooke, Downing St., 13 December 1814, Canada, Public Archives, *Report, 1948*, p. 193; Griffith to Cochrane, Halifax, N.S., 30 November 1814, Cochrane Papers, 2574.

51. Banner, *To the Hartford Convention*, p. 347.

52. Halbert and Ball, *Creek War*, pp. 134 ff.

53. George Woodbine to Cochrane, Pensacola, 9 August 1814, Cochrane Papers, 2328; John Francis and Peter McQueen to Cochrane, Pensacola, 1 September 1814, F.O. 5/139.

54. Nicholls to Juan Ruiz de Apodaca, *Seahorse* off Barrancas, 9 November 1814, F.O. 72/219; Nicholls to Cochrane, Apalachicola Bay, 12 August–17 November 1814, Cochrane Papers, 2328; Frank L. Owsley, Jr., "Jackson's Capture of Pensacola," pp. 181–83.

55. Cochrane to Nicholls, *Tonnant* off Apalachicola, 3 December 1814, Cochrane Papers, 2346; Cochrane to Cockburn, near New Orleans, 6 January 1815, Cochrane Papers, 2349.

56. Pulteney Malcolm to Clementina Malcolm, 19 October 1814, Pulteney Malcolm Papers, National Maritime Museum, Greenwich, England.

57. Wellington to Liverpool, Paris, 9 November 1814, in Wellington, *Supplementary Despatches*, 9:426.

58. Liverpool to Goulburn, Fife House, 21 October 1814, Goulburn Papers, II.

59. Patrick Colquhoun, *A Treatise on the Wealth, Power, and Resources, of the British Empire, in Every Quarter of the World, including the East Indies*, p. 215; *Times* (London), 22 November 1814.

60. Bathurst to Goulburn, Downing St., 27 September 1814, Goulburn Papers, II; Perkins, *Castlereagh and Adams*, pp. 39–127.

61. Castlereagh to British delegation, Foreign Office, 28 July 1814, Goulburn Papers, I.

62. Anglo-American Treaty, Ghent, 24 December 1814, Miller, *Treaties*, 2:574–82.

63. Liverpool to Castlereagh, Fife House, 23 December 1814, Wellington, *Supplementary Despatches*, 9:495.

64. *Times* (London), 11 January 1815.

65. Brown to Liverpool, 29 December 1814, Add. MSS. 38,260.

66. Nicholas Vansittart to Castlereagh, Downing St., 23 December 1814, Add. MSS. 31,231; Bathurst to Goulburn, Downing St., 26 December 1814, Goulburn Papers, III; Sherbrooke to Bathurst, Halifax, N.S., 1 February 1815, C.O. 217/96.

67. Pickering to Samuel Hodgdon, Washington, 25 December 1814, Pickering Papers, XV.

68. Castlereagh to commissioners, Foreign Office, 28 July 1814, Londonderry, *Castlereagh Correspondence*, 10:70–71.

69. Cochrane to Nicholls, *Tonnant*, off Apalachicola River, Cochrane Papers, 2349; Alexander Dickson, "Journal of Operations in Louisiana," p. 13.

70. *Times* (London), 1 February 1815.

71. Thomas McKee to Johnson, Montreal, 26 September 1814, Deputy Supt. Gen., R.G. 10, A 5b, P.A.C.; speech by deputy superintendent general,

Burlington, Upper Can., 24 April 1815, ibid.; Ninian Edwards to Thomas Forsyth, Kaskaskia, 4 December 1814, Thomas Forsyth Papers, Draper MSS., T1, State Historical Society of Wisconsin, Madison.

72. William Russell to Monroe, St. Louis, 20 October 1814, Carter, *Territorial Papers*, 14:797.

73. *Times* (London), 2 June 1814.

74. Liverpool to Bathurst, Walmer Castle, Eng., 15 September 1814, Hist. MSS. Com., *Bathurst MSS.*, p. 288.

75. Liverpool to Canning, Fife House, 28 December 1814, Wellington, *Supplementary Despatches*, 9:514; Bathurst to Prevost, War Dept., 27 December 1814, Claus Papers, X.

76. Johnson to Prevost, 4 April 1812, in Sir John Johnson, *The North American Johnsons: A Short Story of Triumph and Tragedy*, pp. 85–87.

77. An example was Gen. Frederick P. Robinson, a wealthy New York loyalist who in 1814 commanded a brigade under Prevost. Robinson in 1777 had been with the British forces on the lower Hudson awaiting Burgoyne's arrival rather than with the British army which surrendered at Saratoga.

78. Horsman, *Elliott*, pp. 195 ff.

79. Daniel Coxe to Liverpool, Surrey, 27 June 1814, Add. MSS. 38,258; John Sinclair to Liverpool, Edinburgh, 1 May 1814, Add. MSS. 38,257.

80. John Eardley Wilmot, *Historical View of the Commission for Enquiring into the Losses, Services, and Claims of the American Loyalists*. The peace treaty was signed before Eardley Wilmot's work appeared in print.

81. Smyth Stuart to Bathurst, Bloomsbury Square, London, 22 September 1814, C.O. 42/159; Smyth Stuart to Bathurst, Bloomsbury Square, 3 October 1814, ibid.; Edward I. Carlyle, "John Ferdinand Smyth Stuart," pp. 102–3; Ritchie, "Louisiana Campaign," p. 28.

82. Strong to Pickering, Boston, 7 February 1815, Pickering Papers, XXX. Morison, *Otis*, pp. 385–86, 541, asserts that Strong in January, before receiving news of New Orleans and the Treaty of Ghent, had already abandoned notions about secession; but Strong's February 7 letter indicates otherwise.

83. Liverpool to Castlereagh, Fife House, 23 December 1814, Wellington, *Supplementary Despatches*, 9:495; Vansittart to Castlereagh, Downing St., 23 December 1814, Add. MSS. 31,231.

84. Wright, "Note on First Seminole War," pp. 570–74.

85. Edmund Wilson, *Apologies to the Iroquois*, p. 258.

86. Ibid., p. 271.

87. Edward A. Kendall to Duke of York, Surrey, 1 December 1814, C.O. 42/159.

Bibliography

1 • MANUSCRIPTS

Ann Arbor, Michigan. William L. Clements Library.
    Sir Henry Clinton Papers
    Clinton-Gloucester Correspondence
    Henry Goulburn Papers
    David Hartley Papers
    William Knox Papers
    Melville Papers
    Pitt Papers
    Shelburne Papers
    John Graves Simcoe Papers
    Sydney Papers
    Benjamin Vaughan Papers
Atlanta. Georgia Department of Archives and History.
    East and West Florida, 1764–1850
Edinburgh. National Library of Scotland.
    Cochrane Papers
    Sir Robert Liston Papers
    Manuscript 8886
    Melville Papers
Greenwich, England. National Maritime Museum.
    Pulteney Malcolm Papers
    John B. Warren Papers
London. British Museum.
    Additional Manuscripts:
        21,661–21,892 (Sir Frederick Haldimand Papers)
        22,900–22,902 (George Chalmers Correspondence)
        23,670 (Charles Rainsford Correspondence)
        24,322 (Miscellaneous letters, American affairs)
        31,229–31,231 (Bexley Papers)
        33,110–33,111 (Thomas Pelham Papers)
        37,842–37,935 (William Windham Papers)
        38,190–38,489 (Liverpool Papers)
    Grenville Papers (Boconnoc Manuscripts)
London. Public Record Office.
    Admiralty 1 (In-letters)

    Audit Office 12 (American loyalists' claims)
    Audit Office 13 (American loyalists' claims)
    Board of Trade 3 (Out-letters)
    Colonial Office 5 (America and West Indies)
    Colonial Office 23 (Bahamas)
    Colonial Office 42 (Canada)
    Colonial Office 43 (Canada)
    Colonial Office 137 (Jamaica)
    Colonial Office 188 (New Brunswick)
    Colonial Office 217 (Nova Scotia)
    Colonial Office 226 (Prince Edward Island)
    Foreign Office 4 (United States)
    Foreign Office 72 (Spain)
    Foreign Office 115 (United States)
    Foreign Office 353 (Jackson Papers)
    Gifts and Deposits Group 30–8 (Chatham Papers)
    Privy Council 2 (Registers)
    Treasury 77 (East Florida Claims Commission)
    War Office 1 (In-letters)
    War Office 6 (Secretary of State)

Louisville, Kentucky. Filson Club.
    Pontalba Collection

New York City. Columbia University Library.
    John Jay Papers
    Gouverneur Morris Papers

New York City. New York Public Library.
    Bancroft Collection
        America
        America and England
        Correspondence of Peace Commissioners
        Correspondence of Sir John Temple
        George III and Lord North
        Hartley's negotiations
        Henry Strachey Letters
        Letters of George III to Shelburne
    Aaron Burr Papers
    George Chalmers Papers
    Diary or narrative, by a British subject, of a journey from New York City
        . . . to Niagara Falls, 6 August–6 September 1808
    William Hartshorne's diary of a journey from New York to Detroit with
        other Quakers to treat with the Indians, 4 May–17 September 1793
    Indian Papers, Philip Schuyler Papers

Nottingham, England. University of Nottingham Library.
  Portland Manuscripts
Ottawa. Public Archives of Canada.
  Claus Papers
  Deputy Superintendent General, R.G. 10, A5b
  Despatches from the Colonial Office to the Governor General
  Earl of Selkirk Papers
  John Graves Simcoe Papers
  William Smith Diary
  Superintendent General and Inspector General, R.G. 10, A5a
  Superintendent of Indian Affairs, R.G. 10, A4
  Upper Canada, Indian Affairs, M.G. 19
  Edward Winslow Papers (microfilm)
Oxford, England. Bodleian Library.
  North Papers
San Marino, California. Henry E. Huntington Library and Art Gallery.
  Miscellaneous manuscripts
  Townshend Collection
Seville. Archivo General de Indias.
  Cuba
  Estado
Tallahassee. Florida State University Library.
  Sir Guy Carleton Papers, Public Record Office, London (microfilm)
  Lyman Draper Manuscripts, State Historical Society of Wisconsin, Madison (microfilm)
    Joseph Brant Papers
    Thomas Forsyth Papers
    Frontier Wars
    Kings Mountain Papers
    Tecumseh Papers
  East Florida Papers, Library of Congress (microfilm)
  Henry Knox Papers, Massachusetts Historical Society, Boston (microfilm)
  Benjamin Lincoln Papers, Massachusetts Historical Society, Boston (microfilm)
  Timothy Pickering Papers, Massachusetts Historical Society, Boston (microfilm)
  Winthrop Sargent Papers, Massachusetts Historical Society, Boston (microfilm)
  West Florida Papers, Library of Congress (microfilm)
Washington, D.C. Library of Congress.
  Robert Morris Papers
  Spanish transcripts

Williamsburg, Virginia. E. G. Swem Library, College of William and Mary.
    Dunmore Family Papers
Windsor Castle, Windsor, England. Royal Archives.
    Georgian Archive

2 • NEWSPAPERS AND CONTEMPORARY PERIODICALS

Bahama Gazette (Nassau), 1784–1800, 1812–15
Daily Universal Register (London), 1785–87
Gentleman's Magazine (London), 1782–1815
Morning Post and Gazetteer (London), 1798–99
Quebec Gazette, 1783–1815
Royal Gazette and Bahama Advertiser (Nassau), 1804–15
The Scots Magazine (Edinburgh), 1786–1816
Times (London), 1788–1815

3 • BOOKS AND ARTICLES

Abbot, Charles, ed. *The Diary and Correspondence of Charles Abbot, Lord Colchester,
    Speaker of the House of Commons, 1802–1817*. 3 vols. London, 1861.
Abernethy, Thomas P. *The Burr Conspiracy*. New York: Oxford University
    Press, 1954.
————. *Western Lands and the American Revolution*. New York: D. Appleton-
    Century Co., Inc., 1937.
Adams, Ephraim D. *The Influence of Grenville on Pitt's Foreign Policy, 1787–1798*.
    Washington: Carnegie Institution, 1904.
Adams, Henry, ed. *Documents Relating to New–England Federalism, 1800–1815*.
    Boston, 1877.
————. *History of the United States of America*. 9 vols. New York, 1889–91.
Adams, John. *The Works of John Adams, Second President of the United States; with
    a Life of the Author*. Edited by Charles F. Adams. 10 vols. Boston, 1850–56.
Alden, John R. *A History of the American Revolution*. New York: Knopf, 1969.
Allen, Harry C. *The Anglo-American Relationship Since 1783*. London: Adam and
    Charles Black, 1959.
Alvord, Clarence W., ed. *Kaskaskia Records, 1778–1790*. Springfield: Illinois
    State Historical Library, 1909.
————. *The Mississippi Valley in British Politics; a Study of the Trade, Land Specu-
    lation, and Experiments in Imperialism Culminating in the American Revolution*.
    2 vols. Cleveland: Arthur H. Clark Co., 1917.
Aptheker, Herbert. *American Negro Slave Revolts*. New York: Columbia Uni-
    versity Press, 1943.
Armstrong, Francis. *Letters to His Royal Highness the Duke of Sussex, relative to His
    Majesty, and Other Important Matters*. London, 1813.
Aspinall, Arthur. "The Cabinet Council, 1783–1835." *Proceedings of the British
    Academy* 38 (1933), 145–252.

Baily, Francis. *Journal of a Tour in Unsettled Parts of North America in 1796 and 1797*. Edited by Jack D. L. Holmes. Carbondale, Ill.: Southern Illinois University, 1969.

Bakeless, John. *Daniel Boone*. Harrisburgh, Pa.: Stackpole Co., 1965.

Baldwin, Leland D. *Whiskey Rebels: The Story of a Frontier Uprising*. Pittsburgh, Pa.: University of Pittsburgh Press, 1939.

Banks, Ronald F. *Maine Becomes a State: The Movement to Separate Maine from Massachusetts, 1785–1820*. Middletown, Conn.: Wesleyan University Press, 1970.

Banner, James M., Jr. *To the Hartford Convention: The Federalists and the Origins of Party Politics in Massachusetts, 1789–1815*. New York: Knopf, 1969.

Barnes, Donald G. *George III and William Pitt, 1783–1806. A New Interpretation Based upon a Study of Their Unpublished Correspondence*. Stanford University, Calif.: Stanford University Press, 1939.

Baudry des Lozières, Louis N. *Second voyage à la Louisiane, faisant suite au premier de l'auteur de 1794–98. Contenant la vie militaire du général Grondel . . . qui commanda long-temps à la Louisiane . . . un détail sur les productions les plus avantageuses, les plus extraordainaires, de cette belle colonie, et sur ses quartiers les plus ferliles et les plus lucratifs: de nouvelles réflexions sur les colonies en général, et le régime nécessaire aux personnes des colonies pendant la première année de leur arrivée*. Paris, 1803.

Baynton, Benjamin. *Authentic Memoirs of William Augustus Bowles, Esquire, Ambassador from the United Nations of Creeks and Cherokees, to the Court of London*. London, 1791.

Bemis, Samuel F. *Jay's Treaty: A Study in Commerce and Diplomacy*. New York: Macmillan, 1923.

———. *Pinckney's Treaty: America's Advantage from Europe's Distress, 1783–1800*. New Haven, Conn.: Yale University Press, 1960.

———. "Relations between the Vermont Separatists and Great Britain, 1789–1791." *American Historical Review*, 21 (1916), 547–60.

Bowles, John. *Reflections at the Conclusion of the War: Being a Sequel to "Reflections on the Political and Moral State of Society, at the Close of the Eighteenth Century."* London, 1801.

Boyd, Julian P. *Number 7, Alexander Hamilton's Secret Attempts to Control American Foreign Policy, with Supporting Documents*. Princeton, N.J.: Princeton University Press, 1964.

———, ed. *The Papers of Thomas Jefferson*. Princeton, N.J.: Princeton University Press, 1950–.

Boyd, Julian P., and Robert J. Taylor, eds. *The Susquehannah Company Papers*. 11 vols. Ithaca, N.Y.: Cornell University Press, 1930–71.

Brant, Irving, *James Madison*. 6 vols. Indianapolis, 1941–1961.

Brown, Everett S., ed. "Letters from Louisiana, 1813–1814." *Journal of American History* 11 (1925), 570–79.

Buckingham and Chandos, Richard P. Grenville, duke of. *Memoirs of the Court of England, during the Regency, 1811–1820. From Original Family Documents.* 2 vols. London, 1856.

Burnett, Edmund C., ed. *Letters of Members of the Continental Congress.* 8 vols. Washington, D.C.: The Carnegie Institution, 1921–36.

Burr, Aaron. *The Private Journal of Aaron Burr, during His Residence of Four Years in Europe, with Selections from His Correspondence.* Edited by Matthew L. Davis. 2 vols. New York, 1838.

Burt, Alfred L. *The United States, Great Britain and British North America from the Revolution to the Establishment of Peace after the War of 1812.* New Haven, Conn.: Yale University Press, 1940.

Butterfield, Consul W. *History of the Girtys; being a Concise Account of the Girty Brothers—Thomas, Simon, James and George, and of Their Half-brother John Turner—also of the Part Taken by Them in Lord Dunmore's War, in the Western Border War of the Revolution, and in the Indian War of 1790–95; with a Recital of the Principal Events in the West during These Wars.* Cincinnati, 1890.

Campbell, J. V. "Account of a Plot for Obtaining the Lower Peninsula of Michigan from the United States in 1795." Michigan Pioneer and Historical Society, *Historical Collections* 8 (1885), 406–11.

Canada, Public Archives. *Reports.* Ottawa, 1881–.

Cannon, John A. *The Fox-North Coalition: Crisis of the Constitution, 1782–4.* London: Cambridge University Press, 1969.

Carlyle, Edward I. "John Ferdinand Smyth Stuart." *Dictionary of National Biography* 19:102–3.

Carter, Clarence E., ed. *The Territorial Papers of the United States.* Washington: U. S. Govt. Printing Office, 1934–.

Caughey, John W., ed. *East Florida, 1783–1785. A File of Documents Assembled and Many of Them Translated by Joseph Byrne Lockey.* Berkeley, Calif.: University of California Press, 1949.

Caughey, John W. "The Natchez Rebellion of 1781 and Its Aftermath." *Louisiana Historical Quarterly* 16 (1933), 57–83.

Christie, Ian R. *The End of North's Ministry, 1780–1782.* London: Macmillan, 1958.

Cobbett, William. *Letters on the Late War between the United States and Great Britain: Together with Other Miscellaneous Writings, on the Same Subject.* New York, 1815.

———, ed. *The Parliamentary History of England, from the Earliest Period to the Year 1803, from which Last-Mentioned Epoch It Is Continued Downwards in the Work Entitled "Hansard's Parliamentary Debates."* 36 vols. London, 1806–20.

Coleman, Kenneth. *The American Revolution in Georgia, 1763–1789.* Athens: University of Georgia Press, 1958.

Collot, Georges H. Victor. *A Journey in North America, Containing a Survey of the Countries Watered by the Mississippi, Ohio, Missouri, and Other Affluing Rivers;*

with Exact Observations on the Course and Soundings of These Rivers; and on the Towns, Villages, Hamlets and Farms of that Part of the New-World; Followed by Philosophical, Political, Military and Commercial Remarks, and by a Projected Line of Frontiers and General Limits. 2 vols. Paris, 1826.

Colquhoun, Patrick. *A Treatise on the Wealth, Power, and Resources, of the British Empire, in Every Quarter of the World, including the East Indies; the Rise and Progress of the Funding System Explained; with Observations on the National Resources for the Beneficial Employment of a Redundant Population*. London, 1815.

Combs, Jerald A. *The Jay Treaty: Political Battleground of the Founding Fathers*. Berkeley, Calif.: University of California Press, 1970.

Corbitt, Duvon C. "James Colbert and the Spanish Claims to the East Bank of the Mississippi." *Journal of American History* 24 (1938), 457–72.

―――, ed. "Papers Relating to the Georgia-Florida Frontier, 1784–1800." *Georgia Historical Quarterly* 20–25 (1936–41).

Cotterill, Robert S. *History of Pioneer Kentucky*. Cincinnati: Johnson, 1917.

Cox, Isaac J. *The West Florida Controversy, 1798–1813: A Study in American Diplomacy*. Baltimore: Johns Hopkins Press, 1918.

Cruikshank, Ernest A., ed. *The Correspondence of Lieut. Governor John Graves Simcoe, with Allied Documents Relating to His Administration of the Government of Upper Canada*. 5 vols. Toronto: Ontario Historical Society, 1923–31.

―――, and Andrew F. Hunter, eds. *The Correspondence of the Honourable Peter Russell, with Allied Documents Relating to His Administration of the Government of Upper Canada during the Official Term of Lieut.-Governor J. G. Simcoe, While on Leave of Absence*. Toronto: Ontario Historical Society, 1932–.

―――. *The Story of Butler's Rangers and the Settlement of Niagara*. Welland, Ont., 1893.

Darling, Arthur B. *Our Rising Empire, 1763–1803*. Hamden, Conn.: Archon Books, 1962.

Davenport, Frances G., and Charles O. Paullin, eds. *European Treaties Bearing on the History of the United States and Its Dependencies*. 4 vols. Washington, D.C.: Carnegie Institution, 1917–37.

Deane, Silas. *The Deane Papers: Correspondence between Silas Deane, His Brothers and Their Business and Political Associates, 1771–1795*. Hartford, Conn.: Connecticut Historical Society, 1930.

―――. *The Deane Papers, 1774–1790*. Edited by Charles Isham. 5 vols. New York, 1887–90.

De Conde, Alexander. *Entangling Alliances: Politics and Diplomacy under George Washington*. Durham, N.C.: Duke University Press, 1958.

De Vorsey, Louis. *The Indian Boundary in the Southern Colonies, 1763–1775*. Chapel Hill, N.C.: University of North Carolina Press, 1966.

Dickson, Alexander. "Journal of Operations in Louisiana." *Louisiana Historical Quarterly* 44 (1961), 1–110.

Downes, Randolph C. *Council Fires on the Upper Ohio: A Narrative of Indian Affairs in the Upper Ohio Valley until 1795.* Pittsburgh: University of Pittsburgh Press, 1940.

Eardley Wilmot, John. *Historical View of the Commission for Enquiring into the Losses, Services, and Claims of the American Loyalists at the Close of the War between Great Britain and Her Colonies, in 1783; with an Account of the Compensation Granted to Them by Parliament in 1785 and 1788.* London, 1815.

Ehrman, John. *The Younger Pitt: The Years of Acclaim.* New York: Dutton, 1969.

Ernst, Robert. *Rufus King, American Federalist.* Chapel Hill, N.C.: University of North Carolina Press, 1968.

Feiling, Keith G. *The Second Tory Party, 1714–1832.* London: Macmillan, 1951.

Flexner, James T. *Mohawk Baronet: Sir William Johnson of New York.* New York: Harper, 1959.

Foord, Archibald S. "The Waning of 'The Influence of the Crown.'" *English Historical Review* 62 (1947), 484–507.

Ford, Paul L., ed. *The Works of Thomas Jefferson.* 12 vols. New York: Putnam, 1904–1905.

Ford, Worthington C., Gaillard Hunt, John C. Fitzpatrick, and Roscoe R. Hill, eds. *Journals of the Continental Congress, 1774–1789. Edited from the Original Records in the Library of Congress.* 34 vols. Washington: U.S. Government Printing Office, 1904–37.

Fortescue, John W., ed. *The Correspondence of King George the Third from 1760 to December 1783; Printed from the Original Papers in the Royal Archives at Windsor Castle.* 6 vols. London: Macmillan, 1927–28.

————. *A Selection From the Papers of King George III Preserved in the Royal Archives at Windsor Castle, Embracing the Period from the 1st Day of November, 1781 to the 20th Day of December 1783.* 2 vols. Cambridge, England: W. Lewis, 1927.

Fox, Charles James. *Memorials and Correspondence of Charles James Fox.* Edited by John Russell. 2 vols. Philadelphia, 1853.

Freeman, Douglas S. *George Washington, A Biography.* 7 vols. New York: C. Scribner's Sons, 1948–57.

Gayarré, Charles E. A. *History of Louisiana. By Charles Gayarré. With City and Topographical Maps of the State, Ancient and Modern, with a Biography of the Author, by Grace King.* 4 vols. New Orleans: F. F. Hansell and Bro., Ltd., 1903.

Graham, Gerald S., ed. "The Indian Menace and the Retention of the Western Posts." *Canadian Historical Review,* 15 (1934), 46–48.

Great Britain. Foreign Office. *British and Foreign State Papers,* London, 1841—.

Great Britain. Historical Manuscripts Commission. *The Manuscripts of the Earl of Dartmouth. Fourteenth Report.* 3 vols. London: H. M. Stationery Office, 1887–1896.

_____. *Report on the Manuscripts of Earl Bathurst, Preserved at Cirencester Park.* London: H. M. Stationery Office, 1923.

_____. *Report on the Manuscripts of J. B. Fortescue, Esq., Preserved at Dropmore. Fourteenth Report.* 10 vols. London: H. M. Stationery Office, 1892–1927.

Green, Thomas M. *The Spanish Conspiracy. A Review of Early Spanish Movements in the South-west. Containing Proofs of the Intrigues of James Wilkinson and John Brown; of the Complicity Therewith of Judges Sebastian, Wallace, and Innes; the Early Struggles of Kentucky for Autonomy; the Intrigues of Sebastian in 1795–7, and the Legislative Investigation of His Corruption.* Gloucester, Mass.: Peter Smith, 1967.

Greene, Evarts B., and Virginia D. Harrington. *American Population before the Federal Census of 1790.* New York: Columbia University Press, 1932.

Greenslade, Marie T. "William Panton." *Florida Historical Quarterly* 14 (1935), 107–29.

Halbert, Henry S., and Timothy H. Ball. *The Creek War of 1813 and 1814.* Edited by Frank L. Owsley, Jr. University, Ala.: The University of Alabama Press, 1969.

Hansard, Thomas C., ed. *The Parliamentary Debates.* 41 vols. London, 1803–20.

Harlow, Vincent T. *The Founding of the Second British Empire, 1763–1793.* 2 vols. London: Longmans, 1952–64.

Hawkins, Benjamin. *Letters of Benjamin Hawkins, 1796–1806.* Savannah, Ga.: Georgia Historical Society, 1916.

Herndon, G. Melvin. *William Tatham and the Culture of Tobacco.* Coral Gables, Fla.: University of Miami Press, 1969.

Hitsman, J. Mackay. *The Incredible War of 1812: A Military History.* Toronto: University of Toronto Press, 1965.

Holmes, Jack D. L. *Gayoso: The Life of a Spanish Governor in the Mississippi Valley, 1789–1799.* Baton Rouge: Louisiana State University Press, 1965.

Holroyd, John Baker, first earl of Sheffield. *Observations on the Commerce of the American States with Europe and the West Indies, including the Several Articles of Import and Export, and on the Tendency of a Bill Now Depending in Parliament, with Additional Notes on the Commerce of the United States.* Philadelphia, 1783.

Horsman, Reginald. "The British Indian Department and the Abortive Treaty of Lower Sandusky, 1793." *Ohio Historical Quarterly* 70 (1961), 189–213.

_____. "The British Indian Department and the Resistance to General Anthony Wayne, 1793–1795." *Journal of American History* 49 (1962), 269–90.

_____. *Expansion and American Indian Policy, 1783–1812.* East Lansing, Mich.: Michigan State University Press, 1967.

_____. *Matthew Elliott, British Indian Agent.* Detroit: Wayne State University Press, 1964.

Innerarity, John. "Letters of John Innerarity: The Seizure of Pensacola by Andrew Jackson, November 7, 1814." *Florida Historical Quarterly* 9 (1931), 127–34.

Jacobs, James R. *The Beginning of the U. S. Army, 1783–1812*. Princeton, N.J.: Princeton University Press, 1947.

―――. *Tarnished Warrior: Major-General James Wilkinson*. New York: Macmillan, 1938.

James, Dorris C. *Antebellum Natchez*. Baton Rouge: Louisiana State University Press, 1968.

James, James A. *The Life of George Rogers Clark*. Chicago: University of Chicago Press, 1928.

Jellison, Charles A. *Ethan Allen: Frontier Rebel*. Syracuse: Syracuse University Press, 1969.

Johnson, Cecil. *British West Florida, 1763–1783*. New Haven, Conn.: Yale University Press, 1943.

Johnson, John. *The North American Johnsons: A Short Story of Triumph and Tragedy*. London: PRM Publishers, Ltd., 1963.

Johnston, Charles M., ed. *The Valley of the Six Nations: A Collection of Documents on the Indian Lands of the Grand River*. Toronto: University of Toronto, 1964.

Kappler, Charles J., ed. *Indian Affairs. Laws and Treaties*. 2 vols. Washington, D.C.: U.S. Government Printing Office, 1903.

Kaufmann, William W. *British Policy and the Independence of Latin America, 1804–1828*. New Haven, Conn.: Yale University Press, 1951.

Kellogg, Louise P. *The British Régime in Wisconsin and the Northwest*. Madison, Wisc.: State Historical Society of Wisconsin, 1935.

Kerber, Linda K. *Federalists in Dissent: Imagery and Ideology in Jeffersonian America*. Ithaca, N.Y.: Cornell University Press, 1970.

King, Charles R., ed. *The Life and Correspondence of Rufus King, Comprising His Letters Private and Official, His Public Documents, and His Speeches*. 6 vols. New York, 1894–1900.

Kingsford, William. *The History of Canada*. 10 vols. Toronto, 1887–98.

Kinnaird, Lawrence, ed. and trans. *Spain in the Mississippi Valley, 1765–94, Translations of Materials from the Spanish Archives in the Bancroft Library*. 3 vols. Washington, D.C.: U. S. Government Printing Office, 1945.

Knopf, Richard C., ed. *Anthony Wayne, A Name in Arms: Soldier, Diplomat, Defender of Expansion Westward of a Nation; the Wayne-Knox-Pickering-McHenry Correspondence*. Pittsburgh: University of Pittsburgh Press, 1960.

La Rochefoucauld Liancourt, Duc de. *Travels through the United States of North America, the Country of the Iroquois, and Upper Canada, in the Years 1795, 1796, and 1797*. 4 vols. London, 1800.

Lindley, Jacob; Joseph Moore; and Oliver Paxson. "Expedition to Detroit,

1793: The Quakers, the United States Commissioners, and the Proposed Treaty of Peace with the Northwestern Indian Tribes." Michigan Pioneer and Historical Society, *Historical Collections* 17 (1890), 565–671.

Lingelbach, Anna L. "The Inception of the British Board of Trade." *American Historical Review* 30 (1925), 701–27

Livermore, Shaw. *Early American Land Companies: Their Influence on Corporate Development*. New York: Oxford University Press, 1939.

Londonderry, Charles Vane, marquis of, ed. *Memoir and Correspondence of Viscount Castlereagh, Second Marques of Londonderry*. 12 vols. London, 1848 53.

Lycan, Gilbert L. *Alexander Hamilton and American Foreign Policy: A Design for Greatness*. Norman, Okla.: University of Oklahoma Press, 1970.

Lyon, E. Wilson. *Louisiana in French Diplomacy, 1759–1804*. Norman, Okla.: University of Oklahoma Press, 1934.

————, ed. "Moustier's Memoir on Louisiana." *Journal of American History* 22 (1935), 251–66.

Mahon, John K. *The War of 1812*. Gainesville, Fla.: University of Florida Press, 1972.

Malmesbury, 1st earl of. *Diaries and Correspondence of James Harris, First Earl of Malmesbury; Containing an Account of His Missions to the Courts of Madrid, Frederick the Great, Catherine the Second, and the Hague; and His Special Missions to Berlin, Brunswick, and the French Republic*. Edited by 3d earl of Malmesbury. 4 vols. London, 1844.

Malone, Dumas. *Jefferson and His Time*. Boston: Little, Brown, 1948–.

Manning, Helen T. *British Colonial Government after the American Revolution, 1782–1820*. New Haven, Conn.: Yale University Press, 1933.

Manning, William R., ed. *Diplomatic Correspondence of the United States: Canadian Relations, 1784–1860*. 4 vols. Washington: Carnegie Endowment for International Peace, 1940–45.

————. *The Nootka Sound Controversy*. In *Annual Report of the American Historical Association for the Year 1904*. Washington, D.C.: U.S. Government Printing Office, 1905.

Martell, J. S., ed. "A Side Light on Federalist Strategy during the War of 1812." *American Historical Review* 43 (1938), 553–66.

Masterson, William H. *William Blount*. Baton Rouge: Louisiana State University Press, 1954.

McLaughlin, Andrew C. "The Western Posts and British Debts." *American Historical Association Annual Report 1894*, Washington, 1895, pp. 413–44.

Milfort, LeClerc de. *Memoir, or A Quick Glance at My Various Travels and My Sojourn in the Creek Nation*. Edited and translated by Ben C. McCary. Kennesaw, Ga.: Continental Book Company, 1959.

Miller, David Hunter, ed. *Treaties and Other International Acts of the United States of America*. Washington: U. S. Government Printing Office, 1931–.

Miller, John C. *The Federalist Era, 1789–1801*. New York: Harper, 1960.

Mills, Dudley. "The Duke of Wellington and the Peace Negotiations at Ghent in 1814." *Canadian Historical Review* 2 (1921), 19–32.

Miranda, Francisco de. *Archivo del General Miranda*. 15 vols. Caracas: Editorial Sur-América, 1929–38.

Morison, Samuel E. *Harrison Gray Otis, 1755–1848: The Urbane Federalist*. Boston: Houghton Mifflin, 1969.

———. "The Henry-Crillon Affair of 1812. In *By Land and By Sea; Essays and Addresses*. New York: Knopf, 1953.

Morris, Anne C., ed. *The Diary and Letters of Gouverneur Morris, Minister of the United States to France, Member of the Constitutional Convention, etc.* 2 vols. New York, 1888.

Morris, Richard B. *The Peacemakers: The Great Powers and American Independence*. New York: Harper and Row, 1965.

Mowat, Charles L. *East Florida as a British Province, 1763–1784*. Gainesville, Fla.: University of Florida Press, 1964.

Murdoch, Richard K. "A British Report on West Florida and Louisiana, November, 1812." *Florida Historical Quarterly* 43 (1964), 36–51.

———. *The Georgia-Florida Frontier, 1793–1796: Spanish Reaction to French Intrigue and American Designs*. Berkeley, Calif.: University of California Press, 1951.

Namier, Lewis. *England in the Age of the American Revolution*. London: Macmillan, 1930.

———. *The Structure of Politics at the Accession of George III*. London: Macmillan, 1957.

Namier, Lewis, and John Brooke. *The House of Commons, 1754–1790*. 3 vols. New York: Oxford University Press, 1964.

Nasatir, Abraham P. *Spanish War Vessels on the Mississippi, 1792–1796*. New Haven, Conn.: Yale University Press, 1968.

Neel, Joanne L. *Phineas Bond: A Study in Anglo-American Relations, 1786–1812*. Philadelphia: University of Pennsylvania Press, 1968.

Nelson, William H. *The American Tory*. Oxford, England: Clarendon Press, 1961.

Norton, Mary B. *The British Americans: The Loyalist Exiles in England, 1774–1789*. Boston: Little, Brown, 1972.

Orr, George. *The Possession of Louisiana by the French, Considered, as it Effects the Interests of Those Nations More Immediately Concerned, viz. Great Britain, America, Spain and Portugal*. London, 1803.

Owsley, Frank L., Jr. "Jackson's Capture of Pensacola." *Alabama Review* 19 (1966), 175–85.

Palmer, Robert R. *The Age of the Democratic Revolution: A Political History of Europe and America, 1760–1800*. 2 vols. Princeton, N.J.: Princeton University Press, 1959–64.

Pares, Richard. *King George III and the Politicians*. Oxford, England: Clarendon Press, 1953.

Parker, David W., ed. "Secret Reports of John Howe, 1808." *American Historical Review* 17 (1911), 70–102, and 332–54.

Patrick, Rembert W. *Florida Fiasco: Rampant Rebels on the Georgia-Florida Border, 1810–1815*. Athens, Ga.: University of Georgia Press, 1954.

Perkins, Bradford. *Castlereagh and Adams: England and the United States, 1812–1823*. Berkeley, Calif.: University of California Press, 1964.

————. "England and the Louisiana Question." *Huntington Library Quarterly* 18 (1955), 279–95.

————. *The First Rapprochement: England and the United States, 1795–1805*. Philadelphia: University of Pennsylvania Press, 1955.

————. *Prologue to War: England and the United States, 1805–1812*. Berkeley, Calif.: University of California Press, 1961.

Plumer, William, Jr. *Life of William Plumer*. Edited by Andrew P. Peabody. Boston, 1857.

Pritchett, John P. "Selkirk's Views on British Policy toward the Spanish-American Colonies, 1806." *Canadian Historical Review* 24 (1943), 381–96.

Quaife, Milo M., ed. *The John Askin Papers*. 2 vols. Detroit: Detroit Library Commission, 1928–31.

Ritcheson, Charles R. *Aftermath of Revolution: British Policy toward the United States, 1783–1795*. Dallas: Southern Methodist University Press, 1969.

Ritchie, Carson I. A. "The Louisiana Campaign." *Louisiana Historical Quarterly* 44 (1961), 13–121.

Robertson, William S. *The Life of Miranda*. 2 vols. Chapel Hill, N.C.: The University of North Carolina Press, 1929.

Rowland, Dunbar, ed. *Official Letter Books of W. C. C. Claiborne, 1801–1816*. 6 vols. Jackson, Miss.: State Department of Archives and History, 1917.

Rydjord, John. *Foreign Interest in the Independence of New Spain: An Introduction to the War for Independence*. Durham, N.C.: Duke University Press, 1935.

Sakolski, Aaron M. *The Great American Land Bubble: The Amazing Story of Land-Grabbing, Speculations, and Booms from Colonial Days to the Present Time*. New York: Harper and Brothers, 1932.

Savelle, Max. *George Morgan, Colony Builder*. New York: Columbia University Press, 1932.

Siebert, Wilbur H. "The Exodus of Loyalists from Penobscot and the Loyalist Settlements at Passamaquoddy." New Brunswick Historical Society, *Collections* (1914), pp. 485–529.

————. "Kentucky's Struggle with Its Loyalists Proprietors." *Journal of American History* 7 (1920), 113–26.

————, ed. *Loyalists in East Florida, 1774–1785; the Most Important Documents Pertaining Thereto, Edited with an Accompanying Narrative by Wilbur Henry Siebert*. 2 vols. Deland, Fla.: Florida State Historical Society, 1929.

————. "The Loyalists of Pennsylvania." *Ohio State University Bulletin* 24 (1920), 1–117.

————. *The Tory Proprietors of Kentucky Lands*. Columbus: The F. J. Heer Printing Co., 1919.

Smith, Paul H. "The American Loyalists: Notes on Their Organization and Numerical Strength." *William and Mary Quarterly* 25 (1968), 259–77.

————. "Sir Guy Carleton, Peace Negotiations, and the Evacuation of New York." *Canadian Historical Review*, 50 (1969), 245–64.

Smith, William H., ed. *The St. Clair Papers: The Life and Public Services of Arthur St. Clair, Soldier of the Revolutionary War, President of the Continental Congress, and Governor of the North-Western Territory, with His Correspondence and Other Papers*. 2 vols. Cincinnati, 1882.

Smyth, John F. D. *A Tour in the United States of America: Containing an Account of the Present Situation of that Country, the Population, Agriculture, Commerce, Customs, and Manners of the Inhabitants . . . with a Description of the Indian Nations, the General Face of the Country, Mountains, Forests, Rivers, and the Most Beautiful, Grand, and Picturesque Views Throughout that Vast Continent. Likewise Improvements in Husbandry that May Be Adopted with Great Advantage in Europe*. 2 vols. London, 1784.

Sparks, Jared, ed. *Correspondence of the American Revolution: Being Letters of Eminent Men to George Washington*. 4 vols. Boston, 1853.

————. *The Life of Gouverneur Morris, with Selections from His Correspondence and Miscellaneous Papers; Detailing Events in the American Revolution, the French Revolution, and in the Political History of the United States*. 3 vols. Boston, 1832.

Stephens, Alexander, ed. *The Life of General W. A. Bowles, A Native of America– Born of English Parents in Frederick County, Maryland, in the Year 1764*. London, 1803.

Stevens, Benjamin F. *B. F. Stevens's Facsimiles of Manuscripts in European Archives relating to America, 1773–1783. With Descriptions, Editorial Notes, Collations, References and Translations*. 25 vols. Wilmington, Del.: Mellifont Press, 1970.

Stevens, Wayne E. *The Northwest Fur Trade, 1763–1800*. Urbana, Ill.: The University of Illinois, 1928.

Stone, William L. *Life of Joseph Brant-Thayendanegea, including the Border Wars of the American Revolution, and Sketches of the Indian Campaigns of Generals Harmar, St. Clair, and Wayne. And Other Matters Connected with the Indian Relations of the United States and Great Britain from the Peace of 1783 to the Indian Peace of 1795*. 2 vols. New York, 1838.

Sutherland, Stella H. *Population Distribution in Colonial America*. New York: Columbia University Press, 1936.

Swiggett, Howard. *The Extraordinary Mr. Morris*. Garden City, New York: Doubleday, 1952.

Taylor, Robert J. *Western Massachusetts in the Revolution*. Providence, R.I.: Brown University Press, 1954.

Thwaites, Reuben G., and Louise P. Kellogg, eds. *Documentary History of Dunmore's War, 1774; Comp. from the Draper Manuscripts in the Library of the Wisconsin Historical Society*. Madison, Wisc.: Wisconsin Historical Society, 1905.

Tregle, Joseph G., Jr. "Political Reinforcement of Ethnic Dominance in Louisiana, 1812–1845." *The Americanization of the Gulf Coast, 1803–1850*. Edited by Lucius F. Ellsworth, Ted Carageorge, William Coker, and Earle Newton. Pensacola, Fla.: State of Florida, Department of State, 1972, pp. 78–87.

Tucker, Glenn. *Tecumseh, Vision of Glory*. Indianapolis: Bobbs-Merrill, 1956.

Turner, Frederick J., ed. *Correspondence of the French Ministers to the United States, 1791–1797: Annual Report of the American Historical Association for the Year 1903*. Washington, D.C.: U.S. Government Printing Office, 1904.

———. "Documents on the Blount Conspiracy, 1795–1797." *American Historical Review* 10 (1905), 574–606.

———. "English Policy toward America in 1790–1791." *American Historical Review* 7 (1902), 706–35, and 8 (1902), 78–86.

Turner, Lynn W. *William Plumer of New Hampshire, 1759–1850*. Chapel Hill, N.C.: University of North Carolina Press, 1962.

U. S. Bureau of the Census. *Historical Statistics of the United States, Colonial Times to 1957; a Statistical Abstract Supplement*. Washington, D.C., 1960.

U.S. Census Office. *Twelfth Census of the United States, Taken in the Year 1900*. 10 vols. Washington, D.C., 1901–1902.

U. S. Congress. *American State Papers. Documents, Legislative and Executive, of the Congress of the United States*. 38 vols. Washington, D.C., 1832–61.

———. *The Debates and Proceedings in the Congress of the United States; with an Appendix, Containing Important State Papers and Public Documents, and All the Laws of a Public Nature; with a Copious Index. First to Eighteenth Congress. —First Session: Comprising the Period from March 3, 1789, to May 27, 1824, Inclusive. Comp. from Authentic Materials*. 42 vols. Washington, D.C., 1834–56.

———. *The Public Statutes at Large of the United States of America, from the Organization of the Government in 1789, to March 3, 1845*. 8 vols. Boston, 1850–54.

Upton, Leslie F. S. *The Loyal Whig: William Smith of New York and Quebec*. Toronto, Ont.: University of Toronto Press, 1969.

Van Doren, Carl. *Secret History of the American Revolution; an Account of the Conspiracies of Benedict Arnold and Numerous Others, Drawn from the Secret Service Papers of the British Headquarters in North America, Now for the First Time Examined and Made Public*. New York: The Viking Press, 1941.

Wainwright, Nicholas B. *George Croghan, Wilderness Diplomat*. Chapel Hill, N.C.: University of North Carolina Press, 1959.

Wallace, Anthony F. C. *The Death and Rebirth of the Seneca*. New York: Knopf, 1970.

Walpole, Horace. *Journal of the Reign of King George the Third, from the Year 1771 to 1783*. Edited by John Doran. 2 vols. London, 1859.

Washburn, Wilcomb E. "The Moral and Legal Justifications for Dispossessing the Indians." *Seventeenth Century America: Eassays in Colonial History*. Edited by James M. Smith. Chapel Hill, N.C.: University of North Carolina Press, 1959.

Watlington, Patricia. *The Partisan Spirit: Kentucky Politics, 1779–1792*. New York: Atheneum, 1972.

Watson, John Steven. *The Reign of George III, 1760–1815*. Oxford, England: Clarendon Press, 1960.

Webster, Charles K. *The Foreign Policy of Castlereagh, 1812–1815, Britain and the Reconstruction of Europe*. London: G. Bell and Sons, Ltd., 1931.

Wellington, Arthur Wellesley, First Duke of. *Supplementary Despatches and Memoranda of Field Marshal Arthur, Duke of Wellington, K. G.* Edited by Second Duke of Wellington. 15 vols. London, 1858–72.

Wertenbaker, Thomas J. *Father Knickerbocker Rebels: New York City during the Revolution*. New York: C. Scribner's Sons, 1948.

Whitaker, Arthur P. "Alexander McGillivray, 1783–1789." *North Carolina Historical Review* 5 (1928), 181–203.

————, ed. and trans. *Documents Relating to the Commercial Policy of Spain in the Floridas, with Incidental Reference to Louisiana*. Deland, Fla.: Florida State Historical Society, 1931.

————. "The Muscle Shoals Speculation, 1783–1789." *Journal of American History* 13 (1926), 365–86.

————. *The Spanish-American Frontier: 1783–1795: The Westward Movement and the Spanish Retreat in the Mississippi Valley*. Gloucester, Mass.: Peter Smith, 1962.

Whitworth, Charles. *England and Napoleon in 1803: Being the Despatches of Lord Whitworth and Others*. Edited by Oscar Browning, London, 1887.

Wilbur, James B. *Ira Allen, Founder of Vermont, 1751–1814*. 2 vols. Boston: Houghton Mifflin Co., 1928.

Willcox, William B. *Portrait of a General: Sir Henry Clinton in the War of Independence*. New York: Knopf, 1964.

Williams, Samuel C. *History of the Lost State of Franklin*. Johnson City, Tenn.: The Watauga Press, 1924.

Williamson, Chilton. *Vermont in Quandary: 1763–1825*. Montpelier, Vt.: Vermont Historical Society, 1949.

Wilson, Edmund. *Apologies to the Iroquois*. New York: Random House, 1959.

Wood, William C. H., ed. *Select British Documents of the Canadian War of 1812*. 3 vols. Toronto: Champlain Society, 1920–28.

Wraxall, Nathaniel W. *Historical Memoirs of My Own Time*. 2 vols. London, 1815.

Wright, J. Leitch, Jr. *Anglo-Spanish Rivalry in North America*. Athens, Ga.: University of Georgia Press, 1971.

———. "Creek-American Treaty of 1790: Alexander McGillivray and the Diplomacy of the Old Southwest." *Georgia Historical Quarterly* 51 (1967), 379–400.

———. "Lord Dunmore's Loyalist Asylum in the Floridas." *Florida Historical Quarterly* 49 (1971), 370–79.

———. "A Note on the First Seminole War as Seen by the Indians, Negroes, and their British Advisers." *Journal of Southern History* 34 (1968), 565–75.

———. *William Augustus Bowles: Director General of the Creek Nation*. Athens, Ga.: University of Georgia Press, 1967.

Yonge, Charles D. *The Life and Administration of Robert Banks, Second Earl of Liverpool, K. G., Late First Lord of the Treasury. Comp. from Original Documents*. 3 vols. London, 1868.

4 • DISSERTATIONS

Harlan, Rogers C. "A Military History of East Florida during the Governorship of Enrique White: 1796–1811." Master's thesis, Florida State University, 1971.

Starr, J. Barton. "Tories, Dons, and Rebels: The American Revolution in British West Florida." Ph.D. dissertation, Florida State University, 1971.

Index

54948